West Metro Area

W9-DJM-650

(East Metro Area inside back cover)

Parks & Wildlands

A GUIDE TO 170 SPECIAL PLACES IN AND AROUND THE TWIN CITIES

BY KAI JOHN HAGEN

Illustrations by Stephanie Torbert

NODIN PRESS • MINNEAPOLIS

Acknowledgments

I am indebted to a great many people who generously contributed their time and effort to make this book possible. In particular, I'd like to thank my wife, Kirsten Waller, whose patience, assistance, and encouragement were invaluable. I am also grateful to Jon Luoma for his continued support and guidance.

In addition, special thanks go out to the many dozens of people at the Department of Natural Resources, The Nature Conservancy, and the nature centers and parks, who provided information essential to this book. I wish I could list them all.

ISBN-0-931714-35-4

Nodin Press, a division of Micawber's, Inc.
525 North Third Street,
Minneapolis, MN 55401

Cover photograph–Stephanie Torbert

For my grandparents,
Evelyn and George Hagen,
at Valhalla

Contents

Foreword

This book is such a good idea that it is only remarkable no one had the inspiration sooner. It's lucky no one did, because Kai Hagen set about to do it right, and did. The information about places to enjoy nature in and around the Twin Cities in this book is accurate and thorough, highly accessible to any casual nature-seeker, but with a level of detail that more hard-core naturalists will have to appreciate.

The Twin Cities area has been blessed with visionaries who insisted, as far back as early in the century, that natural treasures be sequestered as public areas – the lakes and extensive parklands of Minneapolis and St. Paul, for instance – and, more recently, Hennepin County's Park Reserve System – and, perhaps most remarkably, the only federal wildlife refuge that penetrates a crowded metropolis (the Minnesota Valley National Wildlife Refuge).

Fiscally, the region has been blessed with private and public support for preservation of wild lands, including the patchwork of ecologically unique lands, that constitute some of the best kept nature-secrets in the area, purchased by the non-profit conservation organization, The Nature Conservancy.

Bio-geographically, we lie at one of the great transitional zones on the continent. The last glaciation reached its terminus in the southern counties of the metropolitan area. To the north of the cities, the forest is already in transition to the evergreen boreal taiga that circles the planet and reaches to the Arctic. To the south and east lie the deciduous forests; here and there are remnants of the oak savannas that once interrupted the big woods. And to the west of the cities began great expanses of open prairie that once stretched all the way to the Rockies.

Put all those factors together, and you get a city where, virtually within the shadow of skyscrapers, you can canoe near the shore of an island where dozens of herons and egrets are nesting, wheeling in the air, and stilt-walking the waters. Where condominium dwellers in sight of a major airport can see woodpeckers. Where, within minutes of the urban center, you can come upon a doe and her fawn, a fox, a coyote, or, at water-side, a colony of herons or a flotilla of trumpeter swans.

As Kai Hagen shows in this book, there are bogs and fens, with orchids and carnivorous plants, there are pine woods and hardwood stands and beds of wildflowers abounding within an hour or less of any home in the metropolitan area. There are places for enthusiasts to explore seriously the geologic history of the region or the biota of unique natural areas, and equally places to introduce children to the glories of nature, and places for simple peace, solitude, soughing of wind, and birdsong – perhaps places that, before this book, you had no idea were so close to home.

Without question, this is one of America's best urban and near-urban environments for experiencing an astonishing variety of flora, fauna, landform, and ecosystem. Yet most of us who like to experience nature – whether that means walking in the woods, photographing, birding, studying the environment, or simply enjoying – get stuck in ruts. Perhaps we know of and regularly visit a few places, maybe even a few dozen, but wonder about the universe of other nature walks, streamsides, bits of prairie and woods that we *know* must be out there, somewhere, but don't have time to look for, or – more important – the right reference book to show us. This book, a reference that belongs in the glove compartment as much as the bookcase, will get you there.

Jon R. Luoma
Minneapolis – July, 1988

Introduction

The purpose of this book is to provide a single source of information about the wealth of natural areas that are open to the general public within an hour or so of the Twin Cities. It is designed to introduce you to these places and entice you to explore them.

For each site listed there is information about the facilities available, how to get there, and where to write or call for additional information, but the primary focus is on the diversity of plant communities, wildlife, and landscapes they protect. By using the book and visiting a variety of these areas you will discover that our region is far from uniform, that it is in fact an extraordinary patchwork of highly distinct environments.

When the first settlers came here little more than one and a half centuries ago they found a land we might not easily recognize today. There were bison and black bears, cougars and wolves, eagles and loons. There were dark forests shaded by towering sugar maple and basswood trees and dense oak woods lush with wild fruit and teeming with songbirds. There were sunlit savannas where white-tailed deer ran in large herds and wide-open prairies where windswept grasses sheltered a multitude of colorful wildflowers. Water was everywhere and it was pure and crystal clear. There were lakes set into rocky hills and lakes sprawling across sandy plains. There were countless wetlands overflowing with waterfowl, and there were murky swamps and spongy bogs. Cold streams bursting with trout rushed to join great rivers that flowed through deep gorges or meandered across wide valleys.

Though it was a timeless place, the landscape was young. Little more than 10,000 years ago the last of the glaciers receded from the land we now call Minnesota. For about a million years the massive rivers of ice, some thousands of feet thick, and great torrents of meltwater had reshaped the terrain, leaving behind moraines, eskers, kames, drumlins, till plains, outwash plains, ice-block lakes, and new river valleys.

At first the area was reclaimed by tundra and resembled areas north of the Arctic Circle, but in time the climate warmed and the land was colonized by the plants and animals and Native Americans encountered by the first European explorers.

In every conceivable way we have dramatically modified that pristine landscape. We have razed forests, plowed prairies, drained wetlands, ditched streams, dammed rivers, and polluted our air and water. But some places survived and there were always a few individuals who fought to protect what remained of our natural heritage. The first state park was established nearly a century ago and ever since we have continued to protect natural areas for ourselves and for their own sake. We have also set aside disturbed lands to be reclaimed by natural succession, and we have begun to actively rehabilitate native habitats and restore once-decimated species of wildlife.

The wilderness is gone, yet few other cities in the country are blessed with such a collection of parks and other preserves as the greater Twin Cities metropolitan area. They are places to be enjoyed and cherished, places for wildlife and places to escape the complexities of city life. The more that we come to appreciate their beauty and their irreplaceable value, the more we will understand the importance of protecting them.

While well over a hundred separate areas are included here, there are many others that are not. In general I have been more selective as distance from the Twin Cities increases, although a few particularly noteworthy places farther away are described. New parks – such as Fish Lake and Eagle Lake in Hennepin County – and new facilities not listed here are constantly being developed. In a number of cases, less accessible areas or areas only accessible by boat – such as the large Gores Wildlife Management Area along the Mississippi River – are not included when similar places nearby are more easily reached. Other areas – such as the Cedar Creek Natural History Area in Anoka County – are not listed because they are not open to the general public. Also not described are a number of lengthy trails, some of which connect parks that are highlighted here. The most noteworthy of these trails are the Minnesota Valley Trail, the Minnesota-Wisconsin boundary Trail, the Luce Line Trail, the Cannon Valley Trail, the Sakatah Singing Hills Trail, the North-Hennepin Trail, and the Rice Creek Trail.

Please remember that the natural areas described in this book represent a complex array of public and private properties which have been established for many different reasons. In other words, activities that are appropriate in one place may well be inappropriate in another. It is important to be aware of these differences when selecting a site to visit.

Some areas, such as Nature Conservancy preserves and Scientific and Natural Areas, contain few, if any, facilities and have been set aside to protect natural plant and animal communities for scientific and educational purposes. The highest priority in managing these lands is to insure the perpetuation of significant elements of natural diversity. Obviously many activities are not compatible with the goal of minimizing the threats to these fragile places. The Nature Conservancy, a private, nonprofit organization, has established the largest system of privately owned nature sanctuaries in the world. For a nominal fee you can become a member and support the efforts to preserve our natural heritage. In return you will receive a quarterly magazine published nationally, and a monthly newsletter from the award-winning Minnesota chapter.

In contrast, most state-owned Wildlife Management Areas are managed primarily for wildlife production, public hunting, and trapping. The emphasis on management for wildlife, particularly game species, means that these areas are often highly manipulated environments. Wildlife Management Areas generally have no facilities, but visitors may pursue a number of activities not allowed in many parks, such as hiking off trails (if there are any) and harvesting edible and decorative plants.

Also highly manipulated, State Forests are known as multiple use areas, a category of management that attempts to balance a wide variety of commercial and recreational endeavors in a sustainable manner. The utilization of these public lands ranges from extractive enterprises – mining and lumbering – to activities such as hunting, fishing, and hiking. These woodlands also provide other valuable services, including watershed protection and the preservation of rare and endangered plants and animals. While the emphasis is quite different from that of our state parks, much has been done to accommodate outdoor recreationists. There are often trails, campgrounds, picnic tables, boat launches, and other facilities.

In many ways our state parks are the crown jewels of Minnesota. More than sixty state parks, ranging from a few hundred acres to over 30,000 acres, are scattered about every corner of the state. The parks preserve and reflect the natural beauty and diversity of Minnesota's landscape. From pine forests along the shore of Lake Superior, to broadleaf woodlands and bluffs overlooking the Mississippi River, to tallgrass prairies, our parks are havens for most of the plants and animals native to Minnesota. Besides protecting the natural environment, the parks contain a wide variety of facilities and offer a multitude of experiences and programs throughout the year.

No metropolitan area in the United States, and perhaps the world, has as many nature centers as the Twin Cities. Operated by the state, counties, cities, school systems, and private foundations, a few dozen environmental learning centers, museums, zoos, and natural history areas are hard at work teaching children and adults alike about the natural world around us. Classes, tours, trips, libraries, exhibits, and demonstrations on virtually every aspect of the environment are available to schools, groups, and individuals. Most of these facilities are situated amid protected nature preserves and have interpretive trails, boardwalks, blinds, and observation docks to provide easy access to a great diversity of habitats. Many of our nature centers depend on financial support from individuals and offer memberships in addition to charging small fees for programs. All of them welcome the help of volunteers.

Wherever they live, residents of the Twin Cities metropolitan area are bound to live close to one of the area's many park reserves or regional parks. Altogether there are about forty such parks dispersed throughout the seven-county area, encompassing approximately 45,000 acres of open space. Between them the parks embrace a remarkable collection of landscapes and plant communities characteristic of the region, including maple-basswood forests, oak woodlands, restored prairies, lakes, marshes, bogs, and bottomland swamps, as well as glacial hills, outwash plains, and major river valleys. No less astounding is the abundance of wildlife that inhabits these areas. The parks also provide a wealth of nature-oriented activities and programs, and a dizzying array of recreational facilities.

In addition, there are scores of other county and municipal parks, a great many of which contain natural areas to explore. These parks range from highly developed recreational parks with small nature study areas to sizable tracts of undeveloped wildlands amid suburban neighborhoods and rural farmland.

Before you head out...

Any excursion into the out-of-doors, even a short walk at a local park, can be more rewarding if you plan in advance. There is no need to burden yourself with enough supplies for an African safari, but a few selected items carried in a small pack or camera case can help make your trip more enjoyable.

One of the most important things to consider is the weather. Even a hike in the rain or cold can be a pleasure if you're prepared. Flexibility is the key – if you can add or shed a layer of clothing, put on gloves, or toss on a rainjacket, you're not likely to get too hot, too cold, or too wet to appreciate what's around you. It can also be useful to bring along a hat and a pair of sunglasses.

Wear broken-in walking shoes or boots. Comfort should be your primary consideration here, as bad footwear can make you miserable. Two pairs of socks are usually more satisfying than one. You may be wearing short pants and a T-shirt on a hot day at home, but in most cases you'll be glad if you changed into long pants and a lightweight long sleeved shirt before hitting the trail.

A few other articles that can be worth their weight in gold are insect repellent, suntan lotion, and lip ointment. It is also a good idea to bring a jug of drinking water and a sack lunch. Other materials that can enhance your experience are binoculars and a field guide or two. Finally, you should obtain a map and any other information that you can about your destination.

On the trail...

Although the greater Twin Cities area is blessed with an abundance of parks and other preserves, most of these special places are vulnerable not only to abuse but also to the impact of crowds of well-meaning visitors. Here are some ways to minimize the impact of your visit:

1. Use trails where they are present. Do not make new trails. In areas where there are no trails, groups should walk abreast, separated by arm's length or more. This avoids trampling vegetation and creating new trails.

2. Avoid walking in boggy or wet areas where soils are saturated and soft. These areas are especially sensitive to trampling of vegetation.

3. If you flush a ground-nesting bird, stop and walk around the nest area. Eggs and nestlings are well concealed and easily crushed.

4. Don't litter. Take out everything you brought in, including gum wrappers and cigarette butts. In fact, consider carrying a bag for trash you find along the trail.

5. Except where permitted, don't pick flowers, or collect wildlife, rocks, or fossils.

6. Do not bring pets, except where specifically allowed, and then only on a leash. Dogs can be a real problem for wildlife.

7. Stay off private property unless you have obtained permission first.

8. Some areas are used by classes or have active research in progress. Do not remove any stakes, poles, signs, or other objects that may be part of an ongoing study.

9. Do not use bikes or any other off-road vehicles except where specifically allowed.

10. Do not enter restricted areas or sanctuaries.

Rules and regulations vary considerably from place to place and it is your responsibility to be aware of them. In general, use common sense and respect the rights of other hikers. The best piece of advice I can offer is to walk quietly and slowly. You may not always see them, but wild animals are usually aware of your presence. The faster you walk and the more noise you make, the less likely you are to encounter wildlife. Fascinating discoveries await the patient and careful observer around every bend in the trail.

Minneapolis Parks

In addition to the Minneapolis areas listed individually – Wirth Park, Minnehaha Park, the Eloise Butler Wildflower Garden and Bird Sanctuary, and the Thomas Sadler Roberts Bird Sanctuary – the City of Lakes contains a great variety of public parks. Most of the park system is composed of highly developed recreation centers or carefully manicured green spaces and gardens. Nevertheless, while there are no expansive wildlands, there are lots of pocket-sized places where woods, wildflowers, and wildlife can be found. For the sake of convenience these places are described in geographical order, beginning at the south end of Wirth Park, heading south through the chain-of-lakes, then east to the Mississippi along Minnehaha Creek, and finally north along the river.

Not many people are familiar with SPRING LAKE but thousands probably see it every day with a glance out their car window as they speed by on Interstate 394. The smallest lake in Minneapolis, Spring Lake covers just 2 acres a few yards south of the Hennepin Avenue exit ramp. It can be reached off Kenwood Parkway, west of Parade Stadium. In spite of the nearby traffic the "lake" is a lovely nature spot. The spring-fed pond is fringed with cattails and surrounded on three sides by about 15 acres of woods and thickets. Raccoons, squirrels, rabbits, and frogs still live here and great egrets are among the birds a visitor might see.

Also situated just south of Interstate 394, near the edge of the city, BROWNIE LAKE is the northern end of the famous chain-of-lakes. Connected by a narrow channel to Cedar Lake, the lake has about 20 acres of open water with a few marshy

21

areas around the edge. It is enclosed by steep hillsides cloaked with mature woodlands. When water is taken from the Mississippi River to raise the waterlevel in the chain-of-lakes, it is pumped into Brownie Lake. It takes over 240,000,000 gallons of water to raise the level one foot.

CEDAR LAKE is the only one of the city's major lakes that is not entirely surrounded by public property, and consequently it is also not surrounded by paved pathways and manicured lawns. All of our highly popular city lakes were once rimmed with broad stretches of marshes, but they were dredged and filled years ago, transforming "mosquito-infested" and "muddy" swamps into the clear and precise shorelines we see now. Squeezed between private residences and a wide railroad right-of-way, the north and northeastern sides of Cedar Lake were largely ignored. As a result, the shoreline of the 190-acre lake is still comprised in part by marshes and woods. Flotillas of waterlilies grace the shallow waters, giving way to little bays filled with cattails and enclosed of small wooded peninsulas. Pockets of woods are also found on the two peninsulas that extend from the developed western side of the lake.

A long man-made channel runs past houses and under city streets to connect Cedar Lake with LAKE OF THE ISLES. In 1889 Lake of the Isles became the first major lake in the city to be reshaped by dredging and filling. Before the facelift the lake consisted of 100 acres of water, 67 acres of marsh, and four islands. After half a million cubic yards of fill were removed, the lake had nearly 120 acres of water with no marsh and only two islands. The process led to a real estate boom and by 1900 Kenwood was almost totally developed. Over the years the two islands – Mike's Island and Raspberry Island – have survived efforts to convert them into a neighborhood for the rich or a Japanese garden. Today the islands are protected as wildlife sanctuaries. Incredibly, large numbers of great egrets and black-crowned night herons raise their young in treetop nests here. The islands are also home to wood ducks, Canada geese, screech owls, and various songbirds. They are off-limits to visitors but the birds can be seen from shore or, better yet, from a canoe.

When the channel between Lake of the Isles and LAKE CALHOUN was completed in 1911, replacing a "swampy morass" that had connected the waters of the two lakes, it set off the largest celebration to that date in the city. Today Lake

Calhoun, the largest lake in the city, is 421 acres of open water surrounded by about 100 acres of landscaped parklands. However, when Gideon Pond, a missionary to the Indians, built the first house in Minneapolis along its shores in 1834, the lake couldn't have been more different than it is now. Set amid a wilderness of wildlife-rich oak woods, savannas, and prairie openings, the marsh-rimmed lake was home to loons and freshwater mussels. On his farthest trip west in 1861, Henry David Thoreau stopped here to fish and take in the scenery. Major resorts came later, then beaches and boulevards, then residential development, and slowly the lake the Indians knew as Med'oza, or Lake of the Loons, disappeared. Still, every spring and fall large numbers of birds, including a few loons, stop here to rest and feed during migration. A paved pathway leads through a few acres of attractive woodlands situated west of the William Berry Parkway just south of the lake.

LAKE HARRIET was never linked to the other lakes because it was discovered to be seven feet lower than neighboring Lake Calhoun. As recently as the Civil War, the land around Lake Harriet was a wild place where bears, deer, and other animal roamed, and plums, grapes, raspberries, and strawberries grew in abundance. According to an early pioneer, the lake was "water of extraordinary cleanness and purity, and its bottom completely covered with beautiful pebbles." Once discovered, Lake Harriet quickly became a popular picnic spot and, in 1880, the horse-drawn trolley line (electrified in 1889) was extended to its shores. More popular than ever, the 353-acre lake and its surrounding attractions still draw large crowds. The adjacent LYNDALE PARK GARDENS includes the second oldest municipal rose garden in the country, an adjoining flower garden with fountains, and a restored rock garden. Thirteen acres of wild woods and wetlands are protected in the THOMAS SADLER ROBERTS BIRD SANCTUARY (described elsewhere).

A tiny creek spills out of the southeast side of Lake Harriet and flows through a narrow strip of woods to nearby MINNEHAHA CREEK. The course of Minnehaha Creek is protected by a greenbelt from the Edina border to its confluence with the Mississippi River in Minnehaha Park. As it winds across the city, the creek passes through a constantly changing mixture of natural woodlands, manicured lawns, and flower gardens. In the vicinity of Minnehaha Parkway and Pleasant

Avenue, a meandering creekbed, pirated channels, and bank-toe erosion reflect the creek's natural tendency to wander in spite of the designs of city planners. At various spots along the creek you can see where large blocks of stones wrapped in wire have been placed to keep it flowing where its "supposed to."

A few blocks south of the creek along Portland Avenue, DIAMOND LAKE appears neglected compared to our other lakes. Squeezed between the road on the east side and houses on the west, and surrounded by a thin strip of trees, the small lake is fringed with perhaps a dozen acres of marsh. Across the road to the north, Pearl Park was once a marshy 29-acre lake, but in 1940, like a number of other shallow lakes in Minneapolis, it was filled in and forgotten

Two-thirds of the way across the city, Minnehaha Creek flows past LAKE NOKOMIS. Originally called Lake Amelia, the lake is now named for Hiawatha's grandmother in Longfellow's poem, "Song of Hiawatha." The shallowest of the major lakes, Lake Nokomis was known as a muddy lake in the middle of a swamp until dredging created the 201 acres of open waters so popular for swimming and sailing today. Another 207 acres of manicured grounds and recreational facilities surround the lake. Minnehaha Creek splits with Minnehaha Parkway here and crosses a public golf course before flowing in and out of LAKE HIAWATHA and continuing roughly eastward to the river.

Situated along the river between Minnehaha Park and the Bureau of Mines, and accessible at the east end of 54th Avenue, is an undeveloped stretch of land known as the MINNEHAHA ANNEX. The property includes land atop the bluffs and extends down to the riverbottom. Informal trails traverse portions of the 70-acre area, which is comprised of exposed limestone bluffs and terraces cut by small ravines. The habitats found here include mature oak woodlands, dense thickets and shrubby clearings, a small marsh, and about eight acres of native prairie.

Between the Ford Bridge and the University of Minnesota, both sides of the Mississippi River gorge are protected from the riverbank to the parkways that wind along the top of the bluffs. Recognized as MISSISSIPPI GORGE REGIONAL PARK, this long strip of land contains a number of hidden attractions. Except for bedrock outcroppings and sheer cliffs, the bluffs and ravines are almost entirely forested. Gnarled oaks and other hardy trees grow with columbines, harebells, and wild roses on exposed areas and steep slopes, while tall sugar maple, basswood, and other trees shelter bloodroot, large-flowered bellwort, and wild ginger in sheltered ravines. Black willow, cottonwood, silver maple, elm, and green ash thrive on the slender, sandy floodplain at the base of the bluffs. The Winchell Trail follows an old Indian footpath through the woods from 44th Street to Franklin Avenue. The woodlands along the river harbor a surprising variety of birds throughout the year, but the best time is in spring and fall when a host of warblers and other birds are moving along the valley.

One block west of the parkway south of 34th Street is an unusual site known as the SEVEN OAKS SINKHOLE. Amid a residential neighborhood a circular roadway (Park Terrace) surrounds the sinkhole, which is part of an underground channel heading east to the river. The deep oval sinkhole is filled with trees and shrubs and an informal trail cuts through the center of it.

Looking across the river from West River Parkway near the Franklin Avenue Bridge, it is possible to see BRIDAL VEIL FALLS, a small cascade that trickles down the eastern bluff. Just south of the University along the east side of the river is an 80-acre tract of woods and open spaces called EAST RIVER FLATS. Above Saint Anthony Falls, between Main Street and the east shore of the river, FATHER HENNEPIN BLUFFS provides access to the river in the heart of the city and offers trails with excellent views of downtown. Settled in the mid-nineteenth century, much of NICOLLET ISLAND is being developed into a historic park. A deck here offers views of Saint Anthony Falls. Just upstream, between Plymouth Avenue and Nicollet Island, the newly developed BOOM ISLAND PARK is the largest riverfront park in Minneapolis.

The newest section of the GREAT RIVER ROAD, which will eventually run the length of the Mississippi River, was opened in the fall of 1987. It is nothing short of remarkable that the city was able to reclaim the west bank of the river between Portland Avenue at Saint Anthony Falls and Plymouth Avenue a mile and a quarter to the north. Comprised largely of parkways and promenades, park benches and planted trees, the park has brought beauty to the forgotten riverbank where the city began. At its northern end the new park loses its formality, and a path and footbridge wind through the woods and over the ravine where Bassett Creek rushes to join the river.

A mile and a half north, west of Marshall Street between 27th and 28th Avenues (N.E.), MARSHALL TERRACE takes in about a dozen acres of woods along the floodplain. Farther upstream and across the river, NORTH MISSISSIPPI PARK stretches for a mile along the river on the east side of Interstate 94. The park is mostly wooded and includes the mouth of Shingle Creek, which winds through Brooklyn Park and Brooklyn Center before entering Minneapolis. As it flows through the neighborhoods at the northern edge of the city, the creek is protected by a narrow greenbelt know as SHINGLE CREEK PARK.

Facilities: There are far too many facilities associated with these area to list them all specifically. You can obtain detailed information from the city about facilities, programs, lessons, and activities. Perhaps the most noteworthy development in the Minneapolis park system is the tremendous network of paved trails that draws crowds of hikers and bikers (and roller skaters, etc.). The trails twist through Wirth Park, wrap around all of the major lakes, follow Minnehaha Creek across the city, and wind along the bluffs overlooking the Mississippi River. A good way to explore the chain-of-lakes is by canoe. Bring your own or rent one at Lake Calhoun (348-5364) or one of the other lakes. The lakes are used for sailing – Harriet, Calhoun, and Nokomis – windsurfing, rowing, and fishing. There are many well-developed picnic areas as well as beaches, concession stands, playgrounds, volleyball courts, ballfields, exercise courses, community centers, golf courses, gardens, and much more. Fishing and boating are also popular activities on the Mississippi, and the parks along the river offer picnic areas, boat launches, overlooks, historical sites, and other attractions.

For additional information:

Minneapolis Park and Recreation Board
310 Fourth Avenue South
Minneapolis, Minnesota 55415
(612) 348-2243
or 348-2226

St. Paul Parks

Besides the St.Paul areas listed individually – Battle Creek Park, Crosby Lake Park, Hidden Falls Park, and Lilydale Park – our state capital contains a diverse collection of public lands. Most of the parks consist of highly developed recreation centers or neatly manicured gardens and green spaces, but you don't need to leave the city to go hiking, canoeing, or birdwatching. For the sake of convenience these places are described in geographical order, beginning near downtown and making a counter-clockwise loop around the city.

Although technically part of the Lilydale-Harriet Island Regional Park, CHEROKEE PARK is generally recognized as a separate area. The park occupies some 68 acres atop the heights opposite downtown and includes another 112 acres on or below the face of the bluff. The narrow strip of land atop the bluff is largely open and includes a picnic area and various athletic facilities, but the bluff itself is a steep slope with woods, thickets, and bedrock outcroppings. Because of the severe angle of the bluff, many areas along the edge have begun to erode, in some places getting quite close to the parkway that borders the park. The park offers excellent views of the Mississippi River and downtown St. Paul.

Also distinct from Lilydale Park, HARRIET ISLAND includes 68 acres of low-lying land along the river directly across from downtown. Up until 1950 the park was a true island, separated from the "mainland" by a channel of the river varying in width from 100 to 200 feet. Named for the first teacher, Harriet Bishop, who came to this area in 1847, the island has long been the site of citywide activities (the annual Riverfest and a recent Winter Carnival have maintained the tradition). However, with the channel filled in, marina basins constructed, a flood protection levee added, and most of the trees removed, the park has lost its natural character.

INDIAN MOUNDS PARK stretches for over a mile along the high bluffs just east of downtown where the river begins a big bend to the south. The park is named for the several Indian burial mounds situated prominently atop the bluff. Away from the bluff the park is comprised of open lawns with shade trees and picnic areas, but from top to bottom the face of the bluff is heavily forested. To the east where the slope is more gentle, there are some well-worn, informal trails that enter the woods. The outstanding views from the overlooks near the mounds take in downtown and a broad sweep of floodplain and bluffs downriver.

Surrounded by industry, railroads, highways, and a barge terminal in the southeastern corner of St. Paul is a most unlikely and remarkable sanctuary. Situated in a 500-acre backwater lake, PIG'S EYE ISLAND is the nesting site of choice for thousands of great blue herons, great egrets, double-crested cormorants, and black-crowned night herons, and yellow-crowned night herons. In fact the island is the largest mixed heron rookery in the state, as well as the largest black-crowned night heron rookery in the country. Unknown to the birds, they nearly lost a battle that was waged for fourteen years on their behalf when a broad coalition of environmental groups and other concerned citizens fought to prevent the area from becoming part of an expanded barge parking lot. In 1984 the battle was won and three years later, in the spring of 1987 as the birds were returning, the issue was permanently laid to rest when the island was designated a state Scientific and Natural Area. The island itself is almost a mile long and up to a half a mile wide and runs up against the Mississippi near Red Rock Drive. Cloaked with large cottonwoods, silver maples, and other trees, the island and its environs are also home to deer, fox, raccoon, beaver, and muskrat. In recent years a growing number of bald eagles have spent part of the winter here. Between April 1 and July 15 the island is off-limits to visitors but the birds can be seen feeding throughout the area.

Managed by Ramsey County, 80-acre BEAVER LAKE PARK straddles the line between St. Paul and Maplewood a little more than a mile north of Interstate Highway 94. The small but scenic lake is rimmed with stretches of cattail and purple loosestrife and there is a tract of woodlands to the north. There is a complete picnic area along the western shore and a few private residences on the southeast side.

Although St. Paul is graced by fewer lakes than Minneapolis, it has taken advantage of those it has. PHALEN LAKE is the largest lake in the city and has the dubious distinction of being the only lake in the state named after an accused murderer. The lake is long and deep and contains 222 acres of open waters adorned with a few flotillas of waterlilies and surrounded by 272 acres of developed parkland. Paved trails for hiking and biking circle the lake but most of the land and a wealth of other facilities are located west of the lake. There are swimming beaches, picnic areas, canoe rentals, a golf course, and much more, set into a landscape of lawns and shade trees. A small lake with some waterlilies and a fringe of cattails is connected by a narrow channel to the northern edge of Lake Phalen. Another manmade channel connects Lake Phalen to a chain of suburban lakes – Keller, Gervais, and Kohlman. Ramsey County manages 165 acres of land adjoining Keller Lake as a regional park and there are a large number of picnic areas along the lake and in the trees across Highway 61.

As long ago as 1850, 70-acre LAKE COMO was popular as a recreational lake and today the lake and its environs are a St. Paul showcase. When the park was still in its natural state the city hired Fredrick Nussbaumer, a German-born landscape architect, to be foreman of the park. He later became the superintendent of all parks in St. Paul but he paid special attention to Como Park. The 378 acres of parkland bordering the lake are home to an exceptional variety of attractions. In addition to the paved pathways, picnic areas, fishing docks, and athletic facilities you might expect to find, there is the famous COMO CONSERVATORY, the COMO ZOO, and the COMO ORDWAY MEMORIAL JAPANESE GARDEN, as well as a small amusement park and various monuments and memorials. A tract of woodlands located south of Horton Avenue in the southwest part of the park has been set aside as a bird sanctuary. A paved trail and a number of informal paths lead through the dense shrubby wood, which consists of bur oak, black cherry, ash, black locust, boxelder, butternut, and scattered white pine with mulberry, honeysuckle, lilac, sumac, and lots of buckthorn in the understory.

The Mississippi River winds through and along the edge of St. Paul for seventeen miles. Much of the shoreline has been acquired and preserved as parkland to form a continuous park system. From the point where the river first reaches the city to Hidden Falls Park almost three miles downstream, the Father of Waters flows between the protected bluffs of MIS-SISSIPPI GORGE REGIONAL PARK. Mississippi River Boulevard parallels the riverway atop the bluffs and passes several scenic overlooks. The bluffs west of the road drop precipitously to the floodplain except where small wooded ravines are cut back into the adjacent neighborhoods. In some places well-worn, informal trails provide access to secluded nature spots.

On either side of Montreal Avenue between Snelling Avenue and Ford Road in the southwest corner of the city is HIGH-LAND PARK. Most of the land in this sizable park is packed with a great variety of athletic facilities. However, the entire southern edge of the area is marked by a belt of wooded hills and small ravines where mature red oak and bur oak stand with black cherry, hackberry, ash, boxelder, and some paper birch. Two pleasant picnic areas are set against the trees atop the hill.

Facilities: There are far too many facilities associated with these places to list them all specifically. You can obtain detailed information from the city about facilities, programs, lessons, and activities. Paved trails for hiking and biking are found primarily in Phalen Park, Como Park, and along the Mississippi River (atop the bluffs until Hidden Falls Park then along the floodplain to Interstate 35E). Boating and fishing are popular all along the river. The park system as a whole contains every sort of recreational and athletic facility you might want to find.

For additional information:

St. Paul Division of Parks and
Recreation
300 City Hall Annex
25 W. 4th Street
St. Paul, Minnesota 55102
(612) 292-7400

Afton State Park

Only fifteen miles as the crow flies from downtown St. Paul, Afton State Park lies along the high bluffs of the scenic St. Croix River in southern Washington County. The park's 1,669 acres are wrapped around the Afton Alps Ski Area and spread across windswept grasslands and forested ravines. To preserve the natural character of the area, development has been kept to a minimum. This is one of the few state parks where camping is limited to primitive, hike-in sites, and even the swimming beach is accessible only by trail. The rugged terrain offers nature-oriented recreation and outstanding views of the St. Croix Valley.

Until fairly recently the rolling uplands were divided into several farms, which had previously replaced the original prairies and oak savannas. The farms are gone but old roads, stone foundations, and lines of planted evergreens, will long mark the location of farmsteads, fields, and pastures. Scattered patches of native grassland escaped conversion to agricultural use and efforts are being made to restore and enlarge these valuable remnants. It wasn't cultivation so much as the suppression of natural fires that led to the disappearance of the savannas. Nevertheless, a few small fragments on dry, south-facing slopes have held off encroaching woodlands. Controlled burning is now being used to rejuvenate the prairie grasses and flowers in both habitats.

The open uplands are cut by deep ravines that drop three hundred feet to the river. Dense woodlands shade the ravines except where sandstone outcroppings jut from the steep slopes. The forest is predominantly oak – bur oak, white oak, red oak, and pin oak - with black cherry, quaking and bigtooth aspen, paper birch, basswood, ironwood, elm, red maple, butternut, and red cedar. Stands of red cedar grow thickly on the well-drained faces and points of the bluffs, where they have probably replaced hillside prairies. Black willow trees border Trout Brook as it flows toward the floodplain, where they grow alongside tall silver maple and cottonwood.

A thriving herd of white-tailed deer lives in the park and there are often as many hoofprints as footprints on the more secluded trails. Badgers, red foxes, and red-tailed hawks hunt the meadows for woodchucks, rabbits, gophers, ground squirrels, and mice. The St. Croix Valley is considered one of the better areas for birdwatching in the region and each season has something different to offer. The stillness of the park in winter is broken by the activities of the pileated woodpecker, great horned owl, ring-necked pheasant, common crow, blue jay, black-capped chickadee, and white-breasted nuthatch. Among the colorful birds that return from southern climes to raise their young in the park each summer are the scarlet tanager, northern oriole, American redstart, ruby-throated hummingbird, indigo bunting, and eastern bluebird. But it is during the spring and fall migrations that birdwatching is best here as countless birds move up and down the valley, including a rich variety of warblers and birds of prey. Bald eagles don't nest in the park but are often seen soaring above the bluffs.

Facilities: Visitors should make their first stop at the Visitor Center, which offers interpretive exhibits, information, restrooms, and a telephone. Eighteen miles of good trails wind through the woods and meadows, plunge into the ravines, and follow along the river. All of these trails are groomed for cross-country skiing but many are not recommended for inexperienced skiers. There are also 5 miles of trails for horseback riding and 4 miles of paved trails for bicycling. There are two picnic areas with toilets and water, one by the parking lot and Visitor Center atop the bluff, and a hike-in site next to the river. The latter is located next to a guarded swimming beach. Fishing is allowed from the riverbank. Twenty-four secluded campsites with toilets and a water pump are accessible only to backpackers and a group camp is available in the southern corner of the park.

How to get there: From St. Paul head east on Interstate Highway 94 toward the St. Croix River. Just before crossing the river, exit onto State Highway 95 and drive south, staying on County Highway 21 when 95 turns right after about 4 miles. Proceed 4 more miles to the intersection of County Highways 21 and 20. The park entrance is on the left.

The park is closed from 10:00 p.m. to 8:00 a.m. except to registered campers. Daily or annual permits are required for all vehicles entering a state park. They may be purchased at the park entrance.

Map key: East 1

For additional information:

Afton State Park Manager
6959 Peller Avenue South
Hastings, Minnesota 55033
(612) 436-5391

Department of Natural Resources
Division of Parks and Recreation
Information Center, Box 40
500 Lafayette Road
St. Paul, Minnesota 55155
(612) 296-6157

Albion Wildlife Management Area

Little known except to hunters, the Albion Wildlife Management Area protects a vibrant wetland habitat two miles south of Annandale in northwestern Wright County. Although the 475-acre preserve includes mixed woods and old fields, the main attraction is the marsh complex visible from the road. There are no trails or boardwalks here and a small boat or canoe is the best way to observe the wetland and its inhabitants.

The broad open water at the heart of the wetland is bordered in separate areas by extensive stretches of sedge meadows, willow thickets, cattails, and phragmites. Some of the birds that raise their young in this mixed habitat are red-necked grebe, mallard, blue-winged teal, red-winged blackbird, long-billed marsh wren, least bittern, and Virginia rail. Among the other birds that may be observed feeding in the marsh are great blue heron, great egret, white pelican, and trumpeter swan.

Low-lying groves of quaking aspen provide an attractive backdrop for the marsh but the surrounding woods are primarily remnant woodlots and former grazing land. Large bur oaks stand out amid small basswood, elm, and ash, as well as thickets of boxelder and dense growths of prickly-ash. The remainder of the uplands are made up of old field grasslands.

Facilities: There are no developed facilities here except for a dirt parking area. State Wildlife Management Areas are managed for three primary reasons: wildlife production, public hunting, and trapping. Other activities, such as birdwatching, are also encouraged but should probably be avoided during the hunting season.

How to get there: From the Twin Cities, take State Highway 55 west through Hennepin County and most of Wright County. At Annandale, turn left onto County Highway 5 and drive south for just less than 3 miles. The WMA is on the left side of the road after the junction with the township road. To reach the parking area turn left onto the township road and look for a turn-off on the right.

For additional information:

Department of Natural Resources
Area Wildlife Manager
P.O. Box 370
St. Cloud, Minnesota 56302
(612) 255-4279

Minnesota Department of Natural
Resources
Section of Wildlife, Box 7
500 Lafayette Road
St. Paul, Minnesota 55155
(612) 296-3344

Map key: West 2

Alimagnet Park

Alimagnet Community Park occupies the southern shoreline of Alimagnet Lake, which straddles the line between the suburbs of Burnsville and Apple Valley. Although half of the 178 acres in Burnsville and a portion of the more than 100 acres in Apple Valley have been developed for a wide variety of recreational activities, the remainder of the land has been left in a natural state.

Beyond the playgrounds and ballfields, trails lead past open meadows and planted pines to an area of wooded hills that wrap around a shallow cove of Alimagnet Lake. Dominated by mature stands of tall white oak and red oak with ironwood, aspen, and black cherry, the woods shelter a scattering of small pothole marshes. Extensive groves of quaking aspen and paper birch grow around the woodland's edge and stretch along much of the lakeshore.

Facilities: The Burnsville side of the park contains an abundance of well-used athletic facilities, including horseshoes and fields for soccer, football, softball, and baseball. There is also playground equipment for children. Separate picnic areas with shelters, tables, and grills are situated near the lake. The Burnsville Department of Parks and Recreation is located just inside the entrance to the park. In Apple Valley there is a volleyball court and a lot of playground equipment, in addition to a picnic area with a shelter, tables, and grills. The trails lead into the woods from both sides of the park and are used by cross-country skiing in winter.

How to get there: The park is just over a mile east of the intersection of Interstate Highways 35W and 35E. From either Interstate, exit onto to County Highway 42 and go east. After a short distance turn north onto County Road 11 and look for the park entrance on the right.

Map key: East 3

For additional information:

City of Burnsville
Park and Recreation Department
1313 East Highway 13
Burnsville, Minnesota 55337
(612) 431-7575

Anoka County Riverfront Park

The Anoka County Riverfront Park is comprised of two distinct parcels of public land along a two mile stretch of the Mississippi River in suburban Fridley. South of the Interstate Highway 694 bridge the park occupies a long strip of well-developed, open uplands separated from the river by a short, steep hill and a narrow band of tall black willow and cottonwood mixed with boxelder, green ash, and elm. "Islands of Peace," the portion of the park north of the Interstate, has been developed by the Foundation for Islands of Peace as a recreation area for the general public, disabled veterans, and blind and handicapped adults and children. The facilities here are nestled into the trees along the river and scattered about Chase's Island. This area also includes Durnam Island, a 57-acre island cloaked by an old bottomland forest, which is accessible by boat only.

Facilities: A park road links all of the facilities in the southern part of the park. Separate trails for hiking and biking run the length of the area and include benches overlooking the river. Two picnic areas offer shelters, tables, grills, water, and restrooms. There is also a field game area, an exercise course, playground equipment, a boat ramp with parking, and a small arboretum.

All of the facilities at Islands of Peace Park are accessible to the handicapped. The reception center contains meeting rooms, a library, fireplace, lounge, and restrooms. A paved trail and a bridge link the center to Chase's Island, which has more paved trails, a shelter, picnic tables, grills, a group fire ring, and a fishing dock. A memorial to American veterans is located next to the parking lot.

How to get there: From Interstate Highway 694, take the exit for East River Road. The entrances for both parts of the park are located off this road just north and south of the Highway.

Map key: West 4

For additional information:

Anoka County Parks and
Recreation
550 Bunker Lake Blvd.
Anoka, Minnesota 55304
(612) 757-3920

Baker Park Reserve

The Hennepin County Parks system was born in 1956 when Morris T. Baker donated 210 acres on Lake Independence as a public park. This park, which has since grown into a 2,600-acre reserve, is now part of an outstanding network of parks that totals more than 24,000 acres. With a wealth of recreational diversions concentrated near the largest natural sand beach in the metropolitan area, and extensive stretches of undeveloped wildlands, Baker Park offers something for everyone.

The park is situated entirely within a range of undulating glacial hills known as a ground moraine. Between the rock-strewn hills are several lakes and marshes which were formed in ice-block depressions or simply in low, water-filled parts of the irregular landscape. The open waters of the shallow lakes give way around the edges to broad stretches of cattail marsh, sedge meadows, and thickets of willow and red-osier dogwood. Such areas are excellent waterfowl habitat and some of them have been channeled and potholed to enhance their production capacity. Lake Katrina, the largest of the lakes, has a floating cattail shoreline with a tendency to develop floating islands of cattails on windy days. A tamarac bog in the southeast corner of the park adds to the diversity of wetland communities.

Most of the uplands are comprised of open meadows that represent abandoned pastures and cropland, but surviving woodlots of various size can be found on hillsides throughout the park. Some of the remnant woodlands offer a good approximation of the original forest. Here you find lovely stands of sugar maple, basswood, red oak, white oak, bitternut hickory, and ironwood, with a deeply shaded understory of gooseberry, ferns, and wildflowers. In contrast, wide-spreading bur oaks grow with red cedar and bigtooth aspen atop exposed rocky knolls. Some of the old fields are being reclaimed by dense young thickets of elm, boxelder, ash, quaking aspen, buckthorn, wild plum, and sumac.

Wildlife flourishes throughout the area, but nowhere as much as the vibrant lakes and wetlands that cover nearly a third of the park. A multitude of birds and other animals live in these watery habitats and many more stop here during the spring and fall migrations. After a century of absence, trumpeter swans now return each year to raise their young in the park. The successful re-introduction of these beautiful birds reflects the commitment of the Hennepin Parks to restore and preserve the county's natural heritage.

Facilities: The park has an extensive system of trails. A 6.2-mile paved trail for biking, hiking, and jogging, makes a loop around the southern half of the park. There are 9 miles of trails for horseback riding and a separate parking area for trailers. Eight miles of trails in the northern half of the park are groomed for cross-country skiing in winter and mowed for hiking the rest of the year. A ski chalet provides rentals, a snack bar, and a warm fire. The reserve has 9 miles of snowmobile trails with link-ups to the metro area trail system. There is a large picnic area on the shore of 828 acre Lake Independence, with tables, grills, water, restrooms, a creative play area, and a sandy swimming beach with lifeguards. Picnickers can rent canoes, paddleboats, bicycles, volleyballs, horseshoes, and game kits at the concession stand. Four separate group picnic areas, all by the lake, may be reserved. There is a boat launch on Lake Independence, as well as access to 32-acre Spurzem Lake at the north end of the park. The Baker Park Golf Course has a 9-hole "executive" length course and a 9 hole "regular" length course, as well as a driving range and a pro shop. Eight group camps are available by reservation. Each has pit toilets, a water pump, and a fire ring, and some include a shelter, electricity, and grills. There is also a modern campground suitable for tents, trailers, or mobile homes, with tables, fire pits, flush toilets, and a dump station. Some sites include electrical hookups.

How to get there: The park is located about 15 miles from Minneapolis next to the town of Maple Plain. Take U.S. Highway 12 (Interstate 394) west from the Cities to the intersection with County Road 29 at the edge of Maple Plain. Turn right (north) onto 29 and follow it as it bends to the right, becoming County Road 19. After it bends back to the left, look for the park entrance on the left. Most of the facilities are located in this area and maps of the rest of the park can be obtained here. There is a nominal daily or annual fee for parking.

For additional information:

Hennepin Parks
12615 County Road 9
Plymouth, Minnesota 55411
(612) 559-9000

Map Key: West 5

Bass Ponds Environmental Study Area

The Long Meadow Lake Unit of the Minnesota Valley National Wildlife Refuge takes in some 2,200 acres of wooded bluffs and watery bottomlands stretching along the Bloomington side of the river between Interstate Highways 35W and 494. Long Meadow Lake itself, which is known as a premier wildlife marsh, dominates the preserve, but because the unit is largely undeveloped and boats are prohibited, most of it is inaccessible. One of the best places to view the marsh is from the Bass Ponds Environmental Study Area, an interesting public use area located just east of the Cedar Avenue Bridge.

In 1926 the Isaak Walton League constructed a number of ponds here to raise largemouth bass for the purpose of supplying fingerlings to the overfished lakes around Minneapolis and throughout the state. This site, at the end of a wooded ravine, was selected because the cold, spring-fed creek could provide enough water to maintain the system of manmade ponds. The flow was directed by a series of dams and pipes so that the water level could be easily manipulated. The ponds remained in operation for three decades until the League's lease could not be renewed. Later, during the 1960s, a gravel company excavated some of the ridge to the southwest; however, the ponds remained intact. The property became a part of the new National Wildlife Refuge after 1976 and restoration of the ponds began in 1981.

The ponds are still used on occasion to raise muskies but today they are manipulated for the benefit of a variety of wildlife. In some years, for example, the water level is dropped to encourage the growth of plants favored by waterfowl. Now nestled amid a regenerated woodland, the ponds are often full of feeding mallard, teal, and wood duck. When a single pond is drained, particularly during migration, large numbers of shorebirds can be seen feasting on the exposed mudflats. White-tailed deer are plentiful in the area and beaver inhabit the largest of the ponds.

The dikes that separate the manmade ponds from Long Meadow Lake provide a good vantage point for observing the broad wetlands and the wildlife there. Ducks, coots, geese, herons, and egrets are the most visible but many other birds, including belted kingfishers and black terns, abound in the marsh. In spring and fall, huge rafts of waterfowl congregate on Long Meadow Lake before continuing north or south.

Facilities: A short, self-guided interpretive trail makes a loop around the ponds. Informative pamphlets are available at the beginning of the trail. A quarter-mile walk along the dike overlooking Long Meadow Lake leads to a boardwalk that winds through part of the marsh to an observation blind at the edge of the open water.

How to get there: The parking lot for the area is situated where 86th Street dead ends in east Bloomington. It is most easily reached by exiting off of Interstate Highway 494 onto 24th Avenue (just east of Cedar Avenue) and heading south about a mile before turning left onto 86th Street.

Map key: West 6

For additional information:

Refuge Manager
Minnesota Valley NWR
4101 E. 80th Street
Bloomington, Minnesota 55425
(612) 854-5900

Battle Creek Regional Park

Battle Creek Regional Park sprawls over 751 acres of wildlands less than five miles from downtown St. Paul. Squeezed between residential communities and crossed by several roads, the park is really a collection of distinct areas stretching from the bluffs overlooking the Mississippi River in the southeastern corner of the city to the rolling hills of Maplewood. There are developed picnic grounds and recreational facilities, as well as an interesting variety of natural areas to be explored.

Named for an 1842 clash between the Ojibway and Dakota Indians, Battle Creek is the primary feature of this urban park. The creek flows through upland neighborhoods in the shade of a narrow greenbelt, then plunges into a deep valley carved into the bluffs before joining the waters of the Mississippi at Pig's Eye Lake. The gradual process of erosion that created the valley and exposed the underlying sandstone became a severe flooding problem when most of the watershed was developed, so today much of the flow is diverted into a storm sewer pipe that parallels the creek below ground. The steep slopes of the valley are covered by woodlands ranging from tall oaks to maple-basswood forest, with a scattering of white pines. South of the creek valley atop the bluffs is a more open mixture of old fields and young woods. Some spots along the bluff offer outstanding views of the broad Mississippi River Valley and downtown St. Paul.

The largest tract of undeveloped land is found in the southeastern portion of the park across McKnight Road in Maplewood. The varied landscape here includes fairly level areas with abandoned fields, second growth woodlands, and planted evergreens, and a stretch of tightly packed hills cloaked by a mature oak forest and dotted with small wetlands. Other sections of the park also contain wooded nature areas, and an extension off the north side of the creek reaches toward Interstate 94 to encompass a cattail marsh surrounded by homes and businesses. Altogether the diverse environs of Battle Creek Park provide a valuable haven for a surprising variety of wildlife, including white-tailed deer, raccoon, red fox, great horned owl, pileated woodpecker, and a host of small mammals and songbirds.

Facilities: There are developed trails in some parts of the park (groomed for cross-country skiing in winter) and many areas are laced by well-worn, informal trails. The main picnic area offers a pavilion, shelters, tables, grills, toilets, playground equipment, and a 2 mile paved bike trail. This trail connects to another 2-mile loop through the woodlands south of Upper Afton Road. There are also ball fields, a community garden, and a tree nursery.

How to get there: All parts of the park can be easily reached by taking the McKnight Road exit off Interstate Highway 94 at the eastern edge of St. Paul and turning south. Trailheads for the developed trails are located on the north side of Lower Afton Road just east of McKnight Road; on the west side of Winthrop Street just south of Upper Afton Road; and in the "Suburban Pond" area at the corner of White Bear Avenue and Suburban Avenue. The main picnic area is situated on the north side of Upper Afton Road just east of McKnight Road. Access to the blufftop is off Battle Creek Road north of Lower Afton Road. The creek crosses Upper Afton Road, dropping into the valley, just west of battle Creek Road.

Map key: East 7

For additional information:

Ramsey County Parks and
Recreation Department
2015 N. Van Dyke Street
Maplewood, Minnesota 55109
(612) 777-1707

Baylor Park

Covering 233 acres adjacent to Eagle Lake in western Carver County, Baylor Park offers a combination of natural attractions and recreational activities. Most of the facilities are located near the 170-acre lake in the southern end of the park. The rest of the area is a patchwork of woods, meadows, and wetlands with a small stream running though it.

For years, cattle grazing in the woods here kept young trees from growing up, creating a familiar park-like setting of mature trees shading an open understory. Once grazing stopped however, a dense growth of small trees and shrubs developed. The absence of middle-aged trees is evidence of the land's past use.

Today much of the woodland is characterized by tall sugar maple, basswood, and bur oak standing above thickets of young elm, ash, swamp white oak, boxelder, hackberry, and aspen, as well as hawthorn, serviceberry, buckthorn, and prickly-ash. Gradually, these young woods are also invading the open areas where milkweeds, thistles, goldenrods, asters, and planted buffalo grass have replaced the cultivated fields of corn for which the original forest was cleared.

A number of tiny wetlands are scattered throughout the park and a floating boardwalk provides a close-up look at an extensive cattail marsh adjoining Eagle Lake.

An attractive stand of sugar maples in the north end of the park is tapped each spring to make maple syrup.

Facilities: About 5 miles of wide trails, including a quarter-mile of floating boardwalk, form interconnecting loops and explore all the park's habitats. All the trails except for the boardwalk are groomed for cross-country skiing. The park offers both tent and RV camping. There are tennis courts, sandy volleyball courts, a softball field, a swimming beach with bathhouse, and a picnic area with tables, grills, water, and playground equipment. A community room in the park barn is available with reservations for group use.

How to get there: From Minneapolis take U.S. Highway 212 or State Highway 5 west to Young America. From the intersection of these two roads, turn north onto County Road 33. Proceed for about 2.5 miles and look for park entrance on the right

The park is open year-round from 8:00 a.m. to 9:00 p.m. or one hour past sunset (whichever is later). There is a nominal daily or annual entrance fee and additional charges for camping, the community room, or ski rental.

Map key: West 8

For additional information:

Carver County Parks
10775 County Road 33
Young America, Minnesota 55397
1-800-642-7275

Beebe Lake Regional Park

One of the most popular parks in Wright County is Beebe Lake Regional Park. Situated on the southern shoreline of Beebe Lake, six miles east of Buffalo, the 64-acre park offers a variety of diversions in an attractive natural setting. Facilities for picnicking, swimming, fishing, and other activities are clustered together by the lake while an easy trail makes a short loop through mature forest and restored prairie.

Largely confined to the sloping land near the lake, the woods provide a retreat to deep shade and cool breezes. Benches have been placed along the trail where you can view the lake and surrounding farmland from the seclusion of the tall trees. The remainder of the park is made up of flat, open fields. These were formerly cultivated, but recently 17 acres were hand-planted with native prairie grasses and flowers.

Facilities: A wide gravel trail makes a half mile loop with benches placed in scenic spots overlooking the lake. The many developments near the lake include a swimming beach with a lifeguard and a bathhouse with modern restrooms and an outdoor shower; a picnic area with a shelter, tables, and grills; as well as a fishing dock, an amphitheater, a creative play area, and volleyball courts. There is also a group campground available by reservation.

How to get there: The park is located on the north side of County Highway 34 between Buffalo and Hanover. From Minneapolis take State Highway 55 to Rockford, then take a right onto County Road 19 just after crossing the Crow River. Almost immediately, take a left onto County 18. After 3 miles take a right onto County 33 and then a quick left onto County 120. Go a little more than 2 miles to County Highway 34. Take another left here and look for the park on the right.

Map key: West 9

For additional information:

Wright County Parks Department
Route 1, Box 97B
Buffalo, Minnesota 55313
(612) 682-3900, ext. 182
339-6881 (Metro)
1-800-362-3667, ext. 182 (Toll Free)

Bethel Wildlife Management Area

Stretching for a mile along the northern edge of Anoka County, the Bethel Wildlife Management Area encompasses 460 acres of oak woods, small prairie remnants, old fields, planted pines, and wetlands. Away from the road, much of the low-lying, sandy landscape is made up of extensive marshes. These wetlands are primarily a mix of open water and cattails with some sedges and bulrushes, fringed with thickets of willow, dogwood, and alder. Waterfowl and other wildlife are plentiful here but easy access is limited.

Facilities: Used mostly by hunters, the area has no marked trails or any other developed facilities. State Wildlife Management Areas are managed primarily for wildlife production, public hunting, and trapping. Other activities, such as birding, mushroom-hunting, and berry-picking, are permitted but should be avoided during the hunting season.

How to get there: From Interstate Highway 694 take State Highway 65 north through Anoka County. After 23 miles turn left (west) onto County Highway 24. Proceed 1.5 miles, then turn right onto County Road 73. Then turn left onto Main Street, crossing the railroad tracks and entering the town of Bethel. Follow Main Street past the small business district and then wend your way northwest by taking a right on Cooper and a left on Broadway, following the bend to the right as it becomes Dogwood. This will bend again to the left and become 245th Street. After a short distance the WMA will be on the left. There are no parking areas but you can pull off to the side of the unpaved road. A good place to enter on foot is where the road bends again to the north.

Map key: West 10

For additional information:

Department of Natural Resources
Area Wildlife Manager
Carlos Avery WMA
Wyoming, Minnesota 55092
(612) 464-2860

Minnesota Department of Natural Resources
Section of Wildlife, Box 7
500 Lafayette Road
St. Paul, Minnesota 55155
(612) 296-3344

Big Willow Park

Big Willow Park in Minnetonka encompasses one of the few protected natural areas along historic Minnehaha Creek as it meanders through the western suburbs on its way to Minneapolis and the Mississippi River. The 97-acre park contains a variety of athletic facilities but most of the area is made up of wetlands, woods, and small clearings. Easy trails crisscross the small park, beginning with a floating boardwalk that crosses a cattail marsh edged by large black willow trees. Marshy lowlands are bordered by pockets of woodland where bur oak, red oak, and other trees stand above a dense growth of small trees and shrubs, including buckthorn, serviceberry, witchhazel, elderberry, viburnum, prickly-ash, hazelnut, gray dogwood, and honeysuckle.

Facilities: The trails here, which include a floating boardwalk and a bridge over Minnehaha Creek, wind though the park. Benches have been placed in spots along the trail. There are a few picnic tables and a satellite toilet. The athletic facilities, which are clustered together near the park entrance, include softball and baseball fields and a soccer field.

How to get there: The park's entrance is located on the north side of Minnetonka Blvd. about a mile and a half west of County Highway 18.

Map key: West 11

For additional information:

Minnetonka Parks and Recreation
Department
14600 Minnetonka Blvd.
Minnetonka, Minnesota 55345
(612) 933-2511

Black Dog Scientific and Natural Area

Named for the chief of the Dakota Indian tribe that inhabited the area when the first settlers arrived in 1853, the Black Dog Scientific and Natural Area protects 130 acres of unique grasslands in the Minnesota River Valley. Less than half a mile east of Interstate Highway 35W, the small preserve contains excellent examples of plant communities that were once common in the valley. Two of these communities, the calcareous fen and the mesic blacksoil prairie, are among the rarest natural communities in Minnesota.

Bisected by power lines and a railroad track, and bordered by thoroughfares, light industry, and residential neighborhoods, this invaluable remnant of our original landscape managed to survive until it was acquired by The Nature Conservancy and the Department of Natural Resources. Nearby oak forests were cut for lumber and fuel, and most of the uplands were cultivated, but the bottomlands, too wet and marshy for cultivation, were used primarily for haying until 1962. Fewer drainage ditches were dug here than on the adjoining farms and the tract also benefited from the farmer's practice of burning the grassland early in the spring every one or two years.

The calcareous fen community was once the dominant type of vegetation at Black Dog Preserve but over the years the fens have been reduced in size and now range from heavily degraded to nearly pristine. A calcareous fen is an endangered grass-sedge dominated plant community with vegetation adapted to its unusual calcium-rich groundwater. Among the specialized plants that typify healthy calcareous fens are twig rush, slender beak-rush, whorled nut rush, fringed gentian, shrubby cinquefoil, and various species of grasses and sedges.

The mesic blacksoil prairie, also known as "tallgrass prairie," is the most productive and species-rich grassland in Minnesota. This prairie once covered great stretches of the state, but the deep, nutrient-rich, loam soils were ideal for farming, and nearly all of it has been converted to agricultural production. Less than 500 acres of undisturbed mesic blacksoil prairie are known to exist in southeastern Minnesota, largely confined to railroad right-of-ways and other places unsuitable for cultiva-

50

tion. The vegetation is dominated by tall grasses – big bluestem, Indian grass, and prairie dropseed – which shelter an abundance of flowers, including blazing star, frost aster, yellow cone flower, Canada tick trefoil, and purple prairie clover.

Bell's vireo is the only rare animal documented on the preserve; however the fen here supports eight different plants classified as endangered or of special concern. The fen and the tallgrass prairie grade almost imperceptibly into disturbed areas, wet meadows, shrub carr, and young woodlands. Man-made changes, such as ditching and fire suppression, have increased the threat from encroaching shrubs and trees. Red-osier dogwood, bog birch, false indigo, long-beaked willow and other shrubs have invaded some areas, while a variety of trees, including cottonwood, paper birch, aspens, and willows, have colonized other areas.

Facilities: There are no developed trails or other facilities here. Part of the preserve has been made into a sanctuary because of its vulnerability, and access to this restricted area is allowed by permit only. You are invited to observe and enjoy the preserve, but please remember that your visit can have an impact on the natural community.

How to get there: From Minneapolis or Interstate Highway 494, head south on Interstate Highway 35W. Just after crossing the Minnesota River into Dakota County, take the Cliff Road exit (County Highway 32) and go east, passing under the Interstate. A little less than a mile from the Interstate, look for a parking lot on the left next to an athletic field. Park in this lot and look for signs marking the preserve across the athletic field and the railroad tracks.

Map key: East 12

For additional information:

Scientific and Natural Areas
Program
Box 7, Minnesota Department of
Natural Resources
500 Lafayette Road, DNR Building
St. Paul, Minnesota 55155
(612) 297-3288

Blackhawk Municipal Park

Blackhawk Park is made up of 40 acres of heavily rolling hills in suburban Eagan. Almost a perfect square, the park takes its name from Blackhawk Lake, a scenic 39-acre lake that skirts the northern boundary. The park's knobby hills are largely grass-covered and open, but woodlands occupy the steeper slopes and a band along the lakeshore. These woodlands range from dense thickets of shrubs and young trees to small pockets of mature oaks, including some lovely, wide-spreading bur oaks.

Facilities: A one-mile-long trail winds about the hills. The trail, which is mowed for hikers in summer and groomed for skiers in winter, offers some nice views of the area. A short paved path leads to a children's play area atop the park's highest hill.

How to get there: From Minneapolis or Interstate Highway 494, take the Cedar Avenue Freeway (77) south. Shortly after crossing the Minnesota River take the Diffley Road exit. Go east on Diffley Road for a little over half a mile to Blackhawk Road. Take Blackhawk Road north just over half a mile, then take a right onto Deerwood Drive. Proceed .2 mile and turn left onto Riverton Avenue. Go .4 mile to Palisade Way. You must park on the street here as there is no parking area.

Map key: East 13

For additional information:

Eagan Parks and Recreation
Department
3830 Pilot Knob Road
P.O. Box 21199
Eagan, Minnesota 55121
(612) 454-8100

Bredesen Park

Encompassing over 200 acres of lowlands where Nine Mile Creek flows under the Crosstown Highway in suburban Edina, Bredesen Park is the happy result of efforts to combine storm water management and wildlife habitat. Originally known as the Mud Lake Area, the park was one of five locations considered as a storage site for storm water along Nine Mile Creek. An early study recommended the construction of a large open lake and recreation area, but following studies led to the creation of a wildlife preserve, which was completed and dedicated in 1985.

Instead of a large lake at the heart of the preserve, there is a broad wetland crammed with cattail, bulrush, sedge, willow, reed grass, and red-osier dogwood. More than two dozen smaller ponds and marshes are scattered about the surrounding woods and thickets. Attractive when in bloom, but a real threat to wetlands and useless to wildlife, purple loosestrife has taken over a couple of ponds near the entrance. The primary wetland complex grades into swampy woodlands of cottonwood, green ash, elm, and boxelder, groves of quaking aspen, a solitary stand of tamarac, and planted weeping willow.

Though only slightly higher, the "uplands" are characterized by a few sizable bur oak and northern pin oak standing above a dense growth of small trees and shrubs. Many of these plants are favored by wildlife, including black cherry, aspen, red cedar, hawthorn, wild plum, pin cherry, buckthorn, high-bush cranberry, nannyberry, snowberry, elderberry, hazelnut, prickly-ash, gooseberry, blackberry, raspberry, woodbine, and wild grape.

White-tailed deer, red fox, raccoon, mink, muskrat, and numerous smaller mammals inhabit the area, but it is the birds that bring the park to life. Canadian geese nest on little islands in the manmade ponds, herons and egrets stalk the shallows, pheasants call from the thickets, and many other birds may be seen nesting or feeding here, such as wood duck, mallard, blue-winged teal, spotted sandpiper, long-billed marsh wren, sora rail, kingfisher, veery, phoebe, catbird, and barn swallow.

Facilities: There are two separate trail systems here. A little less than two miles of wide, gravel nature trails wind through the woods and past the many ponds and marshes inside the fence. A few stationary maps are placed along the trail. Two additional paved trails, one for bicycles, encircle the preserve outside the fence. Restrooms are located by the entrance.

How to get there: Follow the Crosstown Highway (State Highway 62) west into Edina. About one mile past Highway 100, take the Tracy Avenue exit and turn north. Go a couple of blocks and turn left onto Olinger Blvd. just past a community park. Follow this street a few more blocks until it intersects Olinger Road. Turn left here and park in the lot at the end of the road.

Map key: West 14

For additional information:

Edina City Hall
Department of Parks and
Recreation
4801 West 50th Street
Edina, Minnesota 55424
(612) 927-8861

Boot Lake Scientific and Natural Area

The Boot Lake Scientific and Natural Area is located in the northeast corner of Anoka County, adjacent to both the Carlos Avery Wildlife Management Area and Martin-Island-Linwood Regional Park. This undeveloped tract takes in some 400 acres encompassing Boot Lake and protects an unusually well-preserved example of the diverse habitats once common on the Anoka Sandplain.

The lake itself is significant geologically as part of a chain of ice-block basin lakes lying in a subglacially formed feature known as a tunnel valley. These valleys, created before and during the last ice age, are now buried under several hundred feet of glacial drift and outwash. Today buried valleys are occasionally marked by strings of low-lying lakes and marshes, including the one that stretches to the southwest and northeast of Boot Lake.

From Boot Lake to the well-drained uplands, one finds an interesting continuum of plant communities here. The open waters of the shallow lake are fringed with emergent vegetation, such as waterlilies and bulrushes, which grade into cattails, then sedges, then thickets of willow, alder, and red-osier dogwood. The surrounding lowlands support a wet forest of tamarac, paper birch, and red maple, as well as winterberry, sensitive fern, American yew, clintonia, bunchberry, and club mosses. As the land gradually rises away from the lake, there is an abundance of tall white pine, a northern tree seldom found growing naturally near the Twin Cities anymore. Oak forests are predominant on the drier upland sites. Mature red oak and white oak stand with basswood, black cherry, bigtooth aspen, alternate-leaf dogwood, poison sumac, and serviceberry. Dense clumps of hazelnut grow around the edge of the woods where the trees give way to small prairie remnants and old fields.

Facilities: There are no developed trails or other facilities here. The area has been set aside to protect the natural plant and animal communities. The southern side of the area is posted as a sanctuary and closed to visitors. You are invited to observe and enjoy the preserve, but please remember that your visit can have an impact on the natural community.

How to get there: Take Interstate Highway 35W north from Minneapolis or Interstate Highway 35E north from St. Paul. Approximately 8 miles north of where these two highways merge take the Wyoming exit. Turn left (passing over the Interstate) and drive west into Anoka County on County Road 22. Follow 22 for about 8 miles, then turn left onto County Road 17. After a little more than a mile, where the road intersects an entrance for the Carlos Avery Wildlife Management Area, turn left onto an unpaved township road. Proceed down this road for .8 mile, passing the Victor Hill Cemetery, and look for two small signs standing together on the left side of the road. These signs mark a corner of the preserve. Park along the side of the road. The best approach to the lake is to head across the field following an imaginary line perpendicular to the road, and continue through the woods a short distance in the same direction.

Map key: East 15

For additional information:

Scientific and Natural Areas
Program
Box 7, Minnesota Department of
Natural Resources
500 Lafayette Road, DNR Building
St. Paul, Minnesota 55155
(612) 297-3288

Bryant Lake Regional Park

Bryant Lake Regional Park is located in a rapidly developing section of Eden Prairie along the north shore of mile-long Bryant Lake. The park encompasses 230 acres within its boundaries but a portion of that was yet to be acquired. Part of the Hennepin County Park System, its designation as a Regional Park means that it will be extensively developed for outdoor recreation.

The most outstanding natural feature here is the belt of steep, rocky hills that occupies much of the park. Left behind by the glaciers, these prominent hills are among the highest and most rugged in the Twin Cities area. Their recent history as grazing land has left them deforested, resulting in an open, windswept terrain that offers fine views of the lake and surrounding area.

The vegetation reclaiming the hills is typical of abandoned farmland. Non-native flowers such as mullien, yarrow, leafy spurge, and white sweet clover thrive along with native milkweed, hoary vervain, and wild bergamot. Hardy pioneer trees are also becoming established, signifying the return of the woods, including sumac, wild plum, chokecherry, buckthorn, chinese elm, boxelder, prickly-ash, red cedar, and bigtooth aspen.

A level stretch of ground along the lakeshore supports an abundance of large wide-spreading bur oaks as well as a number of tall ash and white oak. A lovely picnic area is situated in the shade of these trees.

Facilties: At present few facilities have been developed within the park but plans call for extensive development of various recreational facilities in the not-too-distant future. Currently a dirt road leads to a boat launch, a swimming beach, and a picnic area. Adjacent to the park is a horse farm run by the Hennepin County Western Suburban Vocational Technical Institute where horses can be rented for use in the park.

How to get there: The park is located between Interstate Highway 494 and U.S. Highway 169. Take 169 (County Road 62) west from the Twin Cities. Shortly past the intersection with County Highway 18 take the Shady Oak Road (County Road 61) exit. Then take the second left (Rowland Road) and continue a short distance to the park entrance on the left.

Map key: West 16

For additional information:

Hennepin Parks
12615 County Road 9
Plymouth, Minnesota 55411
(612) 559-9000

Bunker Hills Regional Park

Bunker Hills Regional Park is situated in the heart of Anoka County where the growing suburbs of Coon Rapids, Blaine, Andover, and Ham Lake intersect. While the park takes in about 1,500 acres of low sandy hills, small lakes, and marshes typical of the Anoka Sandplain, it has been extensively developed and is more of a recreation area than a nature preserve. However, in spite of the remarkable number of county services, offices, and recreational facilities located here, the park does contain a few interesting parcels that provide a glimpse of the original landscape.

The most noteworthy area is in the vicinity of 61-acre Bunker Lake at the northern edge of the park. The lake is bordered by steep-sided sand dunes and low-lying ponds and wetlands. The well-drained dunes still support vestiges of the tall grass prairie and oak savanna that once carpeted much of the area. Mature bur oak and red oak, stunted by the poor soil, share the dunes with hardy shrubs and some native prairie plants. The vegetation becomes noticeably more lush and varied in the well-watered spaces below the dunes. Here the oaks grow taller alongside quaking and big-toothed aspen, paper birch, black cherry, ash, elm, basswood, and other trees and shrubs, including hazelnut, raspberry, winterberry, and wild grape. A few cottonwood and silver maple trees border wet thickets of willow, alder, red-osier dogwood, and sensitive and cinnamon ferns, which give way to sedges, cattails, and small pools of open water.

A small herd of white-tailed deer shares the park with red foxes, raccoons, bull snakes, garter snakes, and four kinds of squirrel. A variety of songbirds, some waterfowl, and a pair of great horned owls nest in the park. During migration Bunker Lake attracts an abundance of waterfowl, which can be easily viewed from an observation deck set into the trees.

Much of the remainder of the park consists of low sandy hills covered with oak trees and evergreen plantations. Wind erosion can have a dramatic impact on this type of soil and the long rows of red pine, scotch pine, jack pine, and white spruce were planted to stabilize the dunes. Although the effort has been successful, the plantations also obscure the underlying dune formations and shade out the native prairie grasses and flowers.

Facilities: The park is crisscrossed by more than 5 miles of trails for hiking and cross-country skiing. The nature trail at Bunker Lake includes small bridges and the observation deck. Bike trails are currently being developed. There are an additional 5 miles of horseback riding trails, and horses can be rented from the county owned stables within the park. The park also runs hay and sleigh rides and pony rides for children. Numerous picnic facilities are scattered throughout the park. There are a few shelters and dozens of tables and grills with access to restrooms and drinking water. Family camping and group camping areas are available, each with tables, firerings, and restrooms. Among the many other facilities there is a swimming beach, ball fields, playground equipment, an indoor and outdoor archery range, an agricultural extension garden that demonstrates how some vegetables do in the sandy soil, a Veterans War Memorial with a World War II era tank, and the Coon Rapids Municipal Golf Course. Recently the county constructed an immense wave pool here. The main building, or activities center, contains a Nature Study Room and houses the County Park Department, the Anoka County Extension Offices, and the Soil and Water Conservation Office. The section of the park west of the railroad tracks contains the Main Park

Maintenance Shop, the Anoka District of Metropolitan Mosquito Control, the Anoka County Law Enforcement Rifle Range, and a fire tower. The portion of the park north of Blaine High School has been preserved as an outdoor environmental education area for the High School and all other area schools.

How to get there: From the Twin Cities exit off of Interstate Highway 694 or U.S. Highway 10 onto State Highway 65 (Central Avenue). Take Highway 65 north just over 5 miles past Highway 10 and turn left onto Main Street (State Highway 242). Go west a little more than 2 miles and look for the park entrance on the right.

The park is open from 7:30 a.m. to 9:30 p.m. except for campers. There is no entry fee but there is a charge for the horse rental, hay rides, sleigh rides, pony rides, and both camping areas.

Map key: West 17

For additional information:

Anoka County Parks Department
550 Bunker Lake Boulevard N.W.
Anoka, Minnesota 55304
(612) 757-3920
or (612) 755-4165 (camping or
picnicking reservations)
or (612) 757- 7010 (horse stables)

Camram Park

In southwestern Burnsville, Camram Park serves as a buffer between fast growing suburbs and a large regional park. Lying adjacent to the rugged Murphy-Hanrehan Park Reserve, the municipal park occupies 150 acres of wooded hills and wetlands. A paved trail leads along a small ridge to scenic picnic sites set amid red oak, aspen, elm, and red cedar, and wide-spreading bur. The steep hill overlooks an expansive cattail marsh rimmed with willow and red-osier dogwood.

Facilities: A short, paved trail makes a loop along the ridge and past the edge of the marsh. The picnic sites atop the hill have tables and grills. A small ball field and playground apparatus are located next to the parking area.

How to get there: Heading south from the Twin Cities on either Interstate Highway 35W or 35E, take the exit for County Road 42 and go west. About 2 miles west of 35W turn left (south) onto the Burnsville Parkway. After almost a mile look for parking lot on the left where the road bends to the right and heads uphill.

Map key: East 18

For additional information:

Burnsville Department of Parks
and Recreation
1313 East Highway 13
Burnsville, Minnesota 55337
(612) 431-7575

Cannon River Wilderness Area

The Cannon River Wilderness Area lies astride a three-mile stretch of the pretty country stream for which it is named. The park contains some 850 acres squeezed into the rolling farmland midway between the towns of Northfield and Faribault in Rice County. Wooded hills and bluffs rising as much as 250 feet above the river enclose a picturesque valley where uncrowded trails wind past scenic overlooks and along the riverbank.

The rugged terrain supports a rich mixture of woodland habitats, ranging from mature oak forest on exposed hillsides and maple-basswood forest in sheltered draws, to second-growth woods and dense thickets on once-farmed lowlands and a belt of bottomland forest on the narrow floodplain. Tiny springs, which emanate from the base of the hills, and scattered meadows, add to the variety of habitats. Here and there the river flows past colorful sandstone cliffs and outcroppings topped with stands of paper birch.

The valley is a haven for most of the animals you might expect to find in the surrounding countryside, including white-tailed deer, red and gray fox, raccoon, woodchuck, striped skunk, cottontail rabbit, gray squirrel, an occasional coyote, pheasant, a few hawks and owls, and an abundance of songbirds. Wild turkeys were introduced in 1979 and small numbers of these large birds still live in the park.

Facilities: There is a small picnic area located next to the parking lot with a shelter, tables, grills, toilets, and a water pump. Four miles of hiking trails, including a footbridge over the river, make it easy to explore the park. The Bluff Trail leads to a scenic overlook with a bench that offers a lovely view of the valley and surrounding hills and farms. Most of the trails are open for cross-country skiing but are not groomed. There are 4 primitive campsites with pit toilets along the river which are used primarily by canoeists. The Cannon River downstream from Faribault is designated as a state recreational and scenic river and there is an access point near the picnic area. A map of the area is available from the County Parks Department.

How to get there: From the Twin Cities head south on Interstate Highway 35. Five miles after entering Rice County, exit at State Highway 19 and drive east about 6 miles to the intersection with State Highway 3 in Northfield. Turn right (south) onto Highway 3 toward Faribault. Go another 7.5 miles on Highway 3 and look for a sign that says "Cannon River County Park." Turn left onto the unpaved Township Road and proceed .8 miles along the river to the park entrance.

A map of the area is available from the County Parks Department. The park is closed nightly at 10:30 p.m. except to campers.

Map key: East 19

For additional information:

Rice County Parks
P.O. Box 40
Faribault, Minnesota 55021
(507) 334-2281 ext. 260

Trails and Waterways Unit
Information Center, Box 40
500 Lafayette Road
St. Paul, Minnesota 55155
(612) 296-6699

Carl Johnson County Forest

Tucked away amid the farmland of western Wright County is the small Carl Johnson County Forest. This 40 acre preserve bordering the North Fork of the Crow River is a lovely place to take a quiet walk. Cloaked by an inviting woodland, the fairly level upland terrain is broken by several small ravines which cut through the steep hill that drops down to the river. Undisturbed for many years, the forest here is composed primarily of stately sugar maple, basswood, and red oak, as well as smaller ironwood and bitternut hickory. Scattered stands of bigtooth aspen and paper birch overlook the river where large silver maples share the floodplain with black willow and green ash. In spring the ground is studded with colorful wildflowers.

Facilities: A one mile hiking trail makes a loop through the forest and leads to a couple of scenic spots above the river where benches have been placed. A large stationary map is located at the trailhead and small ones are found along the trail. There is a picnic table next to the parking area.

How to get there: From the Twin Cities go west on either State Highway 55 or U.S. Route 12. From 55 turn south onto County Highway 5 at Annandale and go about 8 miles to County Highway 35. From U.S. Route 12 turn north onto County 5 a little more than a mile past Howard Lake and go 6 miles to County 35. Travel west on 35 for about 3 miles and turn north onto a dirt road after crossing the river. Continue straight on this road for just over a mile to the parking area.

Map key: West 20

For additional information:

Wright County Parks Department
Route 1, Box 97B
Buffalo, Minnesota 55313
(612) 682-3900 ext. 182
339-6881 (Metro)
1-800-362-3667 ext. 182 (Toll Free)

Carlos Avery Wildlife Management Area

By far the largest expanse of public land in the seven county metropolitan area, the Carlos Avery Wildlife Management Area sprawls over 23,050 acres in northeastern Anoka County and southwestern Chisago County. Although certain sections have been set aside as wildlife sanctuaries, this vast preserve was established primarily for wildlife production, public hunting, and trapping. This emphasis on management, mainly for the benefit of game species, and the resulting manipulation of various plant communities, distinguishes Carlos Avery as a State Wildlife Management Area (WMA). Like most Wildlife Management Areas, Carlos Avery offers relatively few developed facilities, but it is crisscrossed by numerous roads and paths that provide easy access for visitors who come to enjoy a variety of wildlife-related activities.

Though the landscape at Carlos Avery WMA is quite different today than it was in presettlement times, it remains an excellent example of the Anoka Sandplain. The Anoka Sandplain is one of the major geological features of Minnesota, covering a large area between the Mississippi and St. Croix Rivers, north of St. Paul and south of Milaca, east of St. Cloud and west of Chisago City. This broad outwash plain was created over 10,000 years ago at the edge of receding glaciers where streams of glacial meltwater spread, depositing loads of gravel and sand as they meandered toward the St. Croix and Mississippi Rivers. The Anoka Sandplain, which is the largest sand and sand dune area within the state, is generally flat but it is not entirely featureless. There are regions of upland hills that represent pockets of glacial till not completely buried by the outwashed sand; there are also patches of sand dunes formed as strong winds blew across the sands after the meltwater streams ran dry; and most notably, there are countless lakes and marshes that are the result of stranded ice blocks once buried in the sand.

Before the influence of modern man, the area was a rich mosaic of oak savanna, tallgrass prairie, wetlands, and tamarac bog. For a while the land escaped development, largely because the sandy and poorly drained soils were of low fertility and not suited to agriculture. However, in the early 1900's the Crex Carpet Company began managing the marshes for wiregrass used in manufacturing woven rugs. A system of dikes and ditches was constructed to allow water level manipulation, prescribed burning, and mowing. After 1925, a combination of decreasing production and increasing competition led to the bankruptcy of the company and, by 1930, much of the land became tax delinquent.

The Minnesota Conservation Commission recognized the area's potential for wildlife, and land acquisition began in 1933. Initially, the WMA was managed by a federal Emergency Conservation Work camp, and many buildings and wildlife projects were constructed under the federal Public Works Progress Administration during the Great Depression. State resident managers have been assigned to the WMA since 1936.

Today all but a few acres of the original oak savanna and tallgrass prairie have been replaced by a mixture of forests, old fields, pine plantations, and food plots. Oaks dominate the forests, but they are associated with a wide variety of other hardwoods and a dense understory of shrubs. The forest is cut selectively or in small blocks to maintain a diversity of habitats; the old fields are managed to provide grassy nesting cover for upland game birds and waterfowl; and at least 150 acres of corn are planted as winter food for deer and other wildlife.

More than anything else, it is the wetlands that make Carlos Avery WMA worth visiting. Thousands of acres of shallow waters cover the landscape, including 6,000 acres impounded by 21 miles of dikes. These marshes range from dense stands of cattail growing in wet soils to deep, open water wetlands with emergent bulrushes and sedges. Some of the more open sections of cattail marsh contain wild rice, a valuable food source for waterfowl. By utilizing a combination of techniques, such as regulating the water level, prescribed burning, level ditching, and mowing, these wetlands are managed for waterfowl, marsh birds, fur-bearers, and public hunting and trapping.

The most undisturbed tracts at Carlos Avery WMA are the sizable stretches of primeval-looking tamarac swamp that border the Sunrise river. This is the area east of Interstate Highway 35, in Chisago County, known as the Sunrise Unit.

The ample space, diversity of habitats, and careful management make Carlos Avery WMA attractive to a great variety of wildlife. While many animals are legally hunted here, many more are nongame species. Fifty-three mammal species are likely to be found in the WMA, including the white-tailed deer, coyote, badger, red fox, raccoon, striped skunk, and red, gray, and fox squirrels. Muskrat and mink thrive in the marshes, as do smaller numbers of beaver and otter.

Birds are particularly abundant here. Of the 244 species found in the vicinity, about half are year-round or summer residents. Nesting waterfowl include the mallard, blue-winged teal, wood duck, coot, pied-billed grebe, and Canada goose. Among the many other birds lured by the extensive wetlands are the great blue heron, great egret, green-backed heron, American bittern, and belted kingfisher. But the most noteworthy resident of the marshes here is the sandhill crane. This spectacular bird, which stands over three feet tall and has a wingspan of 80 inches, is quite rare near the Twin Cities. Birdwatchers will also find the preserve teeming with shorebirds, warblers, vireos, thrushes, sparrows, woodpeckers, and more. In addition, twenty-one resident and migratory raptors frequent the area, such as the great horned owl, marsh hawk, Cooper's hawk, and occasional bald eagle.

Facilities: The Carlos Avery WMA is staffed by two resident managers and three additional employees. The Carlos Avery Game Farm and regional forestry headquarters are also on the WMA, but they are managed and staffed independently. In addition, an environmental education area with an interpretive trail has been established near the game farm. Hunting is permitted under state regulations, and trapping is allowed with a permit from the manager. Many people choose to explore the area by automobile. There are 57 miles of unpaved roads and numerous parking areas and pull-offs within the preserve. Hiking, snowshoeing, and cross-country skiing are permitted but the more than 23 miles of trails and firebreaks are not marked or groomed. Often the best way to get around on foot is to walk along the dikes. Other activities, such as fishing, nature photography, mushroom-hunting, and berry-picking are also encouraged but should probably be avoided during the hunting season.

How to get there: Because of the sprawling character of the WMA, it is a good idea to obtain a map at the headquarters before exploring the area. To get there from the Twin Cities, take either Interstate Highway 35W or 35E north. Just 8 miles after the two highways intersect, take the Wyoming exit. Take County Highway 22 west from Wyoming. Less than one mile from town, Highway 22 veers north. Continue driving west. After 2.5 miles turn south. From this intersection it is little more than 2 miles to the Carlos Avery WMA headquarters.

Map key: East 21

For additional information:

Carlos Avery WMA
5463 W. Broadway
Forest Lake, Minnesota 55025
(612) 296-5200

Minnesota Department of Natural Resources
Section of Wildlife, Box 7
500 Lafayette Road
St. Paul, Minnesota 55155
(612) 296-3344

Carpenter St. Croix Valley Nature Center

The Carpenter St. Croix Valley Nature Center is situated along the St. Croix River a short distance upstream from its confluence with the Mississippi River. Like the many other nature centers in the metropolitan area, the primary purpose of the Center is environmental education. Unlike most of the others, however, it is open to the general public only during business hours and reservations are requested. Altogether the tract encompasses 325 acres, including 180 acres of leased farmland, a 60 acre apple orchard, and a plantation of red pine.

The area's natural habitats are generally limited to a band of wildlands between the level uplands and the river's edge. There are small remnants of oak savanna and groves of birch and aspen atop the high bluffs; richly varied woodlands filling deep ravines and covering the steep slopes; and bottomland forest along the floodplain. There are also vernal waterfalls, rocky outcroppings, and small caves. Wildlife is abundant here as it is throughout the valley, but never more than in spring and fall when countless thousands of birds – waterfowl, raptors, warblers, and others – follow the river between northern nesting areas and southern climes.

Facilities: Paved and unpaved trails lead through the cultivated uplands and down to the river. There are two large observation decks overlooking the bluff and a ravine. There are numerous buildings on the property. The main administration building is a former residence with a conference room, library, crafts room, offices, and other facilities for staff members and volunteers. The interpretive building is a converted garage with several classrooms. An old maintenance building houses a gift shop and an apple sales area. A 150-year-old homestead has been converted into an intern residence. An 80-year old farmhouse and a 60-year-old barn now serve as a maple syrup shack and a warming house. There are also numerous indoor and outdoor pens used as wildlife rehabilitation holding and retraining pens.

How to get there: From the Twin Cities take U.S. Highway 61 (also U.S. Highway 10) southeast from Interstate Highway 94 or 694. Follow Highway 10 toward Prescott, Wisconsin when it splits with Highway 61 before crossing the Mississippi river to Hastings. After a little more than 2 miles on 10, turn left (north) onto County Road 21 (St. Croix Trail). The entrance is on the right 1.5 miles north of Highway 10.

The center is open from 8:00 a.m. to 5:00 p.m. on weekdays and from noon to 5:00 p.m. on the first and third Sundays of the month. It is closed for all national holidays. All groups are asked to reserve visits one month in advance by calling the office.

Map key: East 22

For additional information:

Carpenter St. Croix Valley
Nature Center
12805 St. Croix Trail
Hastings, Minnesota 55033
(612) 437-4359

Carver Park Reserve

Carver Park Reserve occupies approximately 3,500 acres in Carver County a short distance southwest of Lake Minnetonka. The gently undulating landscape is a lovely composite of lakes, marshes, woodlands, old fields, and tamarac bog. The park includes or borders on ten lakes that range in size up to 470 acres. These lakes and extensive wetlands comprise about a quarter of the reserve; a comparable area is made up of woodlands. The remainder is former farmland, much of which is reverting to forest while some is kept as open grassland to maintain a diversity of habitats for wildlife.

Although the area's history as agricultural land affected even the woodlots that escaped conversion to crops and pastures, the park contains some good examples of the forest, known as the "Big Woods," that once typified the area. Found on drier sites, this is a well developed climax community dominated by stately sugar maple and basswood trees with ironwood common in the understory. In other areas, the forest is in an interim stage of

development with many red oak, bur oak, and aspen mixed in, as well as bitternut hickory, black cherry, and other trees. Old fields in the earlier stages of recovery are characterized by opportunists such as sumac, prickly-ash, honeysuckle, choke-cherry, buckthorn, boxelder, and red cedar. Moist areas bordering the many lakes and wetlands support cottonwood, black willow, and silver maple.

The park also includes a tamarac bog, a swampy mix of woods and wetlands described by Donald Peattie in *A Natural History of Trees* as a place "where one can neither paddle a canoe or walk, nor even touch solid bottom with a ten foot pole." The tamarac, which is the only deciduous conifer in Minnesota, is common to poorly drained soils throughout the north, thriving as far as the Arctic Circle in everything from silted up beaver ponds to vast peat bogs. Carver Park however, is near the southern limit of the trees' range; here the soft, green tamaracs share the bog with green ash, willow, aspen, dogwood, and a great variety other plants adapted to the soggy habitat.

Clearly the most outstanding aspect of Carver Park Reserve is the profusion of wildlife that finds shelter within the park's diverse environs. One of North America's most magnificent birds, the trumpeter swan, has been successfully re-introduced to the park. Once eliminated from Minnesota and hunted nearly to extinction, this graceful giant is now a common sight at Carver. Similar efforts are being made to re-establish osprey, and a fortunate visitor may be treated to the spectacle of one of these fishhawks plunging talons-first into the water for a walleye dinner. The many lakes and wetlands are prime habitat for beaver, mink, muskrat, and otter, and support large populations of birds that nest or feed here, such as Canada goose, wood duck, ruddy duck, mallard, blue-winged teal, hooded merganser, double-crested cormorant, great blue heron, great egret, and green-backed heron, as well as least bittern, Virginia and sora rail, Forster's tern, and yellow-headed blackbird. The woods and fields are home to deer, red and grey fox, raccoon, striped and spotted skunk; badger; red, grey, fox, and flying squirrel, woodchuck, cottontail rabbit, and numerous species of owls, hawks, and woodpeckers. In addition, Carver Park contains one of the richest populations of songbirds in the Twin Cities area, including the dickcissel, meadowlark, bobolink, willow flycatcher, blue-gray gnatcatcher, sedge wren, northern oriole, scarlet tanager, veery, wood thrush, and bluebird; a careful observer may also see various warblers, sparrows, vireos, and more.

Facilities: Visitors should make the Lowry Nature Center their first stop. This partially earth-sheltered building contains exhibits, classrooms, offices, restrooms, and a bird feeding station. Park employees here can answer your questions and provide you with maps. An excellent network of well marked trails with observation decks and floating boardwalks radiates from the building, providing easy access to a wide variety of habitats. An additional 8 miles of paved trails for hiking and biking are accessible to the handicapped. Bicycles can be rented at the Nature Center. There are 6 miles of horseback riding trails with water and rest areas. In winter the park's trails are groomed for cross-country skiers and some are open to snowmobilers. Skis can be rented here. There is also a skating pond and a sliding hill. A waterfowl viewing blind overlooks a lovely expanse of wetlands in the Fred E. King Waterfowl Sanctuary. Four lakes with boat launches offer boating, canoeing, and fishing. There is a group camp and a large family campground, with sites for tents, trailers, and motor homes. The campground has tables, grills, toilets, and a swimming beach. Two separate picnic areas, a reserved group site and an open area, have ball fields, volleyball courts, horseshoe pits, and toilets.

How to get there: The park is sandwiched between State Highway 7 and State Highway 5. From Minneapolis take Highway 7 west for about 20 miles to County Road 11 and turn left. Nearly all of the parks facilities are reached from this road.

The Lowry Nature Center is open from 8:00 a.m. to 5:00 p.m. on weekdays and from 8:00 a.m. to sunset on weekends. Daily or annual permits are required for all cars entering a Hennepin County park.

Map key: West 23

For additional information:

Carver Park Reserve
7025 Victoria Drive
Excelsior, Minnesota 55331
(612) 472-4911

Hennepin Parks
12615 County Road 9
Plymouth, Minnesota 55411
(612) 559-9000

Central Park

Nestled into the suburban neighborhoods of south Blooming-ton is an appealing natural area known as Central Park. Though comprised of only 148 acres it encompasses an interesting variety of habitats and offers an unexpected sense of solitude. The park is long and narrow, bordering both sides of Nine Mile Creek as it winds its way to the Minnesota River. Elsewhere, Nine Mile Creek is a slowly meandering stream that flows through numerous lakes and broad marshes. However, within the park it enters a deep ravine that slices through the tall bluffs overlooking the Minnesota River Valley.

A well-marked trail follows the creek the full length of the park, gradually descending into the ravine and leading to the river bottoms. Along this trail you can see ample evidence of the continuing forces of erosion that have created the ravine over the centuries. In many places the ever-shifting stream has washed away portions of the trail, toppled decades-old trees, and exposed sections of the steep hillside by undercutting its base. Look also for the low, wet areas that are abandoned stretches of the creek bed. This process has been hastened by suburban development within the watershed drained by Nine Mile Creek. Historically the rain that fell was largely absorbed by the marshes, soils, and plants upstream and then slowly released, maintaining a relatively constant flow. However, today much of the rain runs quickly off buildings, parking lots, and streets, creating floodlike conditions during which most of the erosion occurs.

The topography of the park supports a number of distinct plant communities, as varying amounts of sunlight, wind, and water create what are called microclimates. The well watered area along the stream supports numerous trees, such as bass-wood, butternut, bur oak, elm, ash, boxelder, and hackberry, with a dense understory of smaller trees and shrubs, including mulberry, buckthorn, prickly-ash, red-osier dogwood, honey-suckle, black raspberry, and wild grape. The steep hillsides, which are well drained and not so thickly overgrown, are dominated by oaks with some aspen and black cherry.

A loop off the main trail leads through a cool, shaded side ravine where sugar maple and ironwood thrive and wildflowers, such as bloodroot, wild ginger, and trillium, carpet the ground in spring. A little farther along the trail is an open area atop the bluff that provides scenic views of the ravine. This is a natural opening known as a goat prairie. With slopes of 40 to 50 degrees facing southward, these prairies are natural solar collectors. The continual freezing and thawing cycle from night to day during the winter, and the steep slope's inability to retain moisture, makes it nearly impossible for woody plants to become established. Even the hardy sumac, red cedar, and bur oak that surround the goat prairie are unable to invade the opening. Instead, grasses and flowers commonly found on the prairies, such as the delicate pasque flower that blooms in early spring, prosper here amid the forest.

At the Minnesota River Bottoms the main trail connects the park to a part of the floodplain known as Welter's Wildwood. There are some very large cottonwoods and silver maples here, as well as black willow and green ash, that are able to survive the annual spring floods. The stream flows through this area and joins the Minnesota River at a point nine miles from the confluence with the Mississippi, hence the name, Nine Mile Creek.

Facilities: There are approximately 5 miles of well-marked trails, portions of which are used for cross-country skiing in winter. Benches are placed at scenic points along the bluff. The upstream part of the park connects with Moir Park (across the creek from City Hall) where there is a developed picnic area with two shelters, tables, grills, and restrooms. There is also a ball field, a volleyball court, and a nine "hole" frisbee golf course.

How to get there: From Minneapolis or Interstate Highway 494, take Interstate Highway 35W south. Exit at 106th Street and head west. Just past Humboldt Avenue the road crosses Nine Mile Creek and there is small parking lot on the left. You can pick up the trail here or continue to Morgan Avenue (the next intersection) and take a right. Proceed north a couple of blocks to the Moir Picnic Grounds.

Map key: West 24

For additional information:

Bloomington Park and Recreation
Department
2215 W. Old Shakopee Road
Bloomington, Minnesota 55431
(612) 887-9601

Cleary Lake Regional Park

Cleary Lake Regional Park is one of two sizable parks in Scott County operated by the Hennepin County Parks system through the Scott-Hennepin Park Advisory Board. Located a short distance southeast of Prior Lake, the 1,200-acre park offers visitors a wide selection of recreational activities. Most of the facilities are concentrated near the shores of scenic Cleary Lake, which covers 137 acres at the northern end of the area, while in the southern and western portions of the park there are undeveloped stretches of gently rolling hills to explore.

Open fields and small plantations of spruce and pine are still part of this once-farmed landscape, but the remainder is made up of mature forest, second-growth woodlands, scattered marshes, and small ponds. Broad-canopied oaks dominate the older woodlands where red oak, bur oak, white oak, and northern pin oak stand with basswood, black cherry, and bitternut hickory. Ironwood is particularly abundant here and some are quite large for the species. Red cedar, boxelder, groves of aspen, and other trees, including an abundance of flowering trees and shrubs favored by wildlife, such as serviceberry, choke-cherry, buckthorn, hawthorn, highbush cranberry, and elderberry, have reclaimed some of the old fields. Black willow, green ash, elm, and red-osier dogwood border the numerous cattail marshes and shallow ponds.

Such a patchwork of habitats always attracts plenty of wildlife. The ducks, wading birds, and songbirds are the most conspicuous inhabitants, but the park is also home to woodchucks, rabbits, squirrels, muskrats, chipmunks, gophers, shrews, mice, frogs, and the predators they attract: raccoons, foxes, hawks, and owls. A thriving herd of white-tailed deer also finds refuge in the park and winter visitors will see their well-worn trails everywhere.

Facilities: A paved trail for hiking and biking encircles Cleary Lake in a 3.5 mile loop. Multi-speed bikes, tandem bikes, and toddler seats may be rented. Hikers can explore the rest of the park on mowed trails. In winter more than 9 miles of trails are groomed for skiers. Part of the park is open to exploration by snowshoe and both skis and snowshoes can be rented at the recreation center/snackbar. A nice picnic area is situated by the lake with tables, grills, toilets, and water. A pavilion is available for rent, as are supplies for volleyball, horseshoes, and shuffleboard. A sandy swimming beach on Cleary Lake has lifeguards from Memorial Day to Labor Day. There is also a boat launch for nonmotorized boats, and canoes, rowboats, and paddleboats may be rented. A few separate camping areas can be reserved by groups, including one on a island in Cleary Lake. Lastly, the park has a 9-hole, executive length golf course with a full range of services: leagues, lessons, club and cart rentals, and a clubhouse.

How to get there: From Minneapolis or Interstate Highway 494 take Interstate Highway 35W south. About 4 miles after crossing the Minnesota River, exit onto County Road 42 and head west. Stay on 42 for about 3.5 miles and turn south onto County Road 27. Go south on 27 for another 4 miles or so and look for the park entrance on the right.

The park buildings are open from 7:30 a.m. to 8:00 p.m. on weekdays and from 7:00 a.m. to 8:30 p.m. on weekends. The beaches open daily at 10:00 a.m. There is a nominal daily or annual fee for parking.

Map key: West 25

For additional information:

Cleary Lake Regional Park
18106 Texas Avenue
Prior Lake, Minnesota 55372
(612) 447-2171

Hennepin Parks
12615 County Road 9
Plymouth, Minneosta 55411
(612) 559-9000

Clifton E. French Regional Park

At the north end of Medicine Lake in suburban Plymouth is Clifton E. French Regional Park. Although this 362-acre park is used primarily for recreational activities, it does have some good natural qualities. A long winding inlet of the 900-acre lake, rimmed with cattail marsh, bisects the park. The wetlands act as a valuable nursery for fish throughout the lake and support a variety of other wildlife. Beaver, muskrat, mink, and turtle live here, while birds such as great egret, black-crowned night heron, belted kingfisher, Canada goose, wood duck, mallard, least bittern, red-winged blackbird, and spotted sandpiper nest or feed in the area. The remainder of the park consists of rolling terrain with some mature woods and extensive open areas gradually reverting to woodland. White-tailed deer, red fox, woodchuck, cottontail rabbit, great-horned owl, and red-tailed hawk may be encountered here.

Facilities: There is a network of cross-country ski trails, which is mowed for hikers in the off season. This well developed park offers a number of other diversions. There is a nice swimming beach with benches, restrooms, dressing rooms, and a snack-bar. Also by the lake is a boat launch, volleyball courts, and a picnic area with tables and grills. Park visitors can rent bicycles, rowboats, canoes, aquabikes, cane fishing poles, and in winter, cross-country skis. In winter there is skating on the frozen lake and sledding on a steep hillside.

How to get there: The park is located on County Road 9 (Rockford Road) less than one mile east of Interstate Highway 494 and about 2 miles west of County Highway 18.

The beach, snack-bar, and rentals are open from 10:00 a.m. to 8:30 p.m. from Memorial Day to Labor Day. During the winter, ski trails and rental are open daily from 8:00 a.m. to sunset. There is a nominal fee for parking that can be paid on a daily or annual basis.

Map key: West 26

For additional information:

Clifton E. French Regional Park
12615 County Rod 9
Plymouth, Minnesota 55441
(612) 559-9000

Collinwood County Park

Extending for a mile along the eastern shoreline of 637-acre Collinwood Lake, this Wright County park offers a variety of outdoor activities for the entire family. The recreational facilities are located by the lake at the northern end of the 308-acre park, leaving lots of undeveloped space to the south where trails wind through a mixture of woods, fields, and wetlands. While abandoned fields and second-growth forests make up most of the gently rolling uplands, a lovely band of mature woodlands occupies the steeper hills bordering the lake. In the park's southern reaches, the trail leads past a marshy bay of Collinwood Lake and smaller cattail-rimmed Chelgren Lake. Muskrats, painted turtles, and leopard frogs inhabit the wetlands and great egrets and great blue herons come to fish the shallow waters.

Facilities: Over 3 miles of trails are mowed for hikers and groomed for cross-country skiers. Benches have been placed along the trail in scenic spots overlooking the broad lake. A stationary map is located by the parking lot and a few more at trail junctions. Also overlooking the lake is a picnic area with a shelter, tables, grills, water, and toilets. There are modern camping facilities with electricity and showers. In addition, there is a guarded swimming beach, a creative play area, and a boat launch. Fees are charged for use of the camping facilities, the picnic shelter, and the boat launch. The park has a full-time resident manager.

How to get there: From Minneapolis take U.S. Highway 12 west through Hennepin County and most of Wright County. About 2.5 miles west of the intersection with County Highway 3 in Cokato, turn left (south) onto dirt road. Proceed for 2 miles, crossing County Highway 31, to park entrance.

Map key: West 27

For additional information:

Wright County Parks Department
Route 1, Box 97B
Buffalo, Minnesota 55313
(612) 682-3900, ext. 182
339-6881 (Metro)
1-800-362-3667, ext. 182 (Toll Free)

Coon Lake Park

Embracing 2,000 feet of shoreline on the largest lake in Anoka County, Coon Lake Park offers a variety of outdoor activities within its 125 acres. The small park is divided by the South Branch of the Sunrise River, which flows out of the lake here. In addition, visitors will find woodlands, planted red and white pines, open fields, small ponds, cattail marsh, and tamarac bog.

Facilities: There is a short hiking trail but the county is planning to develop a more extensive nature trail with boardwalks to provide a close-up look at the marshes and tamarac bog. A portion of the shoreline has been developed into a swimming beach with a bathhouse and restrooms, and a boat launch area with parking. Several picnic areas are scattered about with shelters, tables, grills, and drinking water. There are also ball fields and playground equipment.

How to get there: Heading north through Anoka County on State Highway 65, turn right onto County Highway 22 (18 miles north of Interstate Highway 694). Follow Highway 22 east about 5 miles and turn right onto County Highway 17. Stay on 17 as it bends twice to the right and then look for the park entrance on the right.

Map key: East 28

For additional information:

Anoka County Parks and
Recreation
550 Bunker Lake Blvd.
Anoka, Minnesota 55304
(612) 757-3920

Coon Rapids Dam Regional Park

Located less than 10 miles upstream from Minneapolis, Coon Rapids Dam Regional Park consists of 360 scenic acres on both sides of the Mississippi River. The centerpiece of the park is the 1,000-foot dam that was built in 1914 and generated power for the area until 1965. A handicapped accessible walkway across the dam connects the Hennepin and Anoka County sections of the park and provides an excellent view of the river. Visitors to the area can choose from a wide range of recreational activities or simply explore the natural environment of bottom-land forest, oak woods, oak savanna, prairie, and old fields.

Early this century the little town of Coon Creek was situated in what is now the park and, during the construction of the dam, as many as 1,000 men worked here. Today the 40 buildings that made up the town are gone and nature has reclaimed the land, but a close look will reveal evidence of the area's history. Here and there you can find a number of familiar plants, such as spruce and white pine, lilac, purple iris, and day lilies, that are commonly grown in our urban environments. These and others are not native to the park but are living reminders of its more civilized past.

The Anoka County side of the park also contains restored areas of dry sand prairie and oak savanna. These are hemmed in by a woodland comprised primarily of red, white, and bur oak, as well as aspen and a number of smaller trees and shrubs favored by the local wildlife, such as buckthorn, prickly-ash, hazelnut, red-berried elder, honeysuckle, chokecherry, and wild grape. In contrast, the flood-prone areas along the river and the numerous islands are cloaked with water-tolerant hardwoods, including cottonwood, silver maple, and boxelder.

Many animals live along the banks of the river and in the park's varied upland environs, Deer, red fox, raccoon, woodchuck, weasel, and rabbit, as well as gray, red, and fox squirrels live here. Mink, muskrat, beaver, and otter inhabit the river, along with painted, snapping, and softshell turtles. Great horned owl, pileated woodpecker, kingfisher, Canada goose, mallard, and wood duck are among the birds that nest in the park. Spring and fall migrations bring a great many other birds through the area, including bufflehead, common goldeneye, blue and green-winged teal, common merganser, and osprey.

Many visitors to the park come to fish the waters of the Mississippi River, which can be done from the shore, one of three platform decks, or boats. Catfish, walleye, northern, smallmouth bass, and crappie are plentiful. Exotics such as eels, silvery drum, and carp are caught as well. The park also hosts an annual Carp Festival in June, a day of games, activities, and a carp fishing contest.

Anoka County has more recently acquired and developed an additional 250 acres or so along the east side of the river between the Hennepin County park and the new North Crosstown Highway Bridge. This area includes woodlands, old fields, the final stretch of meandering Coon Creek, and a manmade lake.

Across West River Road from the park, in Brooklyn Center, a city-owned Natural Environment Area contains shallow ponds and marshes, old fields, shrubby thickets, and groves of young trees. A short trail leads from the parking lot past the watery habitats where you can see ample evidence of beaver activity. A quiet and patient observer may well see a beaver here.

Facilities: Visitors should make their first stop at the Visitor Center which includes live animal exhibits, an aquarium displaying native fish, an observation deck, offices, and restrooms. There are 3 main trails, including an interpretive trail, which total 4.5 miles and traverse all habitats within the park on both sides of the river. The trails are groomed for cross-country skiers in the winter and you can rent skis and snowshoes. There are picnic tables near the river and a large picnic shelter, which must be reserved. There is a campsite for bicyclists and a separate primitive site for canoeists. The park also includes a fishing deck and a boat launch. Canoes may be rented at the visitors center.

The park is the eastern trailhead for the 7.2 mile North Hennepin Corridor Trail which is used for hiking, biking, and horseback riding. The trail connects Coon Rapids Dam Regional Park with the huge Elm Creek Park Reserve. The newer Anoka County expansion to the south has, or will soon have, hiking and cross-country skiing trails, a paved bike trail, 2 separate picnic areas, game fields, a boat launch, a riverbank overlook, fishing docks on the river and the trout pond, restrooms, and a parkway.

How to get there: The park can be reached from either side of the river. In Anoka County take East River Road north from Interstate Highway 694. Just after merging with Coon Rapids Boulevard take a left on Egret Boulevard, which leads to the park. In Hennepin County take West River Road north from 694 until you see a sign for the park.

The park is open daily from 5:00 a.m. to 11:00 p.m. The Visitors Center is open from 8:00 a.m. to 9:00 p.m. during the summer and from 9:00 a.m. to 5:00 p.m. during the winter. From May to September 24-hour, walk-in fishing is allowed.

Map key: West 29

For additional information:

Coon Rapids Dam Regional Park
9750 Egret Boulevard
Coon Rapids, Minnesota 55433
(612) 757-4700

Anoka County Parks and
Recreation
550 Bunker Lake Blvd.
Anoka, Minnesota 55304
(612) 757-3920

Hennepin Parks
12615 County Road 9
Plymouth, Minnesota 55411
(612) 559-9000

Cottage Grove Ravine Regional Park

Cottage Grove Ravine Regional Park, formerly known as South Washington County Park, is situated near the Mississippi River about eight miles southeast of St. Paul. The park includes 300 acres of moraine hills split down the middle by a ravine that drains into a 25-acre lake. The most rugged areas, particularly the steep slopes along the ravine, support mature woodlands, while the more gently rolling areas exhibit various stages of natural succession as the park recovers from its previous use as grazing land for livestock.

At the northern end of the park the trails lead through a mixture of old fields and plantations of spruce and pine. Although the fields are still open, one can observe the encroachment of sumac, boxelder, choke cherry, and red cedar. These trees enjoy the sunlight and are often among the first to invade trees enjoy the sunlight and are often among the first to invade once grazing has ceased. Red cedar, commonly found in old fields and poor soils throughout the eastern half of the country, supplied the world with pencil wood for nearly a century.

Much of the park is characterized by scattered oaks standing above a virtually impenetrable thicket of saplings and shrubs, such as hackberry, buckthorn, mulberry, honeysuckle, hazelnut, elderberry, prickly-ash, gooseberry, blackberry, raspberry, and wild grape. These plants provide wildlife with an abundant source of food during the summer months. The hills at the center of the park are cloaked by an older forest dominated by large bur oak and red oak, as well as ironwood, paper birch, aspen, elm, and some basswood.

Facilities: More than 5 miles of wide trails for hiking and cross-country skiing explore the park. There is a large stationary map by the parking lot and smaller ones where trails intersect. A developed picnic area near the lake includes tables, grills, a shelter with fireplace and restrooms, drinking water, and a creative play area.

How to get there: Take U.S. Highway 61 south from St. Paul or Interstate Highway 494. Exit at County Road 19 and take the frontage road east to the park entrance. There is a nominal daily or annual fee for parking.

Map key: East 30

For additional information:

Washington County Parks
Department
11660 Myeron Road North
Stillwater, Minnesota 55082
(612) 731-3851

Cranberry Wildlife Management Area

The Cranberry Wildlife Management Area is a 355-acre tract of wetlands and woods adjacent to mile-long Lory Lake at the northern edge of Isanti County. As the name suggests, the site was formerly occupied by a commercial cranberry operation. At that time a system of dikes was constructed, converting much of the area's wetlands into large shallow pools in which the water level could be precisely controlled. The pools have since been restored to wetlands and today the dikes are used to control the water level for the benefit of wildlife. Informal trails along the dikes allow visitors to penetrate the marsh and provide good vantage points for observing its inhabitants.

Broad stretches of cattails, interspersed with waterlilies and open water, are bordered by thickets of willow, alder, and dogwood, as well as small groves of aspen and a variety of other trees, such as paper birch, ash, and elm. Mallard, blue-winged teal, coot, and ring-necked duck make their nests here, and a pair of common loons regularly raise their young on Lory Lake. Patient observers may also see muskrat, mink, and beaver.

A mixture of young woods and grassy openings occupies the land east of the marsh. This area was almost entirely logged a few years ago in order to improve the habitat for game species, such as deer, pheasant, and ruffed grouse, which enjoy the new growth and dense cover.

In comparison, there is a small, and particularly attractive, parcel of mature forest at the north end of Lory Lake. Tall red oak, white oak, and white pine form a lofty canopy here. However, the dominance of smaller sugar maples in the understory, along with some basswood and ironwood, is evidence that the oaks, though impressive, are only a stage in the forest's development. Bitternut hickory, blue beech, yellow birch, and alternate-leaf dogwood enhance the diversity of the wood, while both quaking and big-toothed aspen prosper around its edges.

Facilities: There are no developed facilities here except for designated parking areas. State Wildlife Management Areas are managed for three primary reasons: wildlife production, public hunting, and trapping. Other activities, such as hiking, birding, and berry-picking are also encouraged but should probably be avoided during the hunting season.

How to get there: From Cambridge, take State Highway 95 west. About 4.5 miles past the Rum River, veer right (north) onto County Highway 1. After 6.5 miles this becomes County Road 63. Following 63, go north one mile, west a half mile, north one mile, east a half mile, and north again for one mile. At the intersection with County Highway 4, take a left. After less than a mile, take a right (north). Cranberry WMA is to the left, look for a dirt access road to the parking area. To reach the north side continue to the next intersection and take a left. South of this road is another dirt access road and (slightly farther) a small pull-off parking area by the mature wood.

Map key: East 31

For additional information:

Department of Natural Resources
Area Wildlife Manager
915 South Highway 65
Cambridge, Minnesota 55008
(612) 689-2832

Minnesota Department of Natural Resources
Section of Wildlife, Box 7
500 Lafayette Road
St. Paul, Minnesota 55155
(612) 296-3344

Crosby Farm Nature Area

Minutes from downtown St. Paul, the Crosby Farm Nature Area occupies a few hundred acres of bluffs and bottomlands across from Fort Snelling at the confluence of the Mississippi and Minnesota Rivers. Portions of the area were still being farmed as recently as the 1950s, but today small plantations of spruce and pine are all that remain. Although subject to a variety of external influences, such as overhead air traffic, Interstate Highway 35E, and river barge traffic, the park is an oasis of natural habitats amid an urban landscape.

The steep valley wall that separates the park from the busy city above is cloaked by a mixed broadleaf woodland and punctuated by rocky outcroppings. A combination of urban run-off and groundwater seepage at the base of the escarpment flows into marshy Upper Pond and the larger Crosby Lake. Upper Pond and its soggy fringes are thick with duckweed, arrowhead, bulrush, cattail, sedge, Joe-Pye weed, water hemlock, and wild iris, and surrounded by willow, speckled alder, skunk currant, and red-osier dogwood. Upper Pond drains into Crosby Lake, which is generally open except for an abundance of white and yellow waterlily.

Nearer the river, the rest of the area is comprised of bottomland hardwoods dotted with several marshy openings. Cottonwood and silver maple dominate, along with black willow, green ash, American elm, and boxelder. Green-headed coneflowers, stinging nettles, tall bellflower, germander, river grape, and bur cucumber thrive in the spacious understory. A number of immense cottonwood trees can be seen along the paved trail that winds through the floodplain.

White-tailed deer are plentiful here, as they are throughout the river valleys. Red fox, striped skunk, raccoon, woodchuck, cottontail rabbit, white-footed deer mouse, and northern water shrew also inhabit the park. Muskrat, mink, snapping turtle, smooth softshell turtle, and pickerel frog live in the pond and lake where herons and egrets come to fish. Among the many birds that one might see here are wood duck, screech owl, ruby-throated hummingbird, belted kingfisher, tree swallow, swamp sparrow, catbird, goldfinch, and Brewer's blackbird. In springtime, the Nature Area is a good place to look for migrating warblers.

Facilities: More than 8 miles of trails wind through the park. The main trail is a 2.2 mile length of wide blacktop for hiking and biking that traverses the park and connects with the trail in Hidden Falls Park. A long section of boardwalk leads across the marsh to an observation deck on Upper Pond. A variety of other trails, ranging from gravel to woodchip to dirt, explore other areas, including one that follows along the face of the bluff. Some of these trails are groomed for cross-country skiing in winter. There is also a picnic area with mowed fields, a stone shelter with a firepit, and satellite toilets.

How to get there: The park is located in the southwest corner of St. Paul. The entrance to the area is at the intersection of Gannon and Shepard Roads just east of State Highway 5. If you follow Mississippi River Blvd. south, the entrance will be on your right just after passing over Highway 5. There is an overlook at this turnoff that offers an excellent view of Fort Snelling and the Mendota Bridge. Follow this small road down the hill and past a marina until it dead-ends at the Nature Area's parking lot.

Map key: East 32

For additional information:

St. Paul Park and Recreation
300 City Hall Annex
25 West 4th Street
St. Paul, Minnesota 55102
(612) 292-7400

Crow-Hassan Park Reserve

Situated in northwestern Hennepin County, the Crow-Hassan Park Reserve encompasses 2,600 acres along a seven-mile stretch of the meandering Crow River. About half of the reserve is gently undulating with wet basins separated by low knolls and ridges. The rest, which overlies the Dayton Outwash Plain, is comprised of elevated flats of sandy alluvium punctuated by smaller marshy depressions with short, steep slopes.

Once covered by hardwood forests with prairie openings on the sandiest soils, the park is made up largely of reclaimed farmland. The recovering landscape is a mixture of mature woodlands, second-growth forests, old fields, pine plantations, restored prairie, small lakes, and marshes.

87

Perhaps the most interesting feature here is the 600 acre expanse of old fields that has been planted with a variety of native prairie grasses. Recreating a prairie from scratch, even a small one, is a painstaking task that requires years of effort. Even then it is virtually impossible to match the complexity and richness of species contained in an undisturbed prairie. But that is not the intent at Crow-Hassan. Instead, the goal has been to reproduce something of the scale of the original prairie. The first plants to be introduced were the dominant grass species of the tallgrass prairie. Big bluestem, little bluestem, Indian grass, sideoats grama, switch grass, and prairie dropseed shelter a scattering of native wildflowers. By late summer, some of these "warm season" grasses attain heights of up to eight feet and visitors may view entire hillsides billowing in the wind.

The old fields not converted to prairie are reverting to woodlands without any help. Advancing thickets of shrubs and small trees, including sumac, prickly-ash, red cedar, wild plum, and aspen, represent the early stages of succession.

White-tailed deer, coyote, red and gray fox, badger, and striped skunk are just a few of the mammals that live here. Muskrat and mink find the ponds and marshes to their liking and otters are occasionally seen along the river. Crow-Hassan is one of the areas where the elegant trumpeter swan has been re-introduced. A wide variety of other waterfowl, raptors, woodpeckers, and songbirds inhabit the diverse environs of the park and make it an excellent site for birdwatching.

Facilities: This sizable park lacks the variety of recreational facilities available at most of the Hennepin County Parks. There is an extensive network of trails and old roads for hiking (11.7 miles), cross-country skiing (10.9 miles), snowmobiling (5 miles), and horseback riding. Two group camps near the river are available by reservation. Fishing is allowed from along the banks of the Crow River.

How to get there: Take Interstate Highway 94 northwest from the Twin Cities, then take the exit for State Highway 101 north towards Elk River. After one mile turn left onto County Road 144 (141st Avenue North). Stay on this road, crossing back over 94, until it ends at County Road 116 (Territorial Road). Turn left here and then take a right after about a half a mile onto County Road 203 (Sylvan Lake Road). Follow this road as it bends to the left and look for signs. The park entrance will be on the right. There is a nominal daily or annual fee for entry to the park.

Map key: West 33

For additional information:

Hennepin Parks
12615 County Road 9
Plymouth, Minnesota 55411
(612) 559-9000

Crystal Lake Park West

This small municipal park protects a band of wooded hills squeezed between Interstate Highway 35 and the largest lake in Burnsville. Its 56 acres wrap around a scenic bay of Crystal Lake rimmed by tall cottonwood trees and pockets of cattail and waterlily. Red oak, bur oak, and basswood, with some ash, paper birch, and small aspen groves cover the steep hillside that borders the lake.

Facilities: An informal trail winds along the shoreline from the parking lot. An intersecting path leads through the woods along the hilltop. A boat launch provides access to the lake and a few picnic tables have been placed nearby.

How to get there: The park is located on the south side of Crystal Lake Road just east of Interstate Highway 35 in Southern Burnsville.

Map key: East 34

For additional information:

Burnsville Department of Parks
and Recreation
1313 East Highway 13
Burnsville, Minnesota 55337
(612) 431-7575

Cylon Wildlife Management Area

The Cylon Wildlife Management Area includes more than 2,000 acres of rich habitats in the northeastern corner of Wisconsin's St. Croix County. Surrounded by rolling farmland, the preserve occupies a low-lying area split by a branch of the Willow River. Although the tract is undeveloped and used primarily by hunters, it is a haven to many nongame species and offers good opportunities for viewing wildlife to those who like to get off the beaten path.

Roughly half of the area is composed of a variety of wetland communities, ranging from small cattail marshes to tamarac swamp. Most of the watery habitat, however, has been created by beavers, whose stick-and-mud dams have drowned a few hundred acres of lowland meadows and woods. Rimmed with willow, alder, red-osier dogwood, sedges, and stands of aspen and silver maple, these shallow ponds are a magnet for waterfowl and other animals. Mature forest, second-growth woodlands, and a few abandoned fields make up the rest of the area. The driest soils are dominated by oaks – red oak, bur oak, and pin oak – mixed with aspen, black cherry, paper birch, basswood, and ironwood, while moist soils support red maple, elm, boxelder, aspen, and scattered stands of large white pine.

The varied landscape here sustains a profusion of wildlife. Beaver are plentiful and share the wetlands, ponds, and Willow River with muskrat, mink, and an occasional river otter, as well as Canada goose, mallard, blue and green-winged teal, wood duck, and hooded merganser. Sandhill cranes, great blue herons, and great egrets are drawn here from nearby nesting areas. The uplands are home to white-tailed deer, coyote, badger, red fox, striped skunk, raccoon, woodchuck, snowshoe hare, and flying squirrel. In recent years an increasing number of black bears have been seen in and around the preserve. Among the many other resident birds are kingfisher, ruffed grouse, pheasant, woodcock, pileated woodpecker, American redstart, yellow warbler, and numerous birds of prey, such as red-tailed hawk, sharp-shinned hawk, Cooper's hawk, barred owl, and great horned owl.

Facilities: There are no facilities here other than a parking lot. A couple of dirt roads penetrate a short distance into the preserve. Long-term plans call for the development of a trail system. In the meantime, some informal tails wind through the area.

How to get there: From the Twin Cities head east into Wisconsin on Interstate Highway 94. About 19 miles past the St. Croix River take the Baldwin exit and drive north on U.S. Highway 63. After almost 12 miles Highway 63 turns east, but continue straight for another 3 miles and turn right (east) onto 222nd Avenue. You can reach the preserve by turning right after 2 miles onto 230th Street, or continue another mile and turn right onto 240th Street (formerly Swamp Road).

Map key: East 35

For additional information:

Area Wildlife Manager
Department of Natural Resources
Box 61
Baldwin, Wisconsin 54002
(715) 684-2914

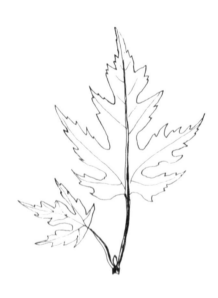

Dalbo Wildlife Management Area

The Dalbo Wildlife Management Area occupies 1,314 acres of undeveloped wildlands in the remote northwestern corner of Isanti County. Situated where the farmlands of central Minnesota blend with the forests of the northeast, the preserve provides a valuable refuge for a surprising variety of birds and mammals. There are no facilities and the area is managed primarily for hunting, but visitors who don't mind the lack of maps and trails can explore the preserve by foot, small boat, or snowshoe.

The landscape at Dalbo is made up primarily of broad expanses of watery flatlands broken up by small upland ridges. Krone Lake occupies about 100 acres in the northeastern corner of the preserve. This shallow lake is rimmed with stretches of wild rice and cattail which merge into a rich mosaic of different wetland communities to the south and west. Throughout the lowlands, dense growths of cattail are interspersed with thickets of willow, alder, and dogwood, patches of sedge meadow, swampy woodlands of paper birch, quaking aspen, and elm, scattered stands of tamarac, and small pools of open water.

Farther west, the wetlands are bordered by rock-strewn uplands that are a combination of mixed woodlands, old fields, and food plots. A portion of the woods here were cut down and the wood sold to encourage the new growth and thickets favored by many game species. Some tall basswood, red oak, and white oak remain alongside bur oak, bitternut hickory, red maple, ironwood, an abundance of aspen and birch, and thickets of sumac, raspberry, gray dogwood, and prickly-ash. A few of the steep-sided ridges stand alone as tree-covered islands in the marsh where the mature woodland has not been so disturbed.

The diverse wetlands supply ample food and shelter for waterfowl and other wildlife. Hooded merganser, wood duck, blue-winged teal, mallard, coot, American bittern, and sora rail raise their young here, while Canada goose, great blue heron, and great egret use the area throughout the summer and fall. Recently, osprey have been regular sights at Dalbo and may well be nesting here. The preserve is heavily used during migration when whistling swans and many other species stop over on their way north and south. Large numbers of muskrat share the lake and marshes with some beaver and mink, as well as an occasional otter. After freeze-up the lowland swamps and thickets become an important wintering area for a sizable population of white-tailed deer. Although seldom seen, coyote inhabit the area and every now and then a black bear wanders this far south.

Facilities: There are no developed facilities except for designated parking areas. A few informal trails do wind through the woods near the southwestern parking lot. Much of the preserve is inaccessible during wet years but can be more extensively explored during dry periods or wintertime. No motors are allowed on Krone Lake and only those willing to haul a small boat or canoe through the cattails can get a close look at the wildlife here. State Wildlife Management Areas are managed for three primary reasons: wildlife production, public hunting, and trapping. Other activities are encouraged but should probably be avoided during the hunting season.

How to get there: From the Twin Cities, take State Highway 65 (Central Avenue) north about 35 miles from Interstate Highway 694 to Cambridge. At Cambridge, turn left onto State Highway 95 and go west for about 9 miles to State Highway 47. Turn right onto 47 and follow it for 5 miles north, one mile west, and another 2.5 miles north to County Highway 16. Turn left onto 16 and go one mile to the junction with County Road 44. To reach the parking area near Krone Lake turn right onto 44 and look for the turnoff on the left where the road bends to the right. To reach the upland parking area continue west on 16 for a little more than 2 miles as it turns right and then bends left. Look for the turn-off on the right just past the bend.

Map key: East 36

For additional information:

Department of Natural Resources
Area Wildlife Manager
915 South Highway 65
Cambridge, Minnesota 55008
(612) 689-2832

Minnesota Department of Natural Resources
Section of Wildlife, Box 7
500 Lafayette Road
St. Paul, Minnesota 55155
(612) 296-3344

Dodge Nature Center

The Thomas Irvine Dodge Nature Center consists of three nearly contiguous tracts of land in West St. Paul, Mendota Heights, and Sunfish Lake. Envisioned as a place where children could experience and learn about nature, the center was established in 1967 when several truck farms were acquired and converted into a nature preserve. Over the years the center has grown to 350 acres while the surrounding farmland has been converted into suburban neighborhoods and shopping centers.

From plowed fields and grazed pastures, the landscape has become a rich patchwork of natural habitats that serve as an outdoor classroom for thousands of students every year. There are mature forests, second-growth woodlands, restored prairies, open meadows, small ponds, scattered wetlands, and flowing streams. Cultivated fields, gardens, pastures, and an orchard are also maintained and incorporated into the teaching process.

These environments provide a valuable sanctuary for an abundance of small mammals, birds, reptiles, amphibians, and insects. Approximately 200 different species of birds have been seen within the boundaries of the Nature Center, about a third of which are known to nest here, including the wood duck, sharp-shinned hawk, woodcock, black-billed cuckoo, screech owl, chimney swift, eastern bluebird, cedar waxwing, ovenbird, and bobolink.

Facilities: Among the most advanced Nature Centers in the country, the Dodge nature Center offers an outstanding array of facilities and programs. A converted farmhouse serves as the main office and contains offices, library, volunteer room, meeting room, and a greenhouse. A schoolhouse has a classroom, workshop, restrooms, and offices. A small museum consists of exhibits, a classroom, a gift shop, and a laboratory with small live animals. There is a model farm with a barn, pasture area for domestic animals, and pens for waterfowl, poultry, and raptors. There is also a beekeeping demonstration shed, a maple syrup evaporation room, and an operating weather station. The trail system leads through the various habitats and includes a boardwalk, floating platform, and a photo blind.

How to get there: From Minneapolis, cross the Minnesota River on the Mendota Bridge and head east on State Highway 110. From St. Paul, cross the Mississippi River on Interstate Highway 35E, and exit onto State Highway 110 heading east. Almost 2 miles east of Interstate 35E, turn left (north) onto Charlton Street (County Road 67). The main entrance is on the left side of the road a short distance past Marie Avenue.

The Nature Center and trails are open to the general public without fees or reservations only 2 days a month – the 2nd Saturday and the 3rd Sunday from noon to 5:00. Groups may visit at other times but there is a small fee and reservations must be made at least 2 weeks in advance.

Map key: East 37

For additional information:

Dodge Nature Center
1795 Charlton Street
West St. Paul, MN 55118
(612) 455-4531

East Twin Lakes County Park

At the western edge of Anoka County, this small park consists of 63 acres with 2,000 feet of frontage on East Twin Lake. Most of the park away from the lake is made up of open fields in which the county intends to plant evergreens, create a few small ponds, and develop additional trails and other facilities. There is a belt of woodlands along the lakeshore where a few big old red oaks and pin oaks stand above a mixture of other trees and some attractive groves of paper birch and quaking aspen.

Facilities: A short footpath winds about the property. Plans call for the construction of a wildlife viewing platform at the edge of the lake. There are a few separate picnic areas with shelters, tables, grills, water, and toilets. A sandy swimming beach with a bathhouse is located near the picnic areas. East Twin Lake is considered an excellent fishing lake and there is boat launch here.

How to get there: From the City of Anoka, head north on State Highway 47. About 2 miles north of U.S. Highway 10, turn left onto County Highway 5. Stay on 5 for about 8 miles, then turn left onto County Highway 22. Stay on this road for almost 2 miles, continuing straight on County Road 65 when 22 turns to the left, and look for the park entrance on the right. If you cross the county line you have gone too far.

Map key: West 38

For additional information:

Anoka County Parks and
Recreation
550 Bunker Lake Blvd.
Anoka, Minnesota 55304
(612) 757-3920

Elm Creek Park Reserve

Sprawling over more than 5,000 acres of gently rolling terrain north of Osseo, the Elm Creek Park Reserve is the largest unit of the remarkable Hennepin County Park System. Like other park "reserves," Elm Creek is managed according to the "80/20" land-use policy. This policy calls for at least 80 percent of the park reserve land to be returned to and maintained in its natural state. As much as 20 percent may be developed for recreational purposes compatible with the natural environment.

Although a little more than half of the park is comprised of formerly cultivated farmlands, the remainder is a richly varied composite of lakes, wetlands, and woods, split by three major streams which together drain close to a third of the county. The park takes its name from Elm Creek, which meanders northward through the heart of the area. It is joined by the waters of Rush Creek, then Diamond Creek, as it flows toward the nearby Mississippi River. The courses of both Elm Creek and Rush Creek are shaded by a typical floodplain forest dominated by tall silver maple and cottonwood, with green ash and boxelder. Near the confluence of these two creeks is a tree-top rookery where great blue herons nest alongside great egrets and black-crowned night herons.

Protected by a long extension of the park, Diamond Creek flows in from the northwest and merges with Elm Creek in the waters of Hayden Lake, the largest of five lakes scattered about the preserve. Each of the lakes occupies a shallow basin rimmed with wetlands that attract a good deal of wildlife. Hayden Lake is surrounded by broad stretches of cattail marsh, sedge meadow, thickets of willow and dogwood, and small stands of tamarac. The lakes, wetlands, and streams here are inhabited by muskrat, mink, a growing number of beaver, an occasional river otter, and a host of birds, such as Canada goose, wood duck, ruddy duck, canvasback, redhead, blue-winged teal, green-backed heron, sora rail, black tern, willow flycatcher, sedge wren, and common yellowthroat.

Although most of the park's uplands were farmed, some parcels of mature woodlands remain, including a fine tract known as Taylor's Woods. These old stands of sugar maple, basswood, red oak, ironwood, bitternut hickory, and white ash offer a glimpse at the forest the early settlers had to clear, an acre at a time, to plant their crops. The forest is now reclaiming many of the old fields but the process is slow. These areas are characterized by thickets of sumac, raspberry, prickly-ash, choke-cherry, red cedar, hawthorne, wild grape, and stands of quaking aspen, which are followed by boxelder, elm, ash, and oak. The park has begun a fascinating project to illustrate this process of succession. At intervals of five years, adjoining plots of old field grasslands one hundred feet by one hundred feet will be allowed to "go wild." In the future, visitors will be able to take a short walk through the history of a forest.

While some animals prefer either forest or open meadows, many others prosper where these habitats overlap and intermingle. The combination of mature forest, young woodlands, dense thickets, and grasslands provides an abundance of food and shelter for an increasing wildlife population. The abandoned woodlots and farmlands at Elm Creek are home to white-tailed deer, coyote, badger, red fox, raccoon, striped skunk, woodchuck, cottontail rabbit, fox squirrel, thirteen-lined ground squirrel, chipmunk, pocket gopher, and white-footed mouse. Among the birds that live here are red-tailed hawk, great horned owl, barred owl, pileated woodpecker, red-bellied woodpecker, tree swallow, rose-breasted grosbeak, eastern wood pewee, great-crested flycatcher, clay-colored sparrow, bobolink, eastern meadowlark, ring-necked pheasant, and bluebird.

The park also contains an area of historical significance. On a sizable hogback ridge at the northeast corner of the park is an assembly of Indian burial mounds that may soon form the basis of a historical and cultural interpretive center.

Facilities: Visitors should make their first stop at the Eastman Nature Center. This excellent facility contains exhibits, classrooms, offices, and restrooms, as well as an herb garden and a pond study area. Park employees here can answer your questions and provide you with maps. A network of well-marked nature trails radiates from the building and winds through a variety of habitats. Altogether there are 14.5 miles of hiking trails, including 9.1 miles of paved trails for biking and hiking. Horseback riders will find many miles of quiet trails running the length of the park. In winter the nature trails and bike trail are open to snowshoeing and there are 11 miles of snowmobiling trails. Skis can be rented here to use on nearly 10 miles of groomed trails. There is also a lighted skating pond and a sliding hill. The trailhead building offers maps, a snackbar, a small shop. In summer you can rent bikes, volleyball and horseshoe equipment, and picnic kits. Next to the building is a Game Fitness Court donated by the Metropolitan Medical Center. The recreation area just up the road from the trailhead building has a large picnic area with tables, grills, water, restrooms, volleyball, and horseshoes; four separate group picnic sites with shelters available by reservation; a sandy swimming beach on a 4-acre man-made pond with lifeguards and changing room; and a creative play area. Two separate group camps are available by reservation.

How to get there: From the Twin Cities, head northwest on Interstate Highway 94 or west on Interstate Highway 694. About 4 miles west of where 94 and 694 merge next to the Mississippi River, exit onto U.S. Highway 169 (State Highway 152) going north. Stay on 169 for about 5 miles, then turn right onto Territorial Road. To get to the trailhead building or recreation area, take the first right. To get to the Nature Center, take the second right onto County Road 121 and another right a mile later onto Elm Creek Road.

The Eastman Nature Center is open from 9:00 a.m. to 8:00 p.m. seven days a week. The beach is open from 9:00 a.m. to 8:30 p.m. between Memorial Day and Labor Day. There is a nominal daily or annual fee for parking.

Map key: West 39

For additional information:

Eastman Nature Center
Elm Creek Park Reserve
13351 Elm Creek Road
Osseo, Minnesota 55369
(612) 420-4300

Hennepin Parks
12615 County Road 9
Plymouth, Minnesota 55419
(612) 559-9000

Eloise Butler Wildflower Garden and Bird Sanctuary

The Eloise Butler Wildflower Garden and Bird Sanctuary is living proof that good things often come in small packages. Consisting of just 20 acres tucked away in Wirth Park, the sanctuary is a hidden treasure where natural beauty and serenity prevail only minutes from downtown Minneapolis. Originally established in 1907, and later named after Eloise Butler, the curator from 1911 to 1933, the garden is carefully managed to preserve and display a wide variety of native plants in a natural setting.

The Sanctuary is roughly bowl shaped, low in the middle with wooded slopes around the outside and an open upland area to the east. Nearly a mile of winding trails lead through mixed broadleaf woodland, mature bog, upland oak woods, and rolling prairie, each of which harbors a distinct array of shrubs and flowers. An excellent guidebook and numerous signs provide visitors with information about many of the plants and their habitats.

The bog is an artificially managed opening at the heart of a low-lying swampy area. A small dam was placed at one end in 1947 and the water has been controlled since that time. Visitors here may be reminded of northern Minnesota as they meander through a mixture of tamarac, balsam fir, white pine, white cedar, black spruce, paper birch, yellow birch, red maple, mountain maple, Carolina buckthorn, winterberry, red-osier dogwood, American yew, highbush cranberry and sensitive fern. Beginning with skunk cabbage and marsh marigold in early spring, a colorful array of water tolerant flowers enlivens this wet lowland, including swamp saxifrage, wild calla, blue and yellow flag iris, forget-me-not, jewelweed, red turtlehead, Jo-Pye weed, and cardinal flower, as well as the carnivorous sundew and pitcher plants, and the showy lady slipper, our state flower.

More akin to regions east and south of the Twin Cities, the surrounding woodlands are a rich blend of basswood, sugar maple, shagbark hickory, black walnut, butternut, eastern hemlock, ironwood, blue beech, hackberry, Kentucky coffee tree, ash, and boxelder. Red oak, white oak, pin oak, and black cherry become more prominent in the drier uplands. The understory of this woodland supports a dense growth of small trees and shrubs, including alternate-leaf dogwood, witchhazel, red elderberry, common bladdernut, leatherwood, black raspberry, pin cherry, common buckthorn, red cedar, prickly-ash, black currant, and hazelnut.

The woods are most popular in springtime before the leaves block out the sunlight. At that time the ground is covered by a spectacular bloom of wildflowers, such as bloodroot, spring beauty, rue anemone, sharp-lobed hepatica, large-flowered bellwort, Virginia bluebell, wild ginger, mayapple, Jack-in-the-pulpit, cut-leafed toothwort, blue cohosh, Jacob's ladder, red baneberry, and yellow lady slipper, in addition to a variety of violets, trilliums, and trout lilies. Here one can also discover a number of ferns with names like cinnamon, interrupted, ostrich, lady, and maidenhair.

In sharp contrast to the woodlands are the few acres of prairie that were established in the 1950s. Aside from a few broad-canopied oaks and the ever encroaching sumac, the landscape is an open one carpeted with many of the grasses and flowers that once characterized a third of Minnesota. Big bluestem, little bluestem, prairie cordgrass, and Indian grass are interspersed with flowers like hoary puccoon, wild lupine, blazing star, compass plant, fringed gentian, purple coneflower, Culver's root, leadplant, giant blue hyssop, and blue-eyed grass.

Within the sanctuary is the Crone Shelter, a rustic cabin named for Mrs. Martha Crone who succeeded Eloise Butler as curator of the garden. The cabin houses a few exhibits, a variety of books on native flora, and a photo album with the pictures and names of flowers currently in bloom at the preserve. Bird feeders outside the cabin attract cardinal, white-breasted nuthatch, black-capped chickadee, common grackle, downy woodpecker, blue jay, and rose-breasted grosbeak.

The Eloise Butler Wildflower Garden and Bird Sanctuary is a place where you come to observe nature in miniature. Walk slowly here and take notice of the subtle details you might pay little attention to elsewhere.

Facilities: Though short, the well-maintained trail system is both lovely and informative. A guidebook and many identifying markers assist those interested in learning more about the plants and habitats. Benches have been placed in numerous spots along the trail. The Crone Shelter offers reading material and exhibits. Toilets are located next to the entrance and a water fountain by the cabin.

How to get there: The Sanctuary is located within Theodore Wirth park, one-half mile north of Highway 12 (Interstate 394) or just south of Glenwood Avenue on Wirth Parkway. Look for a sign next to the entrance road.

The preserve is open daily from 7:30 a.m. to dusk between April 1 and October 31.

Map key: East 40

For additional information:

Minneapolis Park and Recreation
Board
310 Fourth Avenue South
Minneapolis, Minnesota 55415
(612) 348-5702
or call the Crone Shelter:
(612) 348- 5702

Esker Wildlife Management Area

The Esker Wildlife Management Area covers 47 acres squeezed into the rolling farmland of northwestern Rice County. The primary attraction is the geological feature for which it is named, but the preserve also includes a small lake and a marsh that attract waterfowl and other wildlife.

Eskers are long, narrow, sinuous ridges that wind across the landscape. They are composed of sand and gravel laid down by subglacial streams when the great sheets of ice were in retreat. At that time, meltwater ran through a crack or tunnel in the glacier and gravel was deposited in the streambed. Initially hemmed in by the surrounding ice, the gravel streambed remained after the glacier melted. Eskers can range up to 150 feet mained after the glacier melted. Eskers can range up to 150 feet in height, 600 feet in breadth, and many miles in length. Although the unnamed esker here is not nearly so large, it is a good example of this unusual landform.

This small esker stretches for a few hundred feet across the heart of the preserve. Its rock-strewn surface is generally open and grassy with scattered groves of sumac, prickly-ash, and wild plum, along with some chokecherry, hawthorn, and boxelder. The lack of forest cover makes the esker highly visible but one must walk along its spine to get a true sense of its size and shape. From atop the esker there is a nice view of the shallow lake to one side and a vibrant marsh to the other. The remaining terrain is made up of grass covered hills with pockets of woodland, including a stand of large bur oaks near the parking area.

Facilities: There are no developed facilities here except for a small parking area. An informal trail leads from the parking area to the esker. State Wildlife Areas are managed for three primary reasons: wildlife production, public hunting, and trapping. Other activities, such as hiking and birding, are also encouraged but should probably be avoided during the hunting season.

How to get there: The Esker WMA is located just over a half an hour south of Minneapolis about 5 miles east of the town of Lonsdale. Heading south on Interstate Highway 35 take the Northfield exit (State Highway 19). Take 19 west for 2.2 miles and then turn right onto Chester Avenue. Go north on Chester Avenue for 1.3 miles and look for a brown "Public Access" sign marking a small dirt driveway. Proceed carefully along this rutted drive (passing a small residence) for less than a quarter mile to the parking area.

Map key: East 41

For additional information:

Minnesota Department of Natural Resources
Section of Wildlife, Box 7
500 Lafayette Road
St. Paul, Minnesota 55155
(612) 296-3344
or (507) 455-5841 (area manager)

Falls Creek Park

On the outskirts of Faribault, this Rice County park covers 64 acres bordering Falls Creek as it winds toward the nearby Straight River. The pretty country stream cuts into farmed uplands and flows through a wide valley with level terraces and wooded slopes. From creek bottom to hilltop the park exhibits a wide variety of trees and shrubs in a small area. Tall black willow and cottonwood trees grow with elm, boxelder, and green ash along the creek. Adjoining lowlands and sheltered ravines support basswood, sugar maple, ironwood, butternut, hackberry, bitternut hickory and blue beech. Dry hillsides are dominated by oaks – red oak, white oak, and bur oak – mixed with black cherry, paper birch, and aspen. Open spaces are giving way to advancing groves of quaking and bigtooth aspen and dense thickets of raspberry, sumac, prickly ash, and other small trees and shrubs. There are also planted rows of spruce and pine. Stream valleys such as this provide invaluable havens for many of the birds and mammals found in the farm country of southern Minnesota. In recent years beavers have made a remarkable comeback throughout the region and signs of their activity can be seen on most of the larger creeks and even some drainage ditches.

Facilities: A pleasant network of hiking trails winds through the park, from a footbridge over the creek to benches at hilltop overlooks. There is a picnic area next to the parking lot with a shelter, tables, grills, water, toilets, and a playing field.

How to get there: From the Twin Cities head south to Faribault on Interstate Highway 35. Take the exit for State Highway 60 and drive east through Faribault, following 60 as it turns south, then east again. About 1.5 miles after crossing over the Straight River look for the park entrance on the left (just after crossing Falls Creek).

Map key: East 42

For additional information:

Rice County Parks
P.O. Box 40
Faribault, Minnesota 55021
(507) 334-2281 ext. 260

Fort Snelling State Park

In his inauguration address of 1961, Governor Elmer Anderson urged the legislature to act on the "almost incredible" opportunity to create a historical park in the heart of the Twin Cities metropolitan area. That year a bill passed establishing Fort Snelling State Park, with the historic old fort as the centerpiece of a 2,500 acre nature preserve and recreation area. Since then the long neglected fort has been magnificently reconstructed and the park has grown to more the 3,200 acres, becoming the second most visited unit in our outstanding system of state parks.

The fort is situated on a strategic bluff overlooking the rest of the park, which stretches about six miles south along the Minnesota River from its confluence with the Mississippi at historic Pike Island. While the Mississippi River Valley is enclosed by steep bluffs adjacent to the river, the Minnesota River Valley is characterized by a broad floodplain bordered by high, but less steeply sloped bluffs. The present channels of both rivers were excavated by torrents of glacial meltwater at the end of the last ice age, but the much larger Minnesota River Valley was carved by the immense flow of Glacial River Warren. For approximately 2,500 years, the River Warren poured out of Glacial Lake Agassiz in northwestern Minnesota until the retreating ice uncovered another outlet to the north. At that time the valley began to fill with sediments and now the floodplain is underlaid by almost 100 feet of alluvial material near Fort Snelling.

By virtue of its location in the midst of a developed landscape, the park is subject to the effects of a wide variety of urban activities. These include a number of freeways and bridges which cross the interior of the park, a heavy amount of commercial and recreational boat traffic on the river, four high-tension power lines, landing-light towers, and the noise of jet planes landing at the airport. Despite these external influences the park remains as an oasis of natural ecological communities that provide valuable habitat for more than 220 species of wildlife.

Although a variety of human activities, such as logging, farming, and dredging, have had an effect on the park's landscape over the past 150 years, the original vegetation was probably quite similar to what exists here today. From blufftop to bottomlands there are many distinct habitats found within the park, including mixed hardwood forest, rocky outcroppings, remnant prairie and oak savanna, abandoned fields, perched bogs, bottomland forest, marshes, wet meadows, lakes, rivers, and streams.

The predominant plant communities occur within the lowlands between the bluffs. Bottomland hardwoods occupying the drier soils and riverbanks, which are subject to seasonal flooding, include some of the largest cottonwood trees in the state, as well as silver maple, black willow, green ash, and elm. Shallow, spring-fed lakes, expansive cattail marshes, broad sweeps of sedge meadows, and thickets of alder and willow occupy the lowest areas and poorly drained soils in the valley.

The park also protects a few areas of special significance. There are several perched bogs, which harbor such plants as yellow and white lady slippers, swamp saxifrage, wild valerian, marsh marigold, and other species. These "hanging" bogs result from groundwater seepage at the base of the escarpment. Another area of interest is the bed of American lotus in Snelling Lake, a plant of limited distribution in Minnesota that has rather specific habitat requirements. Remnants of upland prairie also exist in isolated areas along the bluffs.

In spite of its location near the center of the Twin Cities, the park is home to an abundance of wildlife. Twenty-nine mammals reside in the area, including red and gray fox, badger, striped skunk, woodchuck, raccoon, opossum, white-tailed jackrabbit, short-tailed weasel, beaver, mink, muskrat, lots of white-tailed deer, and a wealth of smaller squirrels, moles, mice, voles, shrews, and bats. There are also thirteen species of reptiles and amphibians, such as the red-bellied snake, bullsnake, fox snake, leopard frog, spring peeper, American toad, common snapping turtle, spiny softshell turtle, and the threatened Blanding's turtle.

Nearly 200 species of birds either nest in or adjacent to the park or appear here during spring and fall migrations. Some of the birds that might be found nesting or feeding in and around the lakes and wetlands throughout the summer are the common loon, double-crested cormorant, great blue heron, great egret, black-crowned night heron, American bittern, Canada goose, red-necked grebe, pied-billed grebe, mallard, blue-winged teal, wood duck, common gallinule, Wilson's phalarope, Forster's tern, and black tern. Among the many other birds that inhabit the diversity of habitats are Cooper's hawk, red-shouldered hawk, marsh hawk, short-eared owl, saw-whet owl, kestrel, ruffed grouse, bobwhite, whip-poor-will, woodcock, black-billed cuckoo, chimney swift, ruby-throated hummingbird, pileated woodpecker, and red-bellied woodpecker, as well as the alder flycatcher, horned lark, veery, cedar waxwing, prothonotary warbler, cerulean warbler, ovenbird, Connecticut warbler, western meadowlark, brown-headed cowbird, dickcissel, and Henslow's sparrow.

Facilities: Situated by the Mississippi River, the Pike Island Interpretive Center contains exhibits, a touch-and-see area, an audio-visual room, a meeting room, and offices. An 18-mile-long network of hiking trails winds about the park. This includes a long loop through the lowlands east of the river, but this stretch is usually wet and sometimes impassable. The entire 18 miles are groomed for cross-country skiing. Snowmobiling is not allowed but snowshoers may explore freely. There is also a 5 mile paved trail for biking and hiking that connects to Minnehaha Park on the Mississippi River. The large picnic area on "Picnic Island" has shelters, tables, grills, water, and toilets. A guarded swimming beach on Snelling Lake has a concession stand, changing rooms and toilets. There is boat launch on the river, a canoe launch on Snelling Lake. Both the river and the lake are popular fishing spots. Paddling a canoe to Gun Club Lake (two separate lakes connected by a narrow channel amid the lowlands east of the river) is an excellent way to observe wildlife.

The reconstructed fort and a modern visitors center offer an outstanding look at an important part of Minnesota's history. Costumed guides and craftspeople bring the old fort to life. The uplands near the fort have a nine-hole golf course (privately owned), a polo grounds, and baseball fields.

How to get there: The park can be reached in minutes from downtown Minneapolis or St. Paul. The entrance is located at the Post Road exit off State Highway 5 between State Highway 55 and Interstate Highway 494 across from Fort Snelling National Cemetery and the airport. The access road to the fort itself exits off Highway 55 between the Crosstown Highway and the Mendota bridge.

The park is closed from 10:00 p.m. to 8:00 a.m. during the summer. At other times of the year the park may close at sunset. Daily or annual permits are required for all vehicles entering a state park. They may be purchased at the park entrance.

Map key: East 43

For additional information:

Fort Snelling State Park
Post Road and Highway 5
St. Paul, Minnesota 5511
(612) 727-1961
or (612) 726-9247 (Interpretive Center)

Department of Natural Resources
Division of Parks and Recreation
Information Center, Box 40
500 Lafayette Road
(612) 296-4776

Frontenac State Park

A few miles downriver from historic Red Wing, Frontenac State Park occupies about 2,700 acres along the high bluffs overlooking Lake Pepin and the Mississippi River Valley. The area has long been appreciated for its natural beauty and historical significance but early attempts to create a park here failed. Finally, prodded by the efforts of local people who raised funds and purchased an important tract of land, the legislature established the park in 1957. The park wraps around the small village of Frontenac, a quiet river town that had its heyday more than a century ago when steamboats brought the wealthy from as far away as New Orleans to stay at fashionable summer resorts.

The park's terrain is dominated by two bluffs, one "land-locked," rising as much as 400 feet above Lake Pepin. The bluffs are comprised of layers of sedimentary sandstone and limestone that were deposited at the bottom of ancient seas and underlie much of the region. The varied landscape we see today was created more recently when the soft bedrock was carved by the Glacial River Warren. This enormous river flowed for perhaps 3,000 years, draining Glacial Lake Agassiz through what is now the Minnesota River Valley. The lake was larger than any lakes found in the world now and covered parts of three states and three provinces. At its largest the River Warren nearly filled the broad valley and the park's bluffs were islands.

Scenic overlooks offer outstanding views of Lake Pepin and the towering bluffs that line both sides of the valley. Lake Pepin is the result of a natural dam formed by the delta of Wisconsin's Chippewa River. The lake is large – 22 miles long and more than two miles wide – but it is gradually shrinking. Where the Mississippi enters the lake it slows down and deposits loads of sediment. As the sediment accumulates, it transforms the open lake into wildlife-rich marshes and shallow channels separated by wooded islands and shifting sandbars. This slow process has been accelerated by the upstream activities of modern man.

While the park encompasses a variety of habitats, most visitors concentrate their activities around the wooded bluffs bordering Lake Pepin. The steep, north-facing hillsides are cloaked with a mature forest broken only by rocky outcroppings. One of these, a natural arch near the top of the bluff known as In-Yan-Teopa Rock, was a sacred place to the Dakota and Fox Indians who once lived here. The forest is dominated by sizable sugar maple, basswood, and red oak, along with a rich mixture of ironwood, bitternut hickory, elm, white ash, black walnut, butternut, paper birch, serviceberry, buckthorn, and alternate-leaf dogwood. Elderberry abounds in the shaded understory, as do ferns, mosses, and wildflowers, including bloodroot, wild ginger, sharp-lobed hepatica, Dutchman's breeches, squirrel corn, large-flowered trillium, jack-in-the-pulpit, miterwort, and baneberry. A narrow strip of cottonwood, silver maple, and green ash grows at the base of the hill.

Ranging from groves of aspen atop the bluff to young stands of sumac, cottonwood, ash, boxelder, and black locust, much of the rest of the park is comprised of old fields in various stages of succession. A few remnants of native prairie and savanna persist on exposed, south-facing slopes marked by a scattering of wide-spreading bur oaks and tall, warm season grasses. Pleasant Valley Creek runs through the south end of the park, flowing through a long marsh rimmed with arrowhead, cattail, sedges, and purple loosestrife.

Wildlife thrives in the park as it does throughout the valley. White-tailed deer, badger, red fox, gray fox, raccoon, woodchuck, opossum, striped skunk, muskrat, mink, and beaver are some of the mammals that live in the park. The area is also home to a small number of timber rattlesnakes, a poisonous reptile that reaches the northwesternmost part of its range in southern Minnesota. Birders flock to Frontenac each spring to watch the waves of warblers and other birds that migrate along the river. Only eight of the thirty warblers that visit the state stop to raise their young here. Frontenac is one of the few places in Minnesota that provides nesting habitat for the prothonotary warbler. Altogether more than 200 birds can be seen in the area every year, including two of the world's greatest travelers — the sanderling and the ruddy turnstone. In summer, ospreys and turkey vultures are frequently seen, while in winter bald eagles and golden eagles can be observed. Once exterminated throughout the Midwest, the peregrine falcon has been reintroduced to the Mississippi River Valley. One of the most widely distributed birds in the world, this graceful predator can reach speeds of 175 miles an hour when diving at its prey.

The portion of the park west of Highway 61 protects a number of prehistoric habitation sites and burial mounds. These date back more than 2,000 years and represent the northern edge of the Hopewellian culture.

Facilities: Ten miles of hiking trails wind about the park. These range from wide, easy trails through the open uplands to a network of narrow, rocky trails built into the face of the bluff which lead to spectacular overlooks. Six miles of this system, not including the bluff trails, are groomed for cross-country skiing. There are also 10 miles of trails for snowmobiling. A trail center with toilets is located near the park entrance. There is a scenic picnic area atop the bluff with tables, grills, water, toilets, and an enclosed shelter with electricity. Also atop the bluff is a semi-modern campground with showers, flush toilets, and a dump station, and a separate primitive group camp.

How to get there: Take U.S. Highway 61 south from St. Paul or Interstate Highway 494 toward Red Wing. The park is located a few minutes past Red Wing on the left (east) side of the road. Look for signs and turn left onto County Road 2 at Frontenac Station. Go about a mile on 2 to the information building where maps are available.

The park is closed from 10:00 p.m. to 8:00 a.m. except to registered campers. Daily or annual permits are required for all vehicles entering a state park. They may be purchased at the information building.

Map key: East 44

For additional information:

Frontenac State Park Manager
Route 2, Box 134
Lake City, Minnesota 55041
(612)345-3401

Department of Natural Resources
Division of Parks and Recreation
Information Center, Box 40
500 Lafayette Road
St. Paul, Minnesota 55155
(612) 296-4776

Girard Lake Park

One of numerous parks in west Bloomington, Girard Lake Park is made up of some 61 acres. The center of the park is occupied by Lake Girard, a shallow, 17-acre lake choked with waterlilies and rimmed with cattail marsh. The lake is partially surrounded by forested hills. Bur oak and red oak dominate the rock-strewn woodland, but white oak, aspen. black cherry, basswood, and ironwood are also plentiful.

Facilities: A mile-long woodchip trail encircles the lake at the base of the hill and connects to short trails that lead through the woods to the local neighborhood. The trail is used for cross-country skiing in the winter. A mowed field in the northwest corner includes an archery range.

How to get there: The park is located along France Avenue south of the 84th Street intersection. A parking lot is available just east of France off 84th.

Map key: West 45

For additional information:

Bloomington Park and Recreation
Department
2215 W. Old Shakopee Road
Bloomington, Minnesota 55431
(612) 887-9601

Grass Lake Regional Park

Grass Lake Regional Park occupies 450 acres stretched out between Interstate Highway 694 and the south shore of Snail Lake in suburban Shoreview. Local roads split the park into three distinct areas and, while there are plans for future development, all facilities except for trails are located in the northern section known as Snail Lake Park.

Between Snail Lake Park and Gramsie Road the park is split by a low ridge that overlooks a marshy lowland stuffed with cattails and bordered by black willow, aspen, and boxelder. The steep-sided ridge is cloaked by a woodland dominated by tall oaks –primarily red oak, with white oak, bur oak, and pin oak. There is also black cherry, hackberry, elm, ash, and stands of aspen and paper birch, as well as basswood and ironwood on the sheltered face of the hill. The understory is thick with berry-laden shrubs and a lush growth of ferns.

The largest section of the park is south of Gramsie Road and encompasses the lake for which the area is named. Grass Lake is a broad expanse of shallow open waters with a wooded island and a wide fringe of cattail marsh. This productive habitat is alternately surrounded by swampy thickets of willow and dogwood, stands of black willow and cottonwood, small hills covered by a mature oak forest, and old fields.

An isolated stand of bur oak and aspen atop a steep hill on the north side of the basin provides a shady spot to observe wildlife. Among the birds that might be seen from here are great blue heron, great egret, green-backed heron, double-crested cormorant, mallard, blue-winged teal, wood duck, ruddy duck, pied-billed grebe, Canada goose, and red-winged blackbird. The marsh is also inhabited by less conspicuous birds - rails, bitterns, wrens, and sparrows – in addition to muskrat, mink, and painted turtle. White-tailed deer, red fox, raccoon, woodchuck, barred owl, and many smaller mammals and songbirds dwell in the woods and fields.

Facilities: Plans call for the development of a complete and clearly marked trail system. Currently the area is very accessible on an extensive network of informal trails. Cross-country skiing is permitted throughout the park and trails are groomed north of Gramsie Road. Other recreational facilities are situated in Snail Lake Park, a 38-acre segment on the south shore of Snail Lake. A nice picnic area here, set amid tall shade trees, has shelters, tables, grills, water, and toilets. There is also a boat launch, a swimming beach, and playground equipment. Ice fishing and snowmobiling are popular on Snail Lake during the winter.

How to get there: Take Interstate Highway 694 east from Interstate Highway 35W or west from Interstate Highway 35E. About 2.5 miles east of 35W or 2.5 miles west of 35E, exit onto Victoria Street (County Road 52) and head north. Take a right onto Gramsie Road (County Road 97) to reach the southern part of the park. Look for a dirt parking area on the right. To reach Snail Lake Park and the trailhead, continue past Gramsie Road and turn right onto Snail Lake Boulevard (County Road 13). Look for the parking area on the left.

Map key: East 46

For additional information:

Ramsey County Parks and
Recreation Department
2015 N. Van Dyke Street
Maplewood, Minnesota 55109
(612) 777-1707

Harry Larson County Forest

Less than one mile north of Lake Maria State Park is the Harry Larson County Forest. This Wright County preserve contains 170 acres of rolling terrain dotted with small pothole marshes. Except for a little open meadow used as a deer feeding site the area is entirely forested. Tall white oak and red oak are dominant, but the forest supports a wide variety of other hardwoods, such as white ash, ironwood, red maple, black cherry, elm, hackberry, paper birch, and pockets of bigtooth aspen. The rich woodland with its shrubby understory is an attractive haven for an abundance of small mammals and songbirds.

Facilities: Nearly two miles of trails in two interconnected loops enable hikers and cross-country skiers to explore the forest. There is a stationary map at the trailhead. A small picnic area with tables, drinking water, and toilets is located by the parking lot.

How to get there: Take Interstate Highway 94 northwest from the Twin Cities. At Monticello exit onto State Highway 25 and head into town. Before crossing the river turn left onto County Highway 75. After about a half a mile take another left onto County Highway 39. Continue on 35, crossing back over the Interstate, for about 6 miles to County Road 111. Turn right here and proceed 2 miles, passing Lake Maria State Park, and look for the parking lot on the right.

Map key: West 47

For additional information:

Wright County Parks Department
Route 1, Box 97B
Buffalo, Minnesota 55313
(612) 682-3900, ext. 182
339-6881 (Metro)
1-800- 362-3667, ext. 182 (Toll Free)

Hastings Scientific and Natural Area

The Hastings Scientific and Natural Area is a 69 acre tract of land located just inside the city limits of Hastings. More than half of the area is within the floodplain of the Vermillion River near its confluence with the Mississippi River, including a short stretch of the river and a shallow backwater lake. A typical bottomland forest, composed of large silver maple and cotton-wood, as well as elm and green ash, carpets this wet lowland. The upland portion of the preserve contains an undisturbed hardwood forest on the steep north-facing slope that rises from the floodplain. The small, but rich, woodland is dominated by tall sugar maple, basswood, and red oak, with ironwood plentiful in the shaded understory. Paper birch, aspen, and a variety of other trees, such as butternut, hackberry, bitternut hickory, boxelder, and alternate leaf dogwood, are scattered about, adding diversity to this attractive woodland. In addition to the multitude of wildflowers that abound on the richer soils, the talus slopes and outcroppings of dolomite provide a variety of niches for specialized plant species, including several mosses, lichens, liverworts, and ferns.

Facilities: There are no developed facilities or trails within the preserve. A short trail penetrates the woods from the pull-off where you can park your car. Beyond that you should exercise care not to disturb the fragile environment.

How to get there: Hastings is southeast of the Twin Cities and can be reached by taking U.S. Highway 61 south from St. Paul or by taking State Highway 55 southeast from the Mendota Bridge. From the intersection of 61 and 55 in Hastings, go south on 61 less than a mile to State Highway 291. Take a left (east) on 291 and follow it across the Vermillion River and past the Hastings Veterans Home. A little farther on, the road bends to the left just before intersecting County Highway 54. At this bend there is a spot where you can pull your car off the road and park.

Map key: East 48

For additional information:

Scientific and Natural Areas
Program
Box 7, Minnesota Department of
Natural Resources
500 Lafayette Road, DNR Building
St. Paul, Minnesota 55155
(612) 297-3288

Hay Creek Recreation Area

The Official State Highway Map of Minnesota shows a substantial portion of seven southeastern counties as a light shade of green. The green area denotes the statutory boundaries of the Richard J. Dorer Memorial Hardwood State Forest, which encompasses one million acres stretching from nearby Hastings to the Iowa border. Anyone who has traveled through the region, however, knows that the forest exists primarily on paper and most of the "green" area is made up of productive farmland and small towns.

The dream of Richard J. Dorer, one of the most far-sighted and effective of Minnesota's early conservationists, the State Forest was established in 1961 to preserve what remained of the region's rich broadleaf woodlands. Though the original plan called for the gradual acquisition of some 200,000 acres, so far less than a quarter of that has been protected. Isolated parcels exist throughout the "forest" but public use is generally limited to six larger recreation areas. The Hay Creek Recreation Area is the only one within the scope of this book.

Located just two miles south of Red Wing, the Hay Creek Unit was one of the first areas to be purchased. Its eroded, hilly farmlands would benefit from conservation practices and the scenic bluffs and winding trout stream gave it high recreation potential. Acquisition continued through 1970, when the tract attained its present size of almost 1,500 acres. Erosion control dams or diversions were constructed at six sites, and old fields and brushy areas were converted into tree plantations. More than 100,000 seedlings have been planted, including red pine, white pine, jack pine, black locust, white spruce, and black walnut.

Still, most of the area is maintained in a more natural state and a variety of habitats can be found from creek bottom to bluff-top. Cottonwood, black willow, silver maple, green ash, and elm shade the lowlands along Hay Creek, while mature woodlands, second-growth forests, and small prairie remnants cover the rugged hills to the east. The forested hillsides are carpeted by sizable red oak and bur oak, as well as white oak, basswood, butternut, black cherry, bitternut hickory, red cedar, and numerous other trees, including stands of aspen and birch. The dense understory is thick with small trees and shrubs such as serviceberry, alternate-leaf dogwood, buckthorn, elderberry, hazelnut, gooseberry, and black raspberry.

A unique plant community found within the area is the "goat prairie." These are small openings where local conditions have allowed pockets of native prairie to persist on hillsides amid the forest. The combination of heat, a lack of moisture, and the continual cycle of freezing and thawing in winter gives the hardy prairie grasses and flowers the competitive edge on a few steep, south-facing slopes.

The forest here provides shelter and food for a variety of wildlife, including white-tailed deer, spotted skunk, opossum, red fox, barred owl, pileated woodpecker, ruffed grouse, and an abundance of songbirds. Of particular interest are two animals rarely found this close to the Twin Cities, wild turkey and timber rattlesnake. Rattlesnakes are not numerous and offer little or no threat to visitors.

Facilities: Eight miles of hiking trails wind along the creek and through the hills, and lead to scenic vistas overlooking the small valley. Horseback riding is permitted in summer and snowmobiling in winter. The trails are groomed for cross-country skiing but are not recommended for beginners. There is a small picnic area located next to the parking lot with tables, firerings, toilets, and water. A map is available from the Department of Natural Resources.

Minnesota's state forests were established to produce timber and other forest crops, provide outdoor recreation, protect watersheds, and perpetuate rare and distinctive species of flora and fauna. In keeping with this principle of "multiple use", timber is harvested at Hay Creek and the area is open to hunting, fishing. and berry-picking.

How to get there: From Red Wing, go south on State Highway 58 for roughly 4 miles. Then turn right (northwest) onto a dirt township road at the Hay Creek Campground. Follow this road, passing over the creek twice, for a little more than a mile and look for the entrance on the right (if you cross the creek a third time you have gone to far).

For additional information:

Area Forest Supervisor
P.O. Box 69
Lake City, Minnesota 55041
(612) 345-3216

Trails and Waterways Unit
Information Center, Box 40
500 Lafayette Road
St. Paul, Minnesota 55455
(612) 296- 6699

Map key: East 49

Helen Allison Savanna

Helen Allison Savanna is located in northern Anoka County adjacent to the University of Minnesota's Cedar Creek Natural History Area. The preserve encompasses 86 acres of the Anoka Sand Plain and includes one of the few protected oak savannas in the state. The tract was acquired by The Nature Conservancy in 1961 and named for Helen Allison Irvine, Minnesota's "Grass Lady," who wrote *The Key to Grasses of Minnesota*. In 1981 it was designated a state Scientific and Natural Area.

When white settlers first came to the region they discovered large areas that were neither woodland nor grassland, but a unique combination of both. Here the land wore a carpet of prairie grasses and flowers scattered with broad-canopied oaks standing in isolation or in small groves. It is thought that wildfires prevented shrubs and saplings from gradually transforming the savanna into a forest, but some oaks survived because their thick, corky bark protected them from the heat of the fast-moving ground fires. Originally this transitional plant community covered wide swaths of the Midwest. However, land clearing, grazing, and the suppression of wildfires that accompanied settlement eliminated all but a few remnants.

The landscape at Helen Allison Savanna consists of gently rolling sand deposits with fairly steep sand dunes and numerous wet depressions. Bur oak and northern pin oak are the most common trees, while prairie grasses such as porcupine grass, big and little bluestem, sand dropseed, and sand reedgrass, dominate underneath and between the oaks. An ever-changing variety of colorful prairie flowers enlivens the preserve during the spring and summer, beginning with pasque flower, three-flowered avens, and hoary puccoon, and including butterfly-weed, black-eyed susan, spiderwort, prairie rose, leadplant, harebell, bush clover, longbearded hawkweed, and large-flowered penstemon. Interspersed with the savanna are a few sand blowouts colonized by stunted ash trees, sea-beach triple awned grass, and hairy panic grass. Paper birch and quaking aspen can be found bordering the low, wet depressions occupied by Hayden's sedge and common bladderwort.

Throughout the area one can see numerous shrubs, such as sumac, hazelnut, and choke cherry, that are battling to replace the prairie. These and other invading species are controlled by the use of carefully applied burning. Periodic burning is widely recognized as an important tool in maintaining savannas or prairies in the absence of the grazing and wildfires that helped shape them. Helen Allison Savanna was the first Nature Conservancy preserve in the country to be managed with controlled burning.

About 20 acres on the western side of the preserve were once plowed and later planted with pines. The pines have since been removed and the old fields are slowly reverting to prairie.

Facilities: There are no developed facilities at Helen Allison Savanna. As with all Nature Conservancy preserves, the protection of the natural plant and animal communities is the highest priority. Although you are invited to observe and enjoy the preserve, please use care to minimize the impact of your visit.

How to get there: Take State Highway 65 (Central Avenue) north from the Twin Cities. Approximately 22 miles north of Interstate Highway 694 turn right onto County Highway 24. After about one mile turn right onto County Highway 26 and proceed about 3.5 miles. The preserve is located on the right side of the road just before the intersection with County Road 15. To park, turn right onto County Road 15 and drive about a quarter mile to a pull-off on the right.

Map key: East 50

For additional information:

The Nature Conservancy
Minnesota Chapter
1313 Fifth Street, S.E.
Minneapolis, Minnesota 55414
(612) 379-2134

Scientific and Natural Areas
Program
Minnesota Department of Natural Resources
500 Lafayette Road
St. Paul, Minnesota 55155
(612) 297-3288

Hidden Falls Park

At the southwestern edge of the city of St. Paul, Hidden Falls Park borders the last two miles of the scenic Mississippi River gorge before it joins the broad Minnesota River Valley at Fort Snelling. Situated across the river from Minnehaha Park and separated from the neighborhoods above by steep wooded bluffs, the park offers city dwellers an easy escape to secluded pathways and quiet picnic areas.

Most of the area lies within the floodplain, which is widest at the north end of the park. Here a well-worn trail with small footbridges makes a loop through a mature bottomland forest, winding along both the river's edge and the base of the bluff. This swampy woodland is made up of large silver maple trees, with cottonwood, boxelder, elm, green ash, black willow, mulberry, and hackberry. The face of the bluff is cloaked by bur oak, red oak, basswood, hackberry, boxelder, buckthorn, and elderberry, except in the steepest places, where portions of the underlying sandstone are exposed.

The falls for which the area is named is at the head of a narrow glen that cuts back into the developed uplands. A concrete pipe that collects run-off from city streets has replaced the free-flowing stream that once fed the small cascade. Nevertheless, the water spills over the more resistant layers of limestone and shale into an attractive natural bowl carved out of the softer sandstone, then runs between stone walls over a series of small manmade waterfalls as it drops to the river.

Facilities: In addition to the previously mentioned nature trail, a paved trail for hiking and biking runs through most of the area and connects the park to Crosby Farm Park. There is a large picnic area set amid tall shade trees which offers a shelter, tables, grills, water, restrooms, and horseshoe pits. There is a boat launch and a parking lot for trailers. Paved trails for hiking and biking parallel the road atop the bluff, passing numerous benches. A separate overlook with parking spaces and a sweeping view of the river gorge is situated just north of the park entrance.

How to get there: The park entrance is located off Mississippi River Boulevard at Magoffin Avenue less than a mile south of the Ford Bridge and more than a mile north of State Highway 5 (Fort Road).

Map key: East 51

For additional information:

St. Paul Division of Parks and
Recreation
300 City Hall Annex
25 W. 4th St.
St. Paul, Minnesota 55102
(612) 292-7400

High Island Creek Park

Off the beaten path amid the quiet farmland of eastern Sibley County, this 200 acre park straddles a deep, wooded valley carved by High Island Creek as it flows toward the nearby Minnesota River. The region's open fields end abruptly where steep, tree-covered slopes drop sharply down from the level uplands.

From a pleasant picnic area overlooking the valley a wide trail leads downhill, past some additional picnic sites, to the confluence of High Island Creek and one of its many smaller tributaries. The fast-moving stream rushes through a somewhat open, sandy bottomland with stretches of grass, tall cottonwood and black willow trees, and some elm, red cedar, and sumac. The surrounding hillsides are shaded by an attractive mixture of mature sugar maple, red oak, bur oak, and basswood, along with abundant ironwood, quaking and big-tooth aspen, red cedar, paper birch, and some blue beech. You can wander up the narrow ravine to the right where a tiny brook flows past sheer walls and rocky outcroppings. The sheltered slopes, exposed outcroppings, and moist floodplain here create a diversity of habitats for plants such as American yew, horsetail, and numerous kinds of flowers, ferns, mosses, and lichens.

Farther up this ravine, just below the picnic area, a large unstable gully provides a look at the continuing process of erosion that has shaped the park's landscape. Fresh slides have exposed the rock-laden glacial drift that underlies the whole area. Ever since the glaciers retreated, these ravines and valleys have been slowly growing, cutting back into the gentle uplands.

Facilities: There is no real trail system here but an old road leads down to the creek and several informal paths head off in various directions. A picnic area situated between farm fields and the woods offers tables, a shelter, grills, water, and toilets. Overnight camping is allowed but a permit must be acquired.

How to get there: From the Twin Cities head southwest on U.S. Highway 169 along the Minnesota River Valley. At the border between Scott and LeSueur Counties take a right (west) onto State Highway 19. Shortly after crossing the river on 19 turn right (north) onto County Road 6. Stay on 6 for a little more than 3 miles, then turn left (west) onto County Road 12. Drive 2 miles on 12, then turn left onto a dirt road and follow it for 1.3 miles to the park.

Map key: West 52

For additional information:

Department of Public Works
P.O. Box 82
Gaylord, Minnesota 55334
(612) 237-2403

Hyland, Bush, Anderson Lakes Regional Park Reserve

Situated only a few minutes southwest of Minneapolis in west Bloomington and Eden Prairie is an exceedingly complex network of county and municipal parklands known as the Hyland, Bush, Anderson Lakes Regional Park Reserve. Altogether the various tracts encompass more than 2,500 acres of richly diverse habitats split by numerous roads and interspersed with densely populated suburban neighborhoods. While much of the land is maintained as undeveloped nature areas, there are a great variety of recreational facilities available, from ski hills to swimming beaches.

Hyland Lake Park Reserve

With well over 1,000 acres, the Hyland Lake Park Reserve contains nearly half the public land in the vicinity. The area is dominated by a high glacial ridge at the northeast end of the park (Mount Gilboa), which gradually drops down into the rolling landscape surrounding 90-acre Hyland Lake at the south end. West of the ridge the Richardson Nature Center lies at the heart of a hilly patchwork of woodlands, prairie, small lakes, and wetlands.

Covering about 100 acres, the restored prairie here is probably one of the finest examples of a well-developed prairie in the metropolitan area. It has taken years of hard work – planting native grasses and flowers, removing foreign plants, and burning the tract to prevent the invasion of trees and shrubs – to approach the diversity of species found in an undisturbed prairie. Native grasses such as big bluestem, little bluestem, Indian grass, side-oats grama, hairy grama, and June grass shelter a constantly changing array of brightly colored wildflowers, including pasque flower, prairie smoke, butterfly weed, leadplant, giant blue hyssop, harebell, prairie rose, wild bergamot, alum root, prairie larkspur, closed gentian, rough blazing star, and a profusion of sunflowers, goldenrods, and asters.

The adjacent oak forests primarily represent overgrown oak savanna. This is suggested by the paucity of middle-aged trees and the presence of large, broad-canopied bur oaks. A wide-spreading growth pattern is characteristic of trees growing in the open. Today the once-solitary bur oaks are crowded by red oak, basswood, black cherry, elm, boxelder, and a dense, shrubby understory. Several shallow ponds, small marshes, and a tiny fen occupy low areas in and around the woods.

Re-introduced in a number of Hennepin County parks, the trumpeter swan now shares the ponds and wetlands with herons, egrets, geese, and ducks, as well as the sora rail, kingfisher, and red-winged blackbird. Some of the raptors known to nest in the park are great horned owl, barred owl, screech owl, red-tailed hawk, and kestrel. Among the many other birds are the bluebird, eastern kingbird, tree swallow, white-breasted nuthatch, brown thrasher, warbling vireo, common yellowthroat, rose-breasted grosbeak, bobolink, eastern meadowlark, brown-headed cowbird, and goldfinch. The resident mammal population includes a thriving herd of white-tailed deer, badger, raccoon, mink, muskrat, flying squirrel, long-tailed weasel, least weasel, masked shrew, pygmy shrew, pocket gopher, and thirteen-lined ground squirrel.

Facilities: Visitors should make their first stop at the Richardson Nature Center. The main building offers information, exhibits, two classrooms, a kitchen, and restrooms. The adjacent building contains staff offices and a meeting room. A network of well-marked nature trails with overlooks and observation docks fans out from the center and explores the varied habitats. There are an additional 8 miles of hiking trails in the park, including 5 miles of paved bike trails. Almost 11 miles of trails are groomed for cross-country skiing and 7 miles of nature trails and bike trails are used for snowshoeing. Except for the Hyland Hills Downhill Ski Area and the Bush Lake Ski Jump on the northeast side of Mount Gilboa, the rest of the facilities are situated in the southern part of the park near Hyland Lake. The modern Hyland Outdoor Recreation Center contains a snackbar, gift shop, and restrooms. You can buy picnic supplies here, or rent skis, snowshoes, bikes, rowboats, paddleboats, and canoes, or check out equipment for a volleyball or croquet game. The boats are for use on Hyland Lake and there is a boat launch for those who bring their own. A large picnic area and a separate group site overlook the lake and offer shelters, tables, grills, games, and water. Also located by the recreation center is a large creative play area, a fitness court, a small lighted skating rink, and a fishing pier. A primitive group camp is situated south of the lake.

Bush Lake Park

Directly across the road from Hyland Park is the city of Bloomington's Bush Lake Park. The park consists of 160 acres of land stretched out around 190-acre Bush Lake. While there are some wooded hills along the lakeshore and a small interpretive area on the north side of the lake, the park is primarily a popular destination for picnickers, boaters, and swimmers.

Facilities: A few well developed picnic sites are scattered around the lake. There is a sandy swimming beach with lifeguards and a bathhouse. There is also a boat launch, playground equipment, a volleyball court, and horseshoe pits.

Tierney's Woods

Located slightly to the northwest along the western edge of Bloomington is a 145 acre county-owned nature area known as Tierney's Woods. Undeveloped except for trails, the area has been described as one of the best woodlands in southern Hennepin County. Stretching between a marsh-rimmed pond and the meandering shoreline of one of the Anderson Lakes, the tract is comprised of hummocky, wooded hills. The upland forest is characterized by tall basswood trees mixed primarily with mature red oak and white oak. A large number of ironwood and paper birch trees are found here, an unusual composition for the area. There are a few sugar maple and black cherry trees, and thick stands of bigtooth aspen have filled in disturbed places open to the sunlight.

Facilities: The main trail follows an old dirt road into the area from the parking lot and two smaller trails make loops through the woods to either side.

Anderson Lakes

Across County Road 18 from Tierney's Woods in Eden Prairie is the county-owned Anderson Lakes Reserve. The area is made up of 310 acres of land embracing all or part of three lakes which total some 365 acres. The Anderson Lakes contain some of the best waterfowl habitat in southern Hennepin County. The lakes are shallow and fringed with a variety of wetland communities. Among the many birds that raise their young here are Canada goose, mallard, blue-winged teal, wood duck, ruddy duck, red-necked grebe, pied-billed grebe, common gallinule, black tern, and red-winged blackbird. The surrounding uplands are are a mixture of old field grasslands on gently rolling areas and pockets of mature woodlands on the steeper hillsides.

Facilities: Development of the area is in its earliest stages. Plans call for the construction of a trail system (connected by corridor parks to the trails at Hyland Lake and Bush Lake) and long-term plans may include a new nature center. Some good views of the lake are possible from along County Road 18, and portions of the area are accessible by way of the old fields and a few informal trails.

Mount Normandale Lake Park

Mount Normandale Lake Park is situated in the shadow of modern office buildings adjacent to the northeast side of Hyland Lake Park Reserve. This municipal park consists of 50 acres of land wrapped around a shallow 135-acre lake dotted with small islands. The islands and scattered marshes provide nesting areas for waterfowl. Nine Mile Creek enters the lake from the north and exits to the east before flowing through a series of broad, low-lying marshes protected by the city of Bloomington.

Facilities: A paved trail with bridges over the creek makes a loop around the entire lake.

How to get there: All of these areas are located south of Interstate Highway 494 and west of Normandale Boulevard (State Highway 100 extended) roughly 14 miles southwest of downtown Minneapolis. To reach the Hyland Lake Park Reserve, Bush Lake Park, or Mount Normandale Lake Park from Interstate 494, exit south onto Normandale Boulevard and go a half a mile to 84th Street. Turn right at 84th (Mount Normandale Lake Park is left of the road here), and follow it, crossing the railroad tracks, as it becomes East Bush Lake Road. Look for signs marking the entrances for the Richardson Nature Center (on the left), Bush Lake Park (on the right), and the Hyland Outdoor Recreation Center (on the left).

There is a nominal daily or annual fee for all vehicles entering Hyland Lake Park Reserve or Bush Lake Park. Parking permits purchased from either Hennepin Parks or the City of Bloomington will be honored at either park.

To reach Tierney's Woods and Anderson Lakes continue west on Interstate 494 for another 2 miles and exit south onto County Road 18. For Tierney's Woods go a short distance south on 18 before taking a left onto Highwood Drive. Look for the small parking lot on the right after making your turn. Anderson Lakes Reserve abuts the west side of County Road 18 for about 1¼ miles beginning a half a mile south of the Interstate.

Map key: West 53

For additional information:

Richardson Nature Center
Hyland Lake Park Reserve
8737 East Bush Lake Road
Bloomington, Minnesota 55438
(612) 941-7993

Bloomington Park and Recreation
Department
2215 W. Old Shakopee Road
Bloomington, Minnesota 55431
(612) 887-9601

Hennepin Parks
12615 County Road 9
Plymouth, Minnesota 55411
(612) 559-9000

Hyland Outdoor Recreation Center
(612) 941-4362
Hyland Hills Ski Area
(612) 835-4604

Interstate State Park

The Dalles of the St. Croix River has long been appreciated as a place of outstanding natural beauty and fascinating geological history. For almost a century the Dalles area has been preserved in the Interstate Parks of Minnesota and Wisconsin. Established in 1895, the two parks were the first cooperative park venture in the United States. The area received additional recognition in 1968 when the St. Croix was one of the first rivers in the nation to be designated as a Wild and Scenic River by the U.S. Congress. Although Minnesota's Interstate Park contains just 293 acres (one-sixth the size of its Wisconsin counterpart), it offers an abundance of sights and activities.

Between the two parks the placid waters of the St. Croix plunge into a narrow gorge bounded by sheer cliffs towering as much as 150 feet above the river. These cliffs are composed of a dark volcanic rock, called basalt, which was formed roughly one billion years ago by a series of immense, fiery lava flows. It is likely that the layers of lava here are contiguous with lava flows exposed on the south shore of Lake Superior. A few hundred million years later what remained of the lava flows were inundated by shallow seas. Over an equally long period of time, as the seas waxed and waned, several hundred feet of sedimentary sandstone and limestone were deposited atop the basalt. When the seas finally receded, some seventy million years ago, the forces of erosion began to reverse the process, eventually uncovering portions of the older volcanic rock.

Then, one million years ago, the most recent Ice Age began and the region was blanketed time after time by slow moving glaciers several thousand feet thick. The deep freeze lasted until "only" 10,000 years ago when the glaciers withdrew northward, leaving behind a layer of debris known as "till." As the last glacier melted great volumes of meltwater formed both Glacial Lake Duluth (now Lake Superior) and Glacial Lake Grantsburg (now extinct). Blocked by dams of ice to the north, the waters spilled southward via the ancestral St. Croix River, quickly cutting into the glacial till and sedimentary rock before encountering the more resistant basalt. The huge river sliced a path through the hard volcanic rock along a course determined by faults and joints, leaving it confined to a deep, narrow gorge – the Dalles. As the river continued to pour through the valley it cut terraces and ground potholes into the rock. Eventually the waters of the Lake Superior basin were able to drain eastward through what are now the Great Lakes, and the St. Croix and its tributaries diminished to their present size.

The Pothole Trail, which starts next to the Interpretive Center, provides visitors a close-up look at the cliffs and dozens of potholes. These potholes form only in turbulent, fast-flowing rivers where pebbles or boulders trapped in a depression are swirled around and around, enlarging and deepening the hole. The potholes at Interstate Park are among the largest in the world, reaching more than 20 feet in diameter and more than 60 feet in depth. The River Trail begins in the same place and follows along the river for more than a mile, passing scenic overlooks and dropping down to the shoreline on its way to the campground.

Most people concentrate their activities near the river but the Curtain Falls Trail, which winds through forested uplands across U.S. Highway 8, provides a lovely and less crowded alternative. The trail to Curtain Falls starts up a steep-sided ravine with sandstone outcroppings where a woodland of sugar maple, basswood, ironwood, hackberry, bitternut hickory, butternut, yellow birch, and alternate-leaf dogwood shades a lush growth of maidenhair fern and colorful wildflowers. Situated at the head of the ravine, the falls are usually dry but thousands of years of erosion have cut an impressive amphitheater-like bowl in the soft sandstone below. In striking contrast to the woods in the ravine, the well-drained glacial till above the falls supports a forest dominated by tall white pine, red pine, and red oak, with some white oak, red maple, paper birch, and aspen. The trail passes an overlook with a beautiful view of the valley before returning by way of another ravine.

For its size, the park supports a surprising diversity of wildlife. Deer, fox, raccoon, skunk, squirrel, and other animals inhabit the wooded uplands, while beaver, muskrat, mink, and otter live in and around the river. More than 150 different species of birds have been sighted here but few attract as much attention as the bald eagles, ospreys, and turkey vultures that are seen along the river from time to time.

Facilities: Visitors should make their first stop at the Interpretive Center located at the north end of the park, which has restrooms and a small museum about the park and its geology.

The park has only 3 miles of foot trails, described above, but few places pack so much into three short walks. The trails are not open to cross-country skiing. The rest of the facilities are situated near the river at the southern end of the park. There is a picnic area with shelters, tables, grills, water, and toilets; a drive-in boat launch and canoe rental; a semi-modern campground with electricity, a dump station, flush toilets, and showers; a primitive group camp; and fishing from the riverbank. You can tour the Dalles on excursion boats that dock at the park's northern end in Taylors Falls. Cooperation between the two parks has led to complementary recreational development and the Wisconsin park offers some activities not available here (such as swimming and cross-country skiing). The St. Croix River is a state-designated canoe route.

How to get there: The park is about 45 miles northeast of the Twin Cities. From Minneapolis or St. Paul head north on either Interstate Highway 35W or 35E. A few miles after the two highways merge, exit onto U.S. Highway 8. Follow Highway 8 to Taylors Falls, passing through Chisago city and Lindstrom. The park entrance is off Highway 8 in Taylors Falls just before the bridge over the river. You can also get here by taking State Highway 95 north along the river from Stillwater or Interstate Highway 94.

The park is closed from 10:00 p.m. to 8:00 a.m. except to registered campers. Daily or annual permits are required for all vehicles entering a state park. They may be purchased at the park entrance. The Interpretive Center is closed throughout the winter.

Map key: East 54

For additional information:

Interstate Park Manager
Box 254
Taylors Falls, Minnesota 55084
(612) 465-5711

Department of Natural Resources
Division of Parks and Recreation
Information Center, Box 40
500 Lafayette Road
St. Paul, Minnesota 55155
(612) 296-4776

Interstate State Park (Wisconsin)

On opposite sides of the historic river that forms the border between the two states, the Interstate Parks of Minnesota and Wisconsin combine to preserve the strikingly scenic gorge known as the Dalles of the St. Croix. Stretching for about three miles along the eastern bank of the river, Interstate Park was the first state park in Wisconsin and part of the first cooperative park venture in the country. In addition, the park is the western terminus of the 1,000-mile long Ice Age Trail, a National Scenic Trail that winds across the state tracing the entire length of the moraines marking the farthest advance of the last glaciers in Wisconsin.

The park encompasses 1,734 acres, dwarfing its 293-acre counterpart across the river, and contains a wide variety of habitats, including two Scientific and Natural Areas. The St. Croix Dalles Scientific Area is an L-shaped segment of the St. Croix River Gorge located in the northern part of the park. More than 100 feet deep, the main gorge was cut into the ancient volcanic bedrock at the end of the Ice Age by an immense river of glacial meltwater pouring out of Glacial Lake Grantsburg. Because the basalt bedrock was well jointed, it was relatively easily removed by water, frost, and gravity, resulting in the vertical cliffs, unusual pinnacled forms, and talus slopes found here. The area is well known for its cylindrical potholes, which are smaller than those on the Minnesota side but spectacular nevertheless.

Vegetation in the rocky gorge is sparse. Several exposed areas of rounded bedrock, vertical cliffs, and boulder slopes are barren, while similar sites with more moisture support polypody fern, fragile fern, rusty woodsia, mosses, and lichens. Scattered about the rocks is a dry and stunted woodland of white pine, red cedar, bur oak, white oak, black oak, basswood, staghorn sumac, and other trees. Big bluestem, poverty oat grass, bearberry, long-leaved bluets, and blueberry are also characteristic of the rocky areas. Fragrant fern, rare and restricted in Wisconsin, is present.

The 80-acre Interstate Floodplain Forest Scientific and Natural Area contains a mature bottomland forest on what is an island in the St. Croix River during periods of high water. The island is six to ten feet above the river but is flooded from time to time. Silver maple is dominant, with green and black ash, hackberry, American elm, and ironwood, and some slippery elm, black oak, and boxelder. The topography is irregular, with many linear levees and a few wet depressions. A small open marsh is stuffed with bulrush, rice cut grass, cordgrass, and reed canary grass.

From the riverbank to the top of the valley, the remainder of the park contains forested hillsides broken by rocky outcroppings and a level terrace with scattered cattail marshes. The more developed soils here support a rich woodland composed chiefly of sugar maple, basswood, red oak, white oak, and ironwood, mixed with bitternut hickory, butternut, white ash, red maple, hackberry, elm, blue beech, and black cherry. The cool understory is crowded with ferns and wildflowers such as wild ginger, Jack-in-the-pulpit, false Solomon's seal, bottle gentian, columbine, and showy lady slipper.

Like the rest of the valley, Interstate Park is enlivened by an abundance of wildlife. A wide variety of mammals, amphibians, and reptiles live here and at least 200 kinds of birds can be expected to use the park during the year. Among the more than 75 that nest in the area are pied-billed grebe, great blue heron, green-backed heron, wood duck, wild turkey, broad-winged hawk, ruffed grouse, barred owl, yellow-bellied sapsucker, least flycatcher, bank swallow, and red-breasted nuthatch, as well as brown thrasher, wood thrush, golden-crowned kinglet, loggerhead shrike, northern oriole, scarlet tanager, rufous-sided towhee, and vesper sparrow. A dozen different warblers have been known to nest in the park, including prothonotary, golden-winged, yellow, blue-winged, cerulean, chestnut-sided, ovenbird, northern waterthrush, Louisiana waterthrush, mourning, common yellowthroat, and American redstart. Many other warblers and a great many other birds move through the park during spring and fall migrations.

Facilities: Visitors should make their first stop at the Ice Age Interpretive Center located a short distance past the park entrance. The center has offices and restrooms, and features photographs, murals, and other information about the glaciers and their effect on the landscape. The varied terrain can be explored on 8 miles of hiking trails and a 1.1-mile-long nature tail. Ten miles of trails are groomed for cross-country skiing. A number of picnic areas offer shelters, tables, grills, and restrooms. A guarded swimming beach with a bathhouse and concession stand is situated on the shore of Lake O' the Dalles. There is also an amphitheater, a ball field, and a boat launch. There are 3 separate campgrounds: the north campground with flush toilets, showers, and a dump station; the less modern south campground; and a primitive group camp. A state fish hatchery is located at the northern edge of the park.

How to get there: See the directions for Minnesota's Interstate Park. From there cross over the river on U.S. Highway 8 and head uphill a short distance before exiting onto State Highway 35 and turning right (south). Look for the park entrance on the right.

The park is closed from 11:00 p.m. to 6:00 a.m. except to registered campers. Daily or annual permits are required for all vehicles entering a state park. They may be purchased at the park entrance.

Map key: East 55

For additional information:

Interstate State Park
Box 703
St. Croix Falls, Wisconsin 54024
(715) 483-3747

James W. Wilkie Unit

The James W. Wilkie Unit is one of seven separate tracts of land along the Minnesota River between Jordan and Fort Snelling that make up the Minnesota Valley National Wildlife Refuge. The Unit borders Valley Fair Amusement Park on the west and extends downstream for more than five miles along the south side of the river. Many people catch a glimpse of the area every day on their way back and forth to work as they cross through the heart of it on the road leading to the Bloomington Ferry Bridge. Comprised of approximately 1,600 acres, the preserve encompasses three large floodplain lakes, a variety of wetland communities, bottomland forest, and small variety of wetland communities, bottomland forest, and small prairie remnants.

The broad shallow lakes, Blue Lake, Fisher Lake, and Rice Lake, and the surrounding lowlands, provide an excellent habitat for an abundance of wildlife. Open waters are rimmed with floating aquatic plants and stretches of bullrushes, cattails, and wild rice, which lure hundreds of wading birds and waterfowl during the nesting season and thousands more during migration. Among the many birds that stop here on their way through in spring and fall are the gadwall, American wigeon, ring-necked duck, lesser scaup, common goldeneye, bufflehead, hooded merganser, snow goose, and tundra swan.

The bottomlands include expanses of willow fen, mixed with aspen on the higher ground, and floodplain forests composed primarily of cottonwood, some of which are very large. Away from the river, along the southern edge of the preserve, there are small sections of dry land on a sandy terrace above the floodplain that contain remnants of native prairie. Wet prairie also exists within the area but much of it has been squeezed out by reed canary grass.

There is a large and thriving great blue heron rookery in a grove of trees near the western edge of the unit. This section is off limits to visitors during the nesting season in order to protect the skittish colony but the herons can easily be seen feeding throughout the area. Great egret, least bittern, green-backed heron, and black-crowned night-heron also inhabit the preserve, sharing the lakes and wetlands with a large number of muskrat, as well as beaver, mink, an occasional river otter, snapping turtle, smooth softshell turtle, fox snake, and green frog.

Facilities: There are trails here for hiking, horseback riding, and cross-country skiing. Snowmobiles are permitted on the Minnesota Valley Trail which follows the river valley and cuts through the Wilkie Unit. During periods of high water substantial portions of the trail system may be flooded and impassable. The Rice Lake State Wayside has a few picnic tables and sanitation facilities, as well as an access to Rice Lake. Small nonmotorized boats are allowed on Rice Lake only.

How to get there: The Unit is most easily reached by taking Interstate Highway 35W south from Interstate Highway 494. Shortly after crossing the Minnesota River, exit onto State

Highway 13 going west. After almost 5 miles Highway 13 turns off to the left and the road becomes State Highway 101. Stay on 101 and look for the Rice Lake Wayside on the right. To reach the trailhead, continue west on 101, passing the turn-off for State highway 18 (to Bloomington Ferry Bridge). The trailhead is located about half a mile west of this intersection.

The portion of the Unit to the west of the trailhead is closed to visitors from the beginning of March until the end of August to protect the rookery.

Map key: West 56

For additional information:

Refuge Manager
Minnesota Valley National
Wildlife Refuge
4101 East 80th Street
Bloomington, Minnesota 55425
(612) 854-5900

Johanna Lake-Schmidt Park

Johanna Lake-Schmidt Park takes in about 60 acres abutting the shore of Lake Johanna in suburban Arden Hills. A narrow strip of land between the lake and Lake Johanna Boulevard contains a number of facilities but most of the area across the road has been left undeveloped as a nature study area. Hillside woodlands of white oak, bur oak, red oak, basswood, and elm overlook a secluded cattail marsh rimmed with cottonwood, willow, ash, boxelder, and small groves of aspen. A railroad track runs along the northern edge of the property where a few native prairie grasses and flowers persist.

Facilities: There are no developed trails here but the informal trails provide good access. The numerous facilities found on both sides of the road near the lake include a guarded swimming beach, concession building, boat launch, playground equipment, drinking water, toilets, and picnic areas with shelters, tables, and grills.

How to get there: From Interstate Highway 35W, exit onto County Road E2 (County 75) about 3 miles north of State Highway 36 or one exit south of Interstate Highway 694. Head east on E2 and take a right (south) onto New Brighton Road (County 47). Go less than a mile to County Road E and turn left (east). After a short distance this road joins Lake Johanna Boulevard. Turn left and look for parking lots on both sides of the road.

Map key: East 57

For additional information:

Ramsey County Parks and
Recreation Department
2015 N. Van Dyke Avenue
Maplewood, Minnesota 55109
(612) 777-1707

Joy Park

Joy Park occupies 63 acres in the northeastern corner of suburban Maplewood between Silver Lake and Interstate Highway 694. Quiet picnic areas set amid mature trees along the north shore of Silver Lake are the only developed facilities here. The rest of the park, across Joy Road, is an undeveloped nature area composed of young woodlands, open meadows, planted evergreens, and small cattail marshes.

Facilities: There are two separate picnic areas next to the lake, each with a shelter, tables, grills, toilets, drinking water, and playground equipment. There are no developed trails here but informal paths wind through the nature area north of the road.

How to get there: The park is located west of Century Avenue between Interstate Highway 694 and State Highway 36. Just south of 694, or almost a mile north of State Highway 36, go west on Lake Boulevard and look for parking areas on the left.

Map key: East 58

For additional information:

Ramsey County Parks and
Recreation Department
2015 N. Van Dyke Avenue
Maplewood, Minnesota 55109
(612) 777-1707

Kasota Prairie

About three and a half miles south of the town of St. Peter, on a terrace overlooking the Minnesota River, is a small preserve known as Kasota Prairie. Consisting of only 38 acres, the tract is a rare example of the tallgrass prairie that once carpeted much of the region. Kasota Prairie escaped the sod-busting plow partly because the topsoil has an average depth of only 12 inches, below which lies solid bedrock in the form of dolomite limestone. Instead, the prairie was mowed for hay until 1969, when it was purchased by The Nature Conservancy.

For seven decades regular mowing prevented the growth of trees and shrubs that would otherwise have replaced the grassland. It is still possible to see how shrubs succeeded around rocky areas where they were sheltered from mowing. Today the prairie is burned periodically in order to replicate the natural conditions that existed before settlement. Fire is the best defense that such isolated grasslands have against invasion from many undesirable weeds, shrubs, and trees. The native grasses and flowers, which have adapted to fire, grow back quickly from protected root systems while other plants are killed by the flames halting their encroachment. The fire also removes the accumulation of dead vegetation, recycling nutrients and exposing the ground to the warming sun, in effect, fertilizing the soil for the new growth.

Although the fires do keep brush in check, shrubs are an important part of the prairie ecosystem. Kasota Prairie has patches of wild plum, wolfberry, and narrow-leaved meadowsweet. These shrubs provide valuable nesting and perching sites for many open-country birds.

Some of the birds that might be considered unique to the area are the dickcissel, eastern bluebird, bobolink, grasshopper sparrow, savanna sparrow, loggerhead shrike, and upland sandpiper. On rare occasions the western kingbird has also been spotted here. In addition to these species, numerous others may be seen on or near the prairie. Kasota Prairie abuts the high bank of the Minnesota River and in early spring it can be excellent for sighting waves of migrating warblers.

The prairie is in almost continuous flower from April to October. Among the common flowers here are the pasque flower, prairie violet, leadplant, prairie rose, blazing star, pale-spike lobelia, and two species of sunflower. One might also look for rattlesnake master, a member of the parsley family with spiny-edged yucca-like leaves. Rattlesnake master reaches the northern edge of its range at Kasota Prairie.

Facilities: There are no developed facilities at Kasota Prairie. As with all Nature Conservancy preserves, the protection of the natural plant and animal communities is the highest priority. Although you are invited to observe and enjoy the preserve, please use care to minimize the impact of your visit.

How to get there: From St. Peter, go south on State Highway 22 for about one mile (crossing the Minnesota River). Turn right onto County Road 21 and head west through the town of Kasota. This is the only paved road running south of the town. About .8 miles south of the village limits, turn right onto a gravel road which is County Road 101. Go 1.5 miles to reach the preserve, which is almost entirely to the left of the road. Look for Nature Conservancy signs posting the area. There is a small pull-off to the right where you can park your car.

Map key: West 59

For additional information:

The Nature Conservancy
Minnesota Chapter
1313 Fifth Street, S.E.
Minneapolis, Minnesota 55414
(612) 379-2134

Katherine Ordway Natural History Study Area

The Katherine Ordway Natural History Study Area occupies 285 acres along the Mississippi River about ten miles south of St. Paul in Inver Grove Heights. The preserve is owned by Macalester College and operated for students by the school's biology department but it is open to visitors any time by appointment. From well-drained uplands to the river's edge, a narrow path leads past a wide variety of habitats, including native prairie, oak savanna, birch forest, mature oak woodlands, temporary and permanent ponds, numerous springs, and a wetland bog.

The soil is coarse gravel, sand, and clay and has poor water retention. This is the major influence in determining the grassland and oak forest vegetation prevalent in the area. Approximately 20 acres of tall prairie grasses, such as big and little bluestem, Indian grass, side-oats grama, and needle grass, are sprinkled with native flowers, including pasque flower, blue-eyed grass, hoary puccoon, prairie rose, wild bergamot, leadplant, Culver's root, and an abundance of asters, daisies, coneflowers, and sunflowers. This rolling upland prairie is dotted with small seasonal ponds and bordered by groves of sumac and quaking aspen that are advancing outward from shady stands of bur oak and pin oak.

Across the railroad tracks that cut through the area the path descends into mature woodlands, which occupy the bluff overlooking the river. While most of the slope is gradual, portions of the bluff are quite steep. The forest here is dominated by wide-spreading white oak and pin oak with paper birch and black cherry. A dense growth of chokecherry, red and black raspberries, gooseberry, hazelnut, and wild grape fills the sunlit understory, along with wildflowers such as wild geranium, large-flowered bellwort, jack-in-the-pulpit, Dutchman's breeches, rue anemone, and columbine. Cool and moist, the sheltered north-facing section of the bluff supports an attractive stand of paper birch with a ground cover of ferns that resembles the north shore. In contrast, the exposed ridge above contains small remnants of oak savanna where hardy bur oaks and a few prairie plants maintain a foothold in the forest.

At the bottom of the hill the trail passes a year-round spring that has created a small wetland between the woods and River Lake. A wealth of water-loving plants abound here, including red-osier dogwood, Joe-Pye weed, jewelweed, white boneset, skunk cabbage, purple asters, blue flag, arrowhead, and watercress, as well as horsetail, bulrushes, sedges, ferns, and mosses. River Lake is a backwater lake separated from the main flow of the Mississippi by a narrow, wooded peninsula.

The study area provides a home to a variety of wildlife. White-tailed deer, red fox, red and grey squirrels, striped skunk, and raccoon are common. Pocket gophers are plentiful in the prairie. Wood duck, mallard, blue-winged teal, and coot, along with great blue heron, great egret, green-backed heron, and belted kingfisher may be seen feeding in the small ponds and along the riverbottom. Barred owl, great horned owl, and pileated woodpeckers nest in the woods, while indigo bunting, yellow-shafted flicker, brown thrasher, scarlet tanager, northern oriole, eastern kingbird, and bluebird enjoy the open spaces, woods, and shrubby thickets. Springtime brings a host of migrating warblers, vireos, and other birds through the area.

Facilities: There is a narrow dirt trail that winds for 2 miles through the numerous habitats. An excellent trail guide is available. The area is used primarily for study so visitors are requested to remain on the trail and make every effort to minimize the impact of their visit. The small building near the entrance contains offices, restrooms, and a laboratory but it is not generally open to the public.

How to get there: From St. Paul or Interstate Highway 494, take State Highway 56 south from St. Paul (or Interstate 494) or take State Highway 55 southeast from the Mendota Bridge. Just after these two highways merge take a left onto County Road 77. Follow 77 for about a mile (passing under railroad tracks) and watch carefully for the entrance on the right. Drive a short distance down the dirt road to the parking area. The trail begins on the opposite side of the building. Please call for permission before visiting.

Map key: East 60

For additional information:

Katherine Ordway Study Area
9550 Inver Grove Trail
Inver Grove Heights, Minnesota
55075
(612) 455-6204
or (612) 696-6104

Kinnickinnic River State Park

Kinnickinnic State Park sits astride the river for which it is named as it flows through a scenic valley before emptying into the St. Croix River just downstream from Minnesota's Afton State Park. The park encompasses approximately 1,300 acres but, as one of Wisconsin's newest state parks, development is in the early stages and there are few facilities. The narrow valley, cut into glacial drift and the underlying sandstone and limestone, contains a wide variety of habitats within a two mile stretch of the river.

The exposed south-facing slope above the river supports a combination of small prairie openings and dry woods characterized by bur oak and red cedar. In contrast, the sheltered north-facing slope supports a comparatively rich woodland dominated by tall white pine, sugar maple, and red oak, mixed with ironwood, basswood, white oak, hackberry, elm, paper birch, and blue beech. The understory here contains large beds of Canadian yew and walking fern, as well as a profusion of wildflowers, such as bloodroot, sharp-lobed hepatica, large-flowered bellwort, rue anemone, wild ginger, wood strawberry, Jack-in-the pulpit, harebell, columbine, and wild rose.

Running between the steep slopes, the river is shaded by a typical floodplain forest of black willow, silver maple, green ash, cottonwood, and elm. At the mouth of the river, where it joins the slow flowing waters of the St. Croix, a sizable semi-open delta has been deposited by the silt-laden Kinnickinnic, and enlarged by dredge spoil. Behind the delta on the downstream side is a large slough that attracts an abundance of wildlife, including osprey, great blue herons, ducks, gulls, painted and softshell turtles, and more.

Dripping and dry cliffs are found intermittently along the valley. A spectacular example of dripping cliffs can be found in a tributary canyon known as the Devil's Mixing Bowl, which is part of a State Scientific Area. An ephemeral stream flows from farmed uplands and spills into the deep, cool gorge where precipitous limestone walls are festooned with ferns, mosses, lichens, and liverworts.

Facilities: Most of the planned facilities will be developed on the uplands north of the river in a gently rolling area of woodlands, old fields, and prairie remnants. A dirt road leads into this part of the park. A mile-long trail is located here. There is a parking lot next to the river where County Road F crosses the valley and a narrow, informal trail winds for about 2 miles along the river toward the delta. On the delta, there is a primitive campsite with a toilet. The campsight is intended only for boaters.

How to get there: Drive east into Wisconsin on Interstate Highway 94. After crossing the St. Croix River take the second exit (at the top of the hill) and go east a short distance on the frontage road to County Road F. This road crosses the Kinnickinnic about 9 miles south of the Interstate. Turn right onto the road on the north side of the valley and follow it to the end to reach the main entrance to the park.

To reach the Devil's Mixing Bowl, continue across the valley and take the first right on the south side of the river. Take this road for 1 mile and pull over next to an old gravel pit just after crossing a small bridge. From here it is about a half a mile walk along a narrow trail through young woods and old field thickets. The area around the bowl is sensitive and, because of slippery footing and overhanging ledges, can be dangerous. Please stay on the well-worn paths. You might also bring a bag to carry out some of the cans and other litter left here by others.

Map key: East 61

For additional information:

Kinnickinnic State Park Manager
Route 3, Box 262
River Falls, Wisconsin 54022
(715) 425-1129

Kunkel Wildlife Management Area

At the southern end of Mille Lacs County, four miles west of Princeton, the Kunkel Wildlife Management Area encompasses 1,945 acres of low-lying land traversed by Battle Brook, a meandering tributary of the St. Francis River. The stream flows through an intricate network of wetlands and shallow lakes that makes up nearly two-thirds of the flat, sandy landscape. Vast stretches of open water and cattail marsh are interspersed with large areas of sedge, willow, and alder. Little Rice Lake contains an extensive stand of wild rice.

Rising only a few feet above the water level, the uplands support a mixture of oak forests, aspen woods, prairie remnants, food plots, and planted evergreens. Red oak, northern pin oak, and bur oak dominate the woodlands, along with some black cherry, chokecherry, and hazelnut. Scattered remnants of native prairie can still be found. Red cedar, hawthorn, chokecherry, and sumac are invading these small openings but controlled burning is planned to maintain them. Because the plantations of pine and spruce offer few benefits to local wildlife they are gradually being removed. Conversely, over 100 acres of winter rye and corn are planted each year to help animals through the winter. Moist soils support thick stands of quaking aspen and lesser amounts of red maple, elm, and green ash.

The diversity of watery and upland habitats are home to an abundance of wildlife. Deer, coyote, red fox, woodchuck, raccoon, rabbit, and squirrel inhabit the woods and meadows, while beaver, muskrat, mink, otter, leopard frog, and painted turtle live in the marshes and along the creek. Birds are plentiful as well, including pied-billed grebe, mallard, blue-winged teal, wood duck, coot, Canada goose, sora rail, yellow-headed blackbird, short-billed marsh wren, woodcock, and common snipe. Observers may also see ruffed grouse, ring-necked pheasant, red-tailed hawk, sharp-shinned hawk, and broad-winged hawk. In addition, the tract is a refuge for a small breeding population of magnificent sandhill cranes.

Facilities: There are no developed facilities here except for the narrow, sandy roads and numerous informal trails that provide access to the area. State Wildlife Management Areas are managed primarily for wildlife production, public hunting, and trapping. Other activities, such as birdwatching and berry-picking, are encouraged but should probably be avoided during the hunting season.

How to get there: Take Interstate Highway 94 and State Highway 101 or U.S. Highway 10 northwest to Elk River. From there go north on U.S. Highway 169. At Princeton, exit onto State Highway 95 and head west. Proceed 2.7 miles west and then turn left onto a sandy road at the Greenbush Town Hall. Shortly after passing a few trailer homes this road enters the preserve. Within the area a few dead end roads intersect this one.

Map key: West 62

For additional information:

Department of Natural Resources
Minnesota Department of Natural Resources
Area Wildlife Manager
915 South Highway 65
Cambridge, Minnesota 55008
(612) 689-2832

Minnesota Department of Natural Resources
Section of Wildlife, Box 7
500 Lafayette Road
St. Paul, Minnesota 55155
(612) 296-3344

Lake Ann Park

This 98-acre municipal park abuts the south shore of Lake Ann in the suburban town of Chanhassen. While most of the park away from the lake is utilized for athletic fields and other recreational facilities, a low-lying belt of land along the shore offers a shaded walkway with nice views of the lake.

The strip of woodlands near the lake includes a lovely stand of mature sugar maples and a lot of large, wide-spreading bur oaks, mixed with tall basswood and red oak, and thickets of prickly-ash, buckthorn, raspberry, Virginia creeper, and wild grape. Along the shoreline these trees give way to black willow, cottonwood, silver maple, green ash, elm, and red-osier dog-wood. The shallow waters near shore are largely open save for a small cattail marsh and scattered bulrushes.

147

Facilities: A paved trail and a woodchip trail follow the shore-line through the woods as far as Greenwood Shores Park, a little neighborhood park. A few fishing docks are located along the trail. There is a small swimming beach on the lake with plans for a concession building and a bathhouse with restrooms. No motors are allowed on the lake but there is a boat launch and eventually the park will have canoes to rent. Also by the lake is a picnic area with tables and grills. Away from the lake the park's facilities include softball and soccer fields, a volleyball court, and tennis courts.

How to get there: From Interstate Highway 494 take State Highway 5 west through Eden Prairie. The park's entrance is on the north side of Highway 5 about 2 miles into Carver County.

The park is open daily from 7:30 a.m. to dusk.

Map key: West 63

For additional information:

Chanhassen City Hall
Parks and Recreation Department
P.O. Box 147
Chanhassen, MN 55317
(612) 937-1900

Lake Elmo Park Reserve

Situated only minutes from St. Paul, a little more than a mile northeast of the intersection of Interstate Highways 94 and 694, the Lake Elmo Park Reserve is the largest tract of public land in Washington County. This recently developed county park occupies more than 2,000 acres stretching west from the shore of 206-acre Lake Elmo and encompassing all of 143 acre Eagle Point Lake. The topography varies from level to steeply-sloped, but most of the area is made up of gently rolling hills dotted with dozens of smaller ponds and wetlands.

A mixture of native prairie and hardwood forest once flour-ished on the silty loams and sandy soils of the region; however, agricultural activities dominated the area for decades, convert-ing prairies to plowed fields and leaving woodlands only where the land was too steep, poorly drained, or otherwise unsuitable for farming. The farms are gone but it will be a long time before they disappear. While old roads and foundations are the most obvious leftovers, there are also small plantations of pine and spruce, rows of trees where fences used to be, and remnant apple orchards.

Although big bluestem and other native grasses still persist locally, about half of the preserve is carpeted by fields of introduced or "weed" species, such as Kentucky bluegrass, quackgrass, mullein, bull thistle, and common yarrow. Woodchuck, badger, cottontail rabbit, thirteen-lined ground squirrel, pocket gopher, meadow mouse, and pheasant have moved into the fields since plowing stopped. Efforts are being made to re-establish native prairie grasses and flowers on one tract of 60 acres near Eagle Lake and another of 28 acres near Lake Elmo.

Woods and wetlands, together with the two larger lakes, comprise less than a third of the preserve. Nevertheless, they have held the key to survival for wildlife in this intensively cultivated area, providing food and shelter for a surprising diversity of animals. Wildlife is generally concentrated in and around areas that include both woods and wetlands. Combined with surrounding thickets and grasslands, these areas are ideal for many species of birds and mammals.

A rich variety of aquatic plants rim open waters and fill small marshes, including cattail, hardstem bulrush, giant burreed, arrowhead, swamp smartweed, white waterlily, and numerous species of pondweed, duckweed, and other floating species. Most of these provide food and cover for wildlife. Mallard, blue-winged teal, and wood duck commonly nest in the park, while Canada goose, widgeon, ringneck, lesser scaup, redhead, canvasback, and pied-billed grebe use the area during migration. Other water-loving birds found here are great blue heron, green-backed heron, American bittern, sora rail, solitary sandpiper, Wilson's snipe, and black tern. Muskrat, mink, painted turtle, and snapping turtle also thrive in the rich wetlands.

Though none are large, numerous tracts of woodland are scattered around the park, primarily on the hills and wet soils bordering the marshy depressions. Red oak is predominant, followed by bur oak and boxelder, as well as northern pin oak, elm, black cherry, hackberry, birch, aspen, and others. These trees and a dense understory of fruit-bearing shrubs, such as buckthorn, hawthorn, elderberry, prickly gooseberry, snowberry, blackberry, and Virginia creeper, supply food and shelter for forest denizens. White-tailed deer, raccoon, striped skunk, gray fox, chipmunk, three kinds of squirrel, and great horned owl, live here.

Facilities: Nearly 20 miles of trails wind throughout the park. About 8 miles are open to horseback riding and 12 miles are groomed each winter for cross-country skiing. An equestrian center is available for visitors who bring their own horses. There are three separate picnic areas, one with a group shelter and toilets, and all with tables, grills, water, and volleyball courts. A swimming pond is located near one of the picnic areas and there is a boat launch on Lake Elmo. The park has both a walk-in campground and an equestrian campground for horseback riders, each with water and toilets. There is a demonstration farm at the northern end of the preserve.

How to get there: Head east from St. Paul on Interstate Highway 94. Three miles past Interstate Highway 694, take the exit for County Highway 19. Turn left (north) on 19 and go a little more than a mile, crossing County Road 70, to the park entrance. There is a nominal daily or annual fee for entry to the park.

Map key: East 64

For additional information:

Washington County Parks
11660 Myeron Road N.
Stillwater, Minnesota 55082
(612) 731-3851

Lakefront Municipal Park

Lakefront Park contains 126 acres of open space along the well-developed shoreline of Prior Lake, the largest lake in Scott County. About 50 acres of the park's most level land is used for a variety of athletic activities. The remainder is a mixture of habitats wrapped around a seven acre inlet known as "Watzel's Bay."

The most notable natural attraction here is a lovely belt of mature woods carpeting a steep hillside overlooking the meandering lakeshore. This sloping woodland is made up of sizable sugar maple, basswood, and red oak trees, with ironwood in the understory. Elsewhere, the more gently rolling land supports scattered bur oaks, young woods and thickets, old fields, and some plantings of pine and spruce. A shallow pond is set into the trees near the park's entrance.

Facilities: The park has a small network of hiking trails which are also used for cross-country skiing in winter. A wooden walkway and bridge lead down the face of the wooded slope to the lakeshore where there is a swimming beach with a bathhouse and concession stand. A picnic area is located atop the hill with a shelter, tables, and a grill. The athletic facilities include a softball field, 2 soccer/football fields, 2 hockey rinks, a basketball court, and a volleyball court.

How to get there: Heading south from the Cities on Interstate Highway 35W, take the second exit after crossing the Minnesota River onto State Highway 13. Go west a little more than 4 miles and turn left (south) where Highway 13 splits with State Highway 101. Stay on 13 for just over 5 more miles and turn right at 160th Street (County 21). Take another right immediately onto Ridgemont Avenue. After a short distance turn left onto Rutledge and look for the park entrance on the left.There is no fee except for the reservation and use of the picnic shelter.

Map key: West 65

For additional information:

Prior Lake City Hall
Park and Recreation Department
4629 Dakota Street S.E.
Prior Lake, Minnesota 55372
(612) 447-4230

Lake George Regional Park

This 270 acre park extends for a mile along the shoreline of Lake George in northern Anoka County. Weekend crowds are attracted here by the long natural sand beach and various lakeside facilities. Currently, the remainder of the park is an undeveloped tract of mature oak woodlands, old fields, small ponds, and extensive wetland communities. However, the county is planning to build a loop drive through the area and greatly expand the recreational facilities.

Facilities: Picnic shelters, tables, grills, drinking water, restrooms, and a bathhouse are all located amid shade trees near the swimming beach. There is also a public boat launch with parking. Future development will include the parkway, additional picnic areas, fishing docks, ball fields, and a lengthy system of nature trails with boardwalks providing access to the wetlands.

How to get there: From U.S. Highway 10 just east of Anoka, exit onto County Highway 9. Proceed north on 9 for about 11 miles and look for the park entrance on the right. Or take State Highway 65 north 21 miles from Interstate 694 to County Road 74. Take a left onto 74 and go about 5.5 miles west to County Highway 9. Turn left here and look for the park on the left.

Map key: West 66

For additional information:

Anoka County Parks and
Recreation
550 Bunker Lake Blvd.
Anoka, Minnesota 55304
(612) 757-3920

Lake Maria State Park

Sprawling over 1,312 acres of rough, wooded terrain six miles west of Monticello, Lake Maria State Park is the largest expanse of protected wildland in Wright County. The park is situated near the northern edge of the "Big Woods," a lush hardwood forest that once stretched 100 miles to the south and was as much as 40 miles wide. The forest thrived on the calcium and limestone-rich soils deposited over much of south-central Minnesota by the last glacier. Lake Maria State Park preserves something of the scale and character of the original Big Woods.

Hikers and cross-country skiers will enjoy the varied topography here. The eastern half of the park is composed of tightly packed hills cloaked by a rich forest and punctuated by small woodland marshes and steep-sided ice-block ponds. The forest of sugar maple, basswood, red oak, white oak, and ironwood shelters a damp understory where ferns and wildflowers flourish. In spring the ground is dotted with bloodroot, yellow violet, large-flowered bellwort, wood anemone, showy trillium, Virginia bluebell, round-lobed hepatica, showy orchis, and others. To the west the landscape is an open mixture of woods, old fields, wetlands, and shallow lakes, including scenic Lake Maria.

The diversity of habitats makes the park attractive to a profusion of wildlife, including more than 200 bird species that nest here or pass through during migration. The lakes and wetlands lure common loon, wood duck, mallard, teal, great egret, great blue heron, red-winged blackbird, and Franklin's gull. On occasion visitors also see osprey and bald eagle. Other raptors include the marsh hawk, Cooper's hawk, short-eared owl, screech owl, and great horned owl. Among the many songbirds that enliven the park are bluebird, goldfinch, northern oriole, yellowthroat, great crested flycatcher, black-capped chickadee, brown thrasher, rose-breasted grosbeak, wood thrush, and red-eyed vireo. In addition, the pileated woodpecker is a permanent resident, nesting in cavities chiseled deep into dead trees.

Facilities: More than 12 miles of well-maintained hiking trails crisscross the park and are groomed for cross-country skiers. A small interpretive center is kept open in winter for skiers to warm themselves by a wood burning stove. Half of the trail system is open to horseback riding. The park is one of few state parks where backpacking is the only camping allowed. There are 11 secluded walk-in sites in four separate areas near Bjorkland Lake. Large groups may reserve the primitive group camp located in the north end of the park. There is a handicapped accessible picnic area overlooking Maria Lake with tables, grills, water, and toilets. A boat access is located next to the picnic ground.

How to get there: Take Interstate Highway 94 northwest from the Twin Cities. Take the Monticello exit (State Highway 25) and go south for nearly 2 miles to County Road 106. Turn right here and follow 106 for about 6 miles to County Highway 11. Turn right again and proceed about 3.5 miles to the park entrance on the left.

The park is closed from 10:00 p.m. to 8:00 a.m. except to registered campers. Daily or annual permits are required for all vehicles entering a state park. They may be purchased at the park entrance.

Map key: West 67

For additional information:

Lake Maria State Park Manager
Route 1
Monticello, Minnesota 55362
(612) 878-2325

Minnesota Department of Natural Resources
Division of Parks and Recreation
Information Center, Box 40
500 Lafayette Road
St. Paul, Minnesota 55155
(612) 296-4776

Lake Minnewashta Regional Park

Little more than a mile, as the crow flies, from Lake Minnetonka, this Carver County park occupies 350 acres of rolling woods and old fields wrapped around a shallow bay of scenic Lake Minnewashta. Known as "Little Minnie," the marshy inlet separates a natural area of wooded hills and scattered wetlands from the well-developed peninsula where most of the park's recreational facilities are concentrated.

The park's woodlands vary from mature stands dominated by sugar maples or red oaks mixed with basswood, ash, bur oak, black cherry, and ironwood, to young thickets of bitternut hickory, elm, aspen, paper birch, red cedar, buckthorn, and sumac. Along the circle drive that winds past the picnic areas on the peninsula are a few impressive oak trees, including one exceptional old bur oak. The open fields at the southern end of the park are being planted with thousands of seedlings to assist the slow process of succession and recreate the "Big Woods" that once characterized the area. Numerous spots along the trails provide nice views of "Little Minnie" where stretches of cattails give way to open waters dotted with flotillas of waterlilies. A patient observer may see a fair number of the birds and other small animals that are attracted to this productive marsh.

Facilities: Several miles of trails loop through the woods and fields, skirt the marshes, and follow the shoreline. The trails are groomed for cross-country skiing in the winter and most can be hiked the rest of the year. Skis can be rented in the park. Numerous picnic areas with shelters, tables, and grills are available, some with restrooms and water. Near the picnic areas is a swimming beach with a bathhouse, as well as an active play area and "tot lot" for kids. There are two separate boat launches, one with a 15 horsepower restriction and one unrestricted. Plans call for the development of additional facilities, including a small amphitheater, a multi-use center, a paved bicycle path, and a group campground. The park has a resident caretaker.

How to get there: From Interstate Highway 494 take either State Highway 5 west past Chanhassen or State Highway 7 west past Excelsior. Turn left from Hwy. 7 or right from Hwy. 5 onto State Highway 41 and look for the park entrance on the west side of the road.

The park is open from 8:00 a.m. to 9:00 p.m. or one hour past sunset, whichever is later. During the summer lifeguards are on duty from 11:00 a.m. to 5:00 p.m. There is a nominal daily or annual fee for entry to the park.

Map key: West 68

For additional information:

Carver County Parks
10775 County Road 33
Young America, Minnesota 55397
1-800-642-7275

Lake Rebecca Park Reserve

Lake Rebecca Park Reserve occupies 2,262 acres of gently rolling countryside bordering the Crow River at the western edge of Hennepin County. Like many of the larger parks in the Twin Cities area, it is composed primarily of former farmland. For years farmers here cleared forests and drained wetlands, dramatically altering the landscape to meet the needs of a growing country. More recently however, the land was set aside to serve as a refuge for wildlife and to help meet the recreational requirements of the large urban population nearby.

The centerpiece of the park is 290-acre Lake Rebecca, but there are also smaller lakes, restored wetlands, scattered woodlands, and old fields to explore. This diversity of habitats, including a variety of successional stages, supports abundant wildlife. For this reason, while many of the old fields will be allowed to slowly develop into mature woodlands, others will be maintained as open grasslands.

Deer, red and gray fox, badger, raccoon, woodchuck, and skunk are some of the mammals that roam the fields and forests, while beaver, muskrat, and mink dwell in the lakes and wetlands. The trumpeter swan, re-introduced to the area nearly 100 years after being wiped out by hunting and habitat destruction, is a spectacular resident of the park and can be easily observed. Other waterfowl here includes Canada goose, mallard, wood duck, ruddy duck, blue-winged teal, and green-winged teal. Great blue heron, green-backed heron, sora rail, yellow-headed blackbird, and double-crested cormorant are also present. In addition, numerous raptors and songbirds inhabit the varied upland environs of the park. Fall is a good time to visit, as many birds, particularly geese and diving ducks, stop here on the way south. The park is also home to the spring peeper, a tiny frog whose high-pitched chorus is considered to be one of the first signs of spring.

Facilities: An extensive system of trails explores the park's woods, meadows, and wetlands. There are nearly 10 miles of trails for hiking, 7.5 miles of trails for horseback riding, a 6.5-mile paved loop for bicyclists, more than 6 miles of groomed trails for cross-country skiing, and a stretch open to snowmobiling. There are three sizable reservation picnic areas with shelters, tables, electricity (at 2 shelters), volleyball courts, and gamefields. Two of the sites are close to the public beach, creative play area, and toilets. Park visitors may rent bikes, canoes, rowboats, aquabikes, paddleboats, and volleyball equipment. Three campsites provide groups the option to drive or hike to sites with shelter and water. There is a large swimming beach and a boat launch on Lake Rebecca.

How to get there: Take State Highway 55 west from Minneapolis for about 20 miles. Turn left (south) onto County Road 50 just before Rockford and the Crow River. After a couple of bends in the road look for the park entrance on the left.

The rental building is open from 8:00 a.m. to 7:00 p.m. on weekends and holidays. The beach is open from 11:00 a.m. to 7:00 p.m. between Memorial Day and Labor Day. There is a nominal daily or annual fee for entry to the park.

Map key: West 69

For additional information:

Hennepin Parks
12615 County Road 9
Plymouth, Minnesota 55411
(612) 559-9000
or (612) 757-4700 (Lake Rebecca)

Lamprey Pass Wildlife Management Area

Bordering busy Interstate Highway 35 less than twenty miles north of St. Paul, the Lamprey Pass Wildlife Management Area contains one of the largest rookeries in the state. At the heart of this 1,268-acre preserve is a noisy treetop colony where hundreds of great blue herons, great egrets, black-crowned night herons, and double-crested cormorants nest, a combination found nowhere else in Minnesota. The abundant wildlife of Lamprey Pass had an advocate over a century ago but it wasn't until 1981 that the area received the recognition and protection it deserved.

The tract is named for Uri Lamprey, a prominent St. Paul attorney who was appointed by the governor in 1901 to organize and lead the new Game and Fish Commission and is regarded as the father of Minnesota's game laws. A naturalist and a hunter, Lamprey fought for bag limits and never shot more than two or three ducks at a time. In 1881 he purchased a stretch of high ground between Howard and Mud Lakes known as "the pass." It later became the Lamprey Pass Gun Club. Wild rice beds were so lush that hunters sometimes used dynamite to clear enough space for ducks to land.

During the 1970s, interest in the gun club waned and the last caretaker moved off the property. Vandals burned buildings and off-road vehicles raced around the woods and fields. Then, in 1980 a developer announced plans to build an 800-unit recreational vehicle park right on top of the rookery. Fortunately for the birds, this and other proposals were defeated by the efforts of local citizens and the Department of Natural Resources who won the support of the Township Board and the county commissioners. The property was then purchased by The Nature Conservancy, which held onto it until the state could buy the land. Shortly thereafter, the Lamprey Pass Wildlife Management Area became the first major land purchase made with money from the Nongame Wildlife Fund, also known as the "Chickadee Checkoff" on our state income tax refunds.

In addition to protecting the valuable rookery, the preserve provides a home to many other animals. Between and around the broad, shallow lakes that dominate the area is a rich patchwork of mature forest, second-growth woodlands, old field grasslands, food plots, swampy thickets, marshes, and a woodland pond. At least seventy other species of birds raise their young here each summer, including the common loon, mallard, wood duck, blue-winged teal, pied-billed grebe, green-backed heron, kingfisher, Cooper's hawk, red-tailed hawk, great-horned owl, pileated woodpecker, ruffed grouse, pheasant, and dozens of songbirds. White-tailed deer share the woodlands and meadows with red fox, raccoon, woodchuck, cottontail rabbit, and gray squirrel, while mink, muskrat, and beaver inhabit the lakes and wetlands.

Lamprey Pass is also interesting historically. Two groups of three Indian burial mounds each are situated near Howard Lake, and three villages or campsites have been found in the nearby woods and fields. Some pottery was discovered close to the mounds that is thought to have been made by the Hopewell culture of central Illinois about 1,800 years ago. As part of this publicly owned wildlife area, the future of the ancient archaeological sites is secure.

Facilities: There are no developed facilities here other than a parking area and an old road that serves as a footpath. A number of informal trails lead away from the dirt road. Because the nesting colony is sensitive to disturbance, the area between Howard and Mud Lakes and north of the old drainage ditch is maintained as a sanctuary and is off-limits during the nesting season. (The birds, however, can be easily observed feeding throughout the area.) State Wildlife Management Areas are managed for three primary reasons: wildlife production, public hunting, and trapping. Other activities, such as birdwatching, are also encouraged but should probably be avoided during the hunting season.

How to get there: From the Twin Cities head north on either Interstate Highway 35W or 35E. A little more than a mile after these highways merge take the exit for State Highway 97 (and County Highway 23). Turn left and cross over the Interstate, then take an immediate right onto the dirt frontage road. If the road is open take it a short distance to the parking area; if not, park in the "Park and Ride" lot and walk from there.

Map key: East 70

For additional information:

Carlos Avery WMA
5643 W. Broadway
Forest Lake, Minnesota 55025
(612) 464-2860

Minnesota Department of Natural Resources
Section of Wildlife, Box 7
500 Lafayette Road
St. Paul, Minnesota 55155
(612) 296-3344

Lawrence Wayside

The Lawrence State Wayside encompasses some 2,100 acres along the Minnesota River near the town of Belle Plaine. Also known as the Lawrence Unit, it is part of a complicated mosaic of federal, state, and local preserves that protect a precious strip of wildlands stretching from here to Fort Snelling in the heart of the metropolitan area.

The rich alluvial soil along the river supports a well-developed floodplain forest dominated by large cottonwood, silver maple, and black willow, with some American elm, green ash, and boxelder. A number of shallow, spring-fed lakes and a variety of wetland communities are scattered throughout the low-lying areas.

Occupying a sandy terrace above the floodplain, the rest of the park is primarily composed of oak forest and shrubby thickets that represent overgrown oak savanna and old fields. Broad-canopied bur oaks and persistent pockets of prairie grasses are evidence of the native savanna that once characterized these well drained uplands. Much of the area has been covered by almost impenetrable growths of sumac, prickly-ash, hazelnut, gray dogwood, chokecherry, buckthorn, and red cedar, while in other areas, young woodlands of red oak, basswood, black cherry, and groves of aspen have become established.

On a 25-acre parcel, controlled burning is being used to restore a portion of the original landscape. Deep-rooted prairie plants survive, even flourish, after a fire, but the invading woody plants are killed.

161

Wildlife abounds within the river valley. The riverbanks, floodplain lakes, and marshes provide habitat for beaver, musk-rat, mink, snapping turtle, northern water snake, leopard frog, belted kingfisher, and an assortment of rails, herons, and waterfowl. The upland woods, thickets, and grasslands are home to deer, red fox, striped skunk, thirteen-lined ground squirrel, white-footed mouse, common garter snake, an occasional badger or coyote, and a variety of songbirds, including brown thrasher, yellow-breasted chat, indigo bunting, rufous-sided towhee, least flycatcher, and field sparrow.

Facilities: There are many miles of trails here for hikers, cross-country skiers, horseback riders, and snowmobilers, including a stretch of the Minnesota Valley Trail. During periods of high water substantial portions of the trail system may be flooded and impassable. A hard surfaced bicycle path will eventually connect the area with Fort Snelling State Park. The park includes 25 rustic, drive-in campsites, 10 walk-in sites, a number of primitive canoe campsites, and a separate pioneer group camp. There is also a pleasant picnic area with tables, grills, water, and toilets.

How to get there: The area is located a little more than 10 miles southwest of Shakopee in Scott County. From Shakopee take U.S. Highway 169 south along the river valley. At Jordan, take a right onto County Highway 9. After crossing the railroad tracks take a left onto County Road 57 and continue about 2.5 miles to the Wayside. This road leads past entrances to the headquarters, trail center, campground, and picnic area.

Map key: West 71

For additional information:

Park Manager
19825 Park Blvd.
Jordan, Minnesota 55352
(612) 492-6400

Minnesota Department of Natural Resources
Division of Parks and Recreation
Information Center, Box 40
500 Lafayette Road
St. Paul, Minnesota 55155
(612) 296-4776

Lebanon Hills Regional Park

Situated within two of the fastest growing suburbs in the Twin Cities area is Lebanon Hills Regional Park, formerly known as Holland-Jensen Park. Consisting of 2,331 acres in Eagan and Apple Valley, stretching east from the Minnesota Zoo, the park is the largest in Dakota County. The scenic preserve offers a wide variety of outdoor activities amid a landscape of rolling wooded hills and grassy meadows dotted with dozens of lakes, ponds, and marshes.

Many of the area's rock-strewn hills are blanketed by mature oak woodlands. Well drained uplands are alternately dominated by stands of red oak and white oak with an appealing mixture of paper birch and ironwood and an open understory carpeted with wild black currant, meadow rue, and a profusion of interrupted, bracken, lady, and maidenhair ferns. In other places the oaks stand with black cherry, aspen, elm, hackberry, and red maple, above a dense growth of buckthorn, chokecherry, hazelnut, black raspberry, and wild grape.

The park's watery habitats range from small seasonal marshes filled with cattail or sedges to shallow lakes thick with yellow waterlily and arrowhead. Low-lying areas bordering the lakes and wetlands support large black willow, silver maple, and boxelder, along with round-leaved dogwood, alder, elderberry, and jewelweed. Throughout the park, particularly in the less hilly sections, the forest is interspersed with small evergreen plantations and old fields in various stages of succession.

The diversity of habitats with ample shelter and food sources is home to an abundance of wildlife. Lebanon Hills is an excellent place for birdwatching. Red-tailed hawk, sparrow hawk, and pileated woodpecker nest here. Colorful indigo bunting, goldfinch, red-eyed vireo, scarlet tanager, northern oriole, rufous-sided towhee, cardinal, and rose-breasted grosbeak can be seen here, as well as catbird, brown thrasher, blue jay, hairy woodpecker, and several species of warbler. Wood duck, mallard, great egret, and green-backed heron share the ponds and marshes with mink, muskrat, and painted turtles. White-tailed deer, red fox, striped and spotted skunk, raccoon, and woodchuck roam the woods and meadows, in addition to red, gray, and fox squirrels, cottontail rabbits, chipmunks, mice, and shrews.

Facilities: There are extensive trails for hiking and horseback riding in both the eastern and western sections of the park (divided by Pilot Knob Road). Maps are located at trail intersections. Portions of these trails are maintained for cross-country skiing and snowmobiling. Unique to our metropolitan parks is a 2-mile-long (one way) canoe trail which traverses 6 lakes and 5 portages. Horse trailer parking is provided but visitors may also rent horses at the Diamond "T" Ranch on Pilot Knob Road. Picnic tables are situated in spots along the trail. Schultz Lake has a developed swimming beach with a snack bar. Two major picnic sites are located at Holland and Jensen Lakes and are equipped with tables, grills, bathrooms, and running water. The park also contains camping facilities for recreational vehicles and a Youth Group Camp. An archery range is located off Johnny Cake Ridge Road.

How to get there: From the Twin Cities you can take Cliff Road (County Road 32) east from Interstate Highway 35W, Highway 77 (Cedar Avenue), or Interstate Highway 35E. For the nature trail, canoe trail, or horse rental take a right (south) at Pilot Knob Road and look for signs. Stay on Cliff Road to reach separate parking areas for picnicking and hiking (skiing in winter) by Holland Lake, or the swimming beach and hiking at Schultz Lake. Go south on Dodd Road and west a short distance on 120th Street to reach the horse trailer parking lot.

The trails are open daily from 5:00 a.m. to 11:00 p.m. Schultz Beach is open during the summer months between 11:00 a.m. and 8:00 p.m. There is a daily or annual fee for use of the beach (except on Wednesdays, which are free).

Map key: East 72

For additional information:

Dakota County Parks Department
8500 127th Street East
Hastings, Minnesota 55033
(612) 437-6608

Lilydale Regional Park

Lilydale Regional Park includes more than 350 acres of reclaimed open space along the Mississippi River about two miles upstream from downtown St. Paul. Combining portions of both Ramsey and Dakota Counties, the park occupies the bottomlands between the river and the high bluffs. Over the years a variety of human activities have left their mark on the area. The park has a scruffy appearance and there are no facilities as yet, but long term plans call for extensive restoration and development.

The town of Lilydale was once located in what is now the park and a number of the original homes stood here until recent decades. The houses are gone now but narrow lanes, old foundations, lilac bushes, and other leftovers remain. Natural caves in the sandstone bluffs were enlarged and others excavated for commercial uses, such as cheese storage, beer storage, mushroom cultivation, and even a ballroom. Most of these caves have since been filled or barricaded. One of these, Echo Cave, is open to organized groups with permission of the St. Paul Parks Department.

The park was also the site of the Twin City Brick Quarry, where sections of the bluff were mined for clay. The mining exposed some of the underlying Decorah Shale, a layer of sedimentary rock that is rich in fossils, some found nowhere else. A number of schools, museums, and nature centers use the abandoned mine for geological study.

Much of the bluff-face is wooded and there are strips of floodplain forest along the river and the shore of Pickerel Lake. Situated at the base of the bluff, the 100-acre lake, which is fed by natural springs and tiny Ivy Creek, supports a growth of marsh marigold, smartweed, water milfoil, elodea, sazo and narrowleaf pondweed, and an abundance of white waterlilies. Northern pike, black bullhead, bluegill, and more than a dozen other species of fish inhabit the shallow waters. Great blue herons and great egrets come to feed from their rookery at Pig's Eye. Other birds one might see here are the belted kingfisher, red-winged blackbird, bank swallow, Wilson's snipe, pectoral sandpiper, and black tern.

Facilities: There are no facilities here other than a dirt parking area next to the lake, but informal trails and open spaces make it easy to get around. Many people come to fish in the lake or along the riverbank. The park is connected to Harriet Island across the river from downtown St. Paul. That park offers a picnic area with a shelter, tables, grills, water, restrooms, a small boat launch, and open fields.

How to get there: From downtown St. Paul, drive southward across the Wabasha Street Bridge and turn right onto Water Street. Follow Water Street under the High Bridge and along the river. The parking lot next to Pickerel Lake is on the left just past the second railroad trestle.

Map key: East 73

For additional information:

St. Paul Division of Parks and
Recreation
300 City hall Annex
St.Paul, Minnesota 55102
(612) 292-7400

Locke Park

Straddling a couple of major roads and squeezed into the densely populated neighborhoods of suburban Fridley, Locke Park protects a valuable natural area along meandering Rice Creek. The existing 122-acre park has been preserved by the City of Fridley for many years. In conjunction with this park, Anoka County more recently acquired another 100 acres of land along or near the creek to create a continuous trailway connecting Manomin Park on the Mississippi River with the Rice Creek-Rush Lake-Long Lake Regional Park in Ramsey County.

The natural area here is generally limited to the stream valley that gives the park a measure of seclusion. Rice Creek twists back and forth across the small valley between short, steep, wooded hillsides. The woods are mature in some areas but dense young stands of saplings and shrubs are more common. A few lovely old bur oaks occupy the high ground, along with red oak, pin oak, basswood, black cherry, ironwood, and aspen. Some tall black willow and cottonwood grow along the creek with silver maple, elm, boxelder, paper birch, and planted weeping willows. East of Central Avenue, where a low dam blocks the creek, Anoka County land encompasses a broader floodplain with typical bottomland vegetation.

Facilities: A woodchip hiking trail and a paved bike trail wind along the valley, crossing the stream several times on small bridges. Where the stream flows out of the park to the west the trails cut across the uplands. The trails are open for cross-country skiing. The parcel east of Central Avenue has a separate parking area and a shelter with information and restrooms. The rest of the facilities are located north of the creek in Locke Park. There is a picnic area with tables, grills, a shelter, water, and restrooms, as well as a playground and horseshoe pits. When the water level is high enough the creek is used for canoeing. The park is adjacent to the Columbia Ice Arena.

How to get there: Take University Avenue (State Highway 47) north from Minneapolis or Interstate Highway 694. A mile and a half north of 694 the road crosses Rice Creek. Take the next right onto the frontage road, continue north briefly, then turn right onto the park road just past the Columbia Ice Arena. A city bike trail cuts across the creek and the park from the end of this road. To reach the parking area upstream, turn right off University Avenue onto Mississippi Street just over a mile north of 694. Stay on Mississippi for a mile and a quarter, crossing State Highway 65, and turn left at Central Avenue. Go a half a mile north and turn right onto 69th Avenue. Look for the entrance on the right.

Map key: West 74

For additional information:

Fridley Recreation Department
6431 University Avenue N.E.
Fridley, Minnesota 55432
(612) 571-3450

Anoka County Parks Department
550 Bunker Lake Boulevard N.W.
Anoka, Minnesota 55304
(612) 757-3920

Lone Lake Park

This 103-acre municipal park in southeastern Minnetonka has been developed primarily as a recreation area. In addition to its numerous facilities, however, the park includes a few dozen acres of wooded hills, a short stretch of the south branch of Nine Mile Creek, and the lake from which it derives its name. Bordered by a steep, wooded hill, the lake is surrounded by black willow, cottonwood, green ash, silver maple, and paper birch, and contains some cattail and flotillas of huge waterlilies. A mixture of dense woods and shrubby openings extends west of the lake toward Nine Mile Creek.

Facilities: A short trail system for hikers and cross-country skiers explores the park's natural area and an observation dock extends into the small lake. There is a nice picnic area adjoining the lake with a shelter, tables, grills, and satellite toilets. The park's many athletic facilities include a soccer field, softball field, basketball court, a nine-"hole" frisbee golf course, a volleyball court, tennis courts, horseshoe pits, and playground equipment for children.

How to get there: The entrance to the park is located on Shady Oak Road (County Road 61) a few blocks north of County Highway 62 and a little more than a mile south of Excelsior Blvd.

Map key: West 75

For additional information:

Minnetonka Parks and Recreation
Department
14600 Minnetonka Blvd.
Minnetonka, Minnesota 55345
(612) 933-251

Long Lake Regional Park

Long Lake Regional Park occupies approximately 230 acres within the city limits of New Brighton and Moundsview near the intersection of Interstate Highways 35W and 694. The oddly shaped county park stretches between the shorelines of

Long Lake and smaller Rush Lake and includes over a mile of Rice Creek, which flows in and out of Long Lake on its way to the Mississippi River. In addition to protecting valuable open space in this well-developed area, the park contains facilities for a variety of recreational activities.

The rolling landscape is composed of woodlands, abandoned farmland, planted red pines, wetlands, and floodplain along Rice Creek. Patches of woods are dominated by mature red oak, bur oak, and northern pin oak, with quaking aspen and a dense understory of small trees and shrubs. Scattered wetlands also dot the park, including an extensive cattail marsh adjoining Rush Lake. The county has plans to add to the diversity of habitats here by restoring nine acres of old field to native prairie.

Even though it is surrounded by highways, commerce, and houses, and split by railroad tracks, the park is home to white-tailed deer, woodchuck, raccoon, gray squirrel, cottontail rabbit, and other wildlife, including a variety of songbirds and waterfowl.

Facilities: Most of the park's facilities are located next to Long Lake. There is a swimming beach, boat launch, playground apparatus, and a small building with concession, lockers, showers, and restrooms. There is also a picnic area with tables and toilets, and a large group picnic area with a shelter. A system of trails for hiking and cross-country skiing is being developed and will eventually include a floating boardwalk. The park is also the future site of the museum for the New Brighton Area Historical Society.

How to get there: Heading north on Interstate Highway 35W, take the first exit after crossing Interstate Highway 694. This is State Highway 96 (County Road G). Turn left and go west a short distance to Old Highway 8 (Forest Lake Cutoff). Turn left again (south) and look for the park entrance on the right.

Map key: East 76

For additional information:

Ramsey County Parks and
Recreation Department
2015 N. Van Dyke Street
Maplewood, Minnesota 55109
(612) 777-1707

Louisville Swamp and Carver Rapids State Wayside

Situated adjacent to the Renaissance Festival a few miles southwest and upriver from Shakopee, the Louisville Swamp is one of the many separate units that make up the Minnesota Valley National Wildlife Refuge. The preserve takes in more than 2,200 acres wrapped around the 400-acre Carver Rapids State Wayside. Undeveloped except for trails, the two areas combine to form a mosaic of wildlife-rich habitats stretching for more than four miles along the Minnesota River.

Much of the area overlies a broad, sandy terrace above the floodplain characterized by dense oak woodlands, old fields, and tracts of prairie and oak savanna. Except for scattered remnants that persist on exposed hillsides, the native grasslands are found near the parking lot and within the Carver Rapids Wayside. Warm season grasses such as big bluestem, little bluestem, Indian grass, sideoats grama, switchgrass, and hairy grama shelter a constantly changing array of blooming wildflowers. Most of the woods and thickets represent overgrown prairie and savanna, but in a few places old, wide-spreading bur oaks still stand singly and in small groves amid the prairie grasses and flowers. Only the use of controlled burning protects the prairies from invasion by surrounding thickets of red cedar, hawthorn, chokecherry, boxelder, and sumac. Pockets of mature woodlands are dominated by bur oak, with red oak, basswood, black cherry, ironwood, hackberry, bitternut hickory, red cedar, groves of aspen, and an understory of buckthorn, chokecherry, prickly-ash, gooseberry, and raspberry.

The swamp for which the area is named is a vibrant expanse of wetlands where Sand Creek has cut a broad swath through the upland terrace as it winds toward the Minnesota River. The low-lying complex is a lush intermingling of open waters, waterlilies, bulrush beds, cattail marsh, sedge meadow, thickets of willow, alder, and dogwood, and bottomland forests. A great variety of wildlife prospers in this productive environment, including beaver, muskrat, mink, snapping turtle, false map turtle, painted turtle, smooth softshell turtle, northern water snake, fox snake, eastern newt, northern leopard frog, green frog, and spring peeper. Among the many birds that come here to nest or feed are the American bittern, great blue heron, great egret, green-backed heron, black-crowned night heron, Canada goose, pied-billed grebe, wood duck, mallard, blue-winged teal, common moorhen, Virginia rail, black tern, belted kingfisher, and yellow-headed blackbird.

Two pioneer homesteads constructed from local stone in the 1860s still stand here. Both are located along the Mazomani Trail and one has been renovated to serve as trail shelter. Mazomani was chief of one of the bands of Dakotah Indians that inhabited this area before and during the early period of settlement.

Facilities: Nearly 10 miles of well-marked trails provide good access to the various habitats, but low areas along the trail can be flooded during periods of high water. The Mazomani Trail makes a loop around the swamp and connects to a smaller loop through the Carver Rapids Wayside. A completed portion of the Minnesota Valley Trail parallels the river, extending upriver to the Lawrence State Wayside and downriver to Shakopee. Horseback riding is allowed on all but the Mazomani Trail. The entire system is open to cross-country skiers; snowmobilers may use the Minnesota Valley Trail. There is a primitive campsite for canoeists located along the river in the Wayside. At the trailhead next to the parking area is a large stationary map and a supply of pocket maps, as well as some historical and interpretive information. Bow hunting is permitted here from September through December and visitors are recommended to wear red or orange clothing at that time.

How to get there: From Shakopee take U.S. Highway 169 south along the river valley. About 4 miles out of town look for the sign and turn right. The parking lot is a short distance past the railroad tracks. A separate entrance for hunters is almost 3 miles farther south on 169 (a special permit is required for all hunting and trapping).

Both areas are closed from sunset to sunrise except to campers.

Map key: West 77

For additional information:

Refuge Manager
Minnesota Valley National
Wildlife Refuge
4101 East 80th Street
Bloomington, Minnesota 55425
(612) 854-5900

Park Manager
19825 Park Blvd.
Jordan, Minnesota 55352
(612) 492-6400

Loveland Park

Loveland Park is situated atop the bluffs overlooking the town of Newport and the broad Mississippi River Valley. Although the park encloses just 83 acres, a portion of which has been developed for picnicking and athletic activities, it contains an interesting variety of habitats and offers quiet footpaths and pleasing vistas. The undulating uplands behind the bluffs are abandoned pastures where windswept grasses alternate with pockets of planted pines and encroaching thickets of sumac, boxelder, and cottonwood. The upper slopes of the steep bluffs are dominated by large red oak, bur oak, and pin oak, with an abundance of aspen, and some black cherry, basswood, and boxelder. The sunlit understory is thick with small trees and shrubs favored by wildlife, such as hazelnut, buckthorn, choke-cherry, sumac, raspberry, gooseberry, woodbine, and wild grape. This dense growth gives way to stunted oaks and small grassy openings on a few exposed, south-facing, sections of the bluff.

In contrast to the well-drained slopes above, a sheltered stream valley cuts into the bluff at the south end of the park. The intermittent flow of the small stream has carved a smooth, moss-covered gully in the underlying sandstone. The stream is shaded by a spacious woodland of tall basswood and red oak, with a lot of ironwood and some elm and paper birch.

Facilities: More than 2 miles of hiking trails wind the length of the park. The trails are good but poorly marked. The rest of the park's facilities are all situated near the park entrance. There is a picnic area with pavilions, tables, grills, drinking water, and toilets; playground equipment, tennis courts, softball fields, a hockey rink, and a pleasure rink.

How to get there: From Interstate Highway 94 in St. Paul or Interstate Highway 494 just east of the Mississippi River, head south on U.S. Highway 61. A little more than half a mile south of 494 turn left at Glen Road. Follow Glen Road for roughly three quarters of a mile and look for the park entrance on the right.

Map key: East 78

For additional information:

Newport City Hall
596 7th Avenue
Newport, MN 55055
(612) 459-5677

Manomin Park

Located in the City of Fridley, Manomin Park was purchased by Anoka County to preserve scenic open space on the Mississippi River. Although the park is made up of just 15 acres, it includes some 4,500 feet of shoreline along the river and Rice Creek, which empties into the river here. Almost entirely wooded, about half the small park lies on the floodplain, where large cottonwood, silver maple, and black willow trees form a high canopy.

Also on this property, the Anoka County Historical Society maintains the Banfill Tavern, a restored pioneer home that is open to the public for viewing. Banfill Tavern has been placed on the National Register of Historic Sites.

Facilities: A network of walking trails with two footbridges leads throughout the tiny park and provides access to the Mississippi River. There are numerous picnic tables with grills and one shelter. Restrooms and drinking water are available.

How to get there: Manomin Park is located off East River Road about a mile and a half north of Interstate Highway 694. Look for it on the left past the intersection of East River Road and Hartman Circle just north of the creek.

Map key: West 79

For additional information:

Anoka County Park and
Recreation
550 Bunker Lake Blvd.
Anoka, Minnesota, 55304
(612) 757-3920

173

Maplewood Nature Center

Located just east of St. Paul is a small suburban oasis of woods and wetlands known as the Maplewood Nature Center. The preserve encompasses a total of 40 acres, a little over half of which are comprised of open water marshes and woodland ponds. Cattail, arrowhead, and waterlily thrive in the shallow water, while cottonwood, silver maple, boxelder, willow, and red-osier dogwood grow around it. A drier upland area is cloaked in large red and white oaks along with a number of mature black cherry trees and a dense, shrubby understory. The center also includes two small prairie plots: a recently established demonstration area and a hillside remnant. Muskrat and mink may be seen in the marsh, as well as mallard, teal, pied-billed grebe, green-backed heron, and wood duck. Other wildlife includes the great horned owl, woodchuck, raccoon, red and gray squirrel, cottontail rabbit, and chipmunk.

The nature center also manages Jim's Prairie, three acres of undisturbed tallgrass prairie located a few minutes away. Those interested in visiting this rare remnant of Minnesota's past can make arrangements with a naturalist.

Facilities: There is an Interpretive Center by the entrance which has exhibits, offices, and restrooms. The well maintained trail system includes benches, an observation dock, and a floating boardwalk. Tables are available for picnickers. The center has binoculars and snowshoes to rent.

How to get there: Just east of St. Paul take the Century Avenue exit off Interstate Highway 94 and go north. A quarter mile past Minnehaha Avenue take a left at East 7th Street.

The Interpretive Center is open Monday through Saturday from 8:30 a.m. to 4:30 p.m.. The trails are open daily from one-half hour before sunrise to one-half hour after sunset.

Map key: East 80

For more information:

Maplewood Nature Center
2659 East 7th Street
Maplewood, Minnesota 55119
(612) 738-9383

Marsh Lake East Municipal Park

In the middle of Bloomington, Marsh Lake East Municipal Park occupies a low, marshy basin bisected by Nine Mile Creek. The 333 acre preserve is one of a number of such areas that protect the floodplain of this suburban stream from development. Like the others, the park is comprised primarily of wetlands and includes very little of the surrounding uplands. Broad stretches of open water and cattail marsh extend north and south from the creek, giving way around the edge to thickets of willow and dogwood and small stands of cottonwood trees.

There is, however, a finger of small, rocky hills that penetrates the wetlands from the south. The broad-canopied bur oaks that dominate these hills and the prairie grasses and flowers that persist here and there are reminders of the oak savanna that once characterized the area. But the prairie has been squeezed out by dense growths of raspberry, hazelnut, prickly-ash, sumac, hawthorn, and wild grape, as well as a variety of hardy trees, such as aspen, black cherry, and basswood.

Facilities: There are no developed facilities here except for a one mile trail that cuts across the southeast corner of the park. Informal paths diverge from the main trail and lead to points overlooking the marsh where you can view the waterfowl and other birds that are drawn here. The only access to the heart of the park is by canoe on Nine Mile Creek.

How to get there: The park is located across the road from Normandale Junior College. From Interstate Highway 494 take the France Avenue exit and go south a little more than 2 miles to West 98th Street. Turn left (east) here and then turn left again into the parking lot for the Bloomington Ice Gardens. You can pick up the short trail from the northwestern corner of the lot.

For additional information: *Map key:* West 81

Bloomington Parks and
Recreation Department
2215 W. Old Shakopee Road
Bloomington, Minnesota 55431
(612) 887-9601

Martin-Island-Linwood Lakes Regional Park

Martin-Island-Linwood Lakes Regional Park is situated in the northeastern corner of Anoka County adjacent to both the Boot Lake Scientific and Natural Area and the Carlos Avery Wildlife Management Area. The park contains 737 acres of diverse habitats surrounding all of Island Lake and portions of Martin Lake, Tamarac Lake, and Linwood Lake. Plans call for the acquisition of key parcels of land and the development of additional facilities. Although it is managed as a single park, the area is split by county highways into three distinct tracts.

The oldest part of the park encompasses Island Lake and is located north of County Highway 22 and west of County Highway 26 with a developed recreation area across the road on Martin Lake. This section includes upland oak woods, abandoned fields, an old evergreen plantation, and a sizable bog fed by a slow-moving stream that flows from Island Lake to Martin Lake. A long boardwalk winds through the bog and offers a close-up look at this otherwise inaccessible habitat. The swampy area is crammed with willow, alder, dogwood, cattail, sedges, sensitive fern, Joe-Pye weed, and a host of smaller specialized flowers and other plants. Tamarac trees thrive here, while other trees, such as paper birch, yellow birch, aspen, and elm, flourish around the edges.

South of County Highway 22 a park road provides access to Linwood Lake and the rich woodlands along its eastern shoreline. A trail from the parking lot follows the lakeshore south to one of the best remnant stands of native white pine in the metropolitan area. It is interesting to observe the gradual transition in the types of plants from the open waters of Linwood Lake to the low hills nearby. The lake is fringed with pockets of bulrushes and small amounts of wild rice, which grade into cattails, then sedges. These wetlands communities give way to a boggy lowland characterized by tamarac, paper birch, and aspen, with a thick growth of American yew, then to increasing numbers of white pine, red maple, yellow birch, green ash, and elm. On slightly higher ground the woods are dominated by red oak and basswood, with white oak, butternut, hackberry, alternate-leaf dogwood, black cherry, and even some red cedar.

East of Highway 26 at the north end of the park is a smaller parcel bordering Tamarac Lake. This is basically a flat area cloaked by a combination of oak-aspen woods and planted pines overlooking the cattail marshes that rim the shallow lake.

Facilities: The small section along the southernmost shore of Martin Lake has a swimming beach, boat launch, and a picnic area with a shelter, tables, grills, water, and restrooms. Additional picnic facilities are located across the road, as is the trailhead to the bog and Island Lake. This section also includes the 4-H Camp Salie which has 4 cabins, a dining hall, and staff cabins. The only facilities in the Linwood Lake area are the park road to the lake, a boat ramp, and trails. The county plans to add many facilities in the future, including additional picnic areas, another boat launch (Island Lake), another swimming beach (Linwood Lake), parkways, and more trails.

How to get there: From the Twin Cities head north on either Interstate Highway 35W or 35E. Eight miles north of where these two highways merge, take the Wyoming exit (County Highway 22). Turn left, crossing over the highway, and continue almost 5 miles to the intersection of County Highways 22 and 26. To reach Linwood Lake, stay on 22 and look for the access road on the left. Turn right onto 26 to reach the other areas. Drive almost a mile on 26, turn right at the fork, then take an immediate left on a park road to reach the picnic area and boat launch on Martin Lake. Stay on 26 and take the next right to reach the swimming area. To reach the trailhead to the boardwalk and Island Lake, take a sharp left off 26 at the next intersection and look for the parking lot on the left. Currently the trails are well worn but not well marked.

Map key: East 82

For additional information:

Anoka County Parks Department
550 Bunker Lake Boulevard N.W.
Anoka, Minnesota 55304
(612) 757-3920

Mary Schmidt
Crawford Woods

Located approximately five miles east of Buffalo in Wright County, Mary Schmidt Crawford Woods is one of only a few dozen places throughout Minnesota that have been designated as "Scientific and Natural Areas." Acquired with the cooperation of The Nature Conservancy, the preserve encompasses 117 acres of relatively undisturbed woodland on the southwest side of Schmidt Lake (additional acquisitions may yet double or triple its size).

At the time of settlement Wright County was almost entirely blanketed by a rich forest known as the "Big Woods." Today, unlogged or ungrazed examples of this plant community are few and far between. Mary Schmidt Crawford Woods is considered to be the finest remaining stand in the county and one of the best in the region. Typical of the Big Woods, tall sugar maple and basswood trees dominate the landscape here. The exceptional ability of these trees to utilize the sunlight and cast a deep shadow over the ground makes it difficult for less shade tolerant competitors to become established. One notable exception is the American hop hornbeam. Better known as ironwood, this small tree, which rarely grows over 25 feet, thrives in the dimly lit understory and is common throughout the Big Woods. Far from being absent however, an assortment of other trees add variety to the maple-basswood forest, including red oak, bitternut hickory, ash, elm, and hackberry. These trees take advantage of sunlit openings created by the death of an old giant or by the numerous small swamps that dot the preserve.

One of the best times to visit is springtime. In the forest, wildflowers begin blooming soon after the snow melts and peak in May or early June, when the trees have leafed out and once again shade the forest floor. During this brief period, a multitude of delicate flowers enlivens the woods, such as bloodroot, spring beauty, large-flowered bellwort, false rue anemone, round-lobed hepatica, large-flowered trillium, jack-in-the-pulpit, and many more.

Facilities: There are no developed facilities. Mary Schmidt Crawford Woods is set aside to protect natural plant and animal communities for scientific and educational purposes. You are invited to observe and enjoy the area, but please remember that your visit can have an impact on the natural community. Picnic facilities and restrooms are available at Beebe Lake Regional Park 2 miles east on County Highway 34.

How to get there: The preserve is located off County Highway 34 between Buffalo and Hanover. Turn north onto County Road 126 and look for small signs on the right. There is a pull-off on the right where you can park your car. From here an old and overgrown road leads a short distance into the wood.

Map key: West 83

For additional information:

Scientific and Natural Areas
Program
Box 7, Minnesota Department of
Natural Resources
500 Lafayette Road, DNR Building
St. Paul, Minnesota 55155
(612) 297-3288

Minnehaha Park

Since the turn of the century, visitors have come to view Minnehaha Falls, long ago immortalized by Henry Wadsworth Longfellow in his poem "Song of Hiawatha." The picturesque cascade is the centerpiece of a splendid urban park located in the southeast corner of Minneapolis where Minnehaha Creek rushes to join the waters of the Mississippi River. Within its 170 acres or so the park contains bits of Minnesota's history, pleasant picnic sites, lovely vistas, and undeveloped natural areas. The picnic facilities and historic attractions are scattered about the manicured uplands amid groves of tall shade trees, while the park's wildlands are limited to the steep bluffs along the river and the deep gorge below the falls.

After spilling out of Lake Minnetonka, the creek winds through the western suburbs and flows across Minneapolis before reaching the park and plunging into an impressive bowl at the head of the wooded gorge. As Minnehaha Falls has slowly eroded its way up the creek, it has exposed the layers of sedimentary rock that underlie the rest of the city. Just below the loosely consolidated "drift" left behind by the last glacier are three contrasting formations deposited by ancient seas. On the top is the erosion-resistant Platteville Formation, a hard layer of fossil-bearing dolomitic limestone. Beneath the limestone is a soft, thinly bedded layer of grayish-green shale called the Glenwood Formation. Below that is a very thick layer of poorly cemented sand known as the St. Peter Sandstone. One of the world's purest quartz sandstones, it covers a large area of the central United States and may be seen in many places along the Mississippi and Minnesota Rivers.

A short distance downstream from the falls the narrow valley carved by the creek merges with an open glen known as the "deer pen area." At the end of the last ice age, when the Mississippi was a much larger river, the glen was a separate channel brimming with the meltwater from receding glaciers. Stately cottonwoods and large black willow and silver maple trees line the creek from here to the river. Brilliant yellow blooms of wild iris adorn the creekbed in the spring. Soggy spring-fed areas at the base of the valley walls are choked with watercress, skunk cabbage, scouring rush, forget-me-not, turtlehead, sensitive fern, jewelweed, red-osier dogwood, and other water-tolerant plants.

The drier lowlands and adjoining slopes are cloaked by a mixed woodland comprised of red oak, bur oak, basswood, and ironwood, with ash, elm, butternut, hackberry, boxelder, and black locust. A dense growth of small trees and shrubs fills the understory, including buckthorn, prickly-ash, chokecherry, elderberry, serviceberry, hawthorne, mulberry, honeysuckle, sumac, woodbine, and wild grape. Rich in plants favored by wildlife and connected to other areas by the Mississippi River, the gorge is visited by a surprising number of birds not commonly seen in the city.

Facilities: Four different staircases made of local stone lead from the uplands to various spots along the creekbottom and connect to a trail that follows the creek to its confluence with the river across from St. Paul's Hidden Falls Park. A separate paved trail connects the park's southern uplands with nearby Fort Snelling State Park. There are numerous vantage points from which to view the falls. A large picnic area near the falls has tables, grills, restrooms, and water. The Minnehaha Park refectory sells food, drinks, and souvenirs. Additional picnic tables and restrooms are located in the "deer pen area." Just above the falls is a statue of Minnehaha and Hiawatha (Minnehaha was the inspiration for Longfellow's poem). Of special historical significance is the Steven's House, which was moved to park grounds south of the falls. The house was the first frame dwelling erected west of the Mississippi in Minneapolis. A number of other statues and plaques are scattered about the park.

How to get there: The park is located east of Hiawatha Avenue at the eastern end of Minnehaha Parkway and the southern end of West River Parkway (paved bicycle trails parallel both parkways). The Ford Bridge crosses the river from St. Paul just north of the park.

Map key: West 84

For additional information:

Minneapolis Park and Recreation Board
310 4th Avenue South
Minneapolis, Minnesota 55415
(612) 348-2226

Minnesota Landscape Arboretum

Piece by piece, the Minnesota Landscape Arboretum, which was established in 1956, has grown into an exceptional complex spread out over 905 acres of rolling hills in Chanhassen. The arboretum was created with the primary goal of testing plants for landscape use in our region and operates within the Department of Horticultural Science and Landscape Architecture of the University of Minnesota. It has become a dynamic research and education center, as well as a splendid beauty spot that draws thousands of visitors annually.

In addition to its wealth of indoor facilities and outdoor exhibits, a large portion of the property has been kept in a natural state. Miles of excellent trails and boardwalks wind through a variety of distinct plant communities which together harbor approximately 436 species or about one-fourth of the known flora of Minnesota. Many of the native plants along these quiet pathways have been labeled with both their Latin and common name. Birds and other wildlife abound throughout the diverse terrain.

Most of the steeper slopes within the area are cloaked by tall sugar maples, with basswood, red oak, ironwood, and some bitternut hickory, butternut, and alternate-leaf dogwood. One of the first gardens constructed in the arboretum, the Grace B. Dayton Wildflower Garden, displays native flowers along a tiny stream that flows through the maple-basswood forest. Among the dozens of wildflowers blooming here each spring are blood-root, sharp-lobed hepatica, snow trillium, Virginia bluebell, blue cohosh, turtlehead, marsh marigold, Dutchman's breeches, wood lily, starflower, and yellow lady slipper. The shaded hillsides shelter banks of ferns, such as lady fern, Christmas fern, sensitive fern, royal fern, and maidenhair fern. An entirely different woodland is found on more exposed, well-drained knolls where bur oak, red oak, and white oak stand with aspen, black cherry, elm, red cedar, buckthorn, and a dense undergrowth of shrubs.

On another hillock the arboretum has recreated one of the state's most threatened ecosystems. Established in 1965, the Bennett Prairie is an attempt to present the plants that existed on the tallgrass prairies before the settlers arrived. Big blue-stem, little bluestem, and Indian grass dominate the 12 acre grassland along with cord grass, needle grass, June grass, side-oats grama, and others. From snowmelt to snowfall, something is always in bloom on the prairie, including pasque flower, hoary puccoon, prairie smoke, purple prairie clover, butterfly weed, blue-eyed grass, leadplant, downy gentian, blazing star, and a host of asters, daisies, goldenrods, and sunflowers.

Nestled into the low areas between the hills are a diversity of watery habitats, including shallow ponds, extensive marshes choked with cattail and phragmites, and a bog. A boardwalk through the bog offers visitors a close-up look at this soggy environment and the plants that live here, such as tamarac, quaking aspen, yellow birch, alder, willow, red-osier dogwood, sedges, sensitive fern, swamp saxifrage, and pitcher plant.

Facilities: Hikers can explore the natural areas on more than 5 miles of interconnected trails and floating boardwalks. Some trails are used for cross-country skiing The handsome building near the entrance, known as the Leon C. Snyder Education and Research Building, houses a tearoom, the Linden Tree giftshop, Anderson Horticultural Library, Meyer-Deats Conservatory, classrooms, research facilities, conference areas, an auditorium, and offices. Located in the vicinity of this building are the Morgan Terrace, McKnight Overlook, a manmade pool with a cascade and overlook, the Cloistered Garden, Knot Garden, Kitchen Herb Garden, Elizabeth Slade Perrenial Garden, and a collection of dwarf conifers. Also nearby are the Palma Wilson Rose Garden, Francis De Vos Home Demonstration Garden, Japanese Garden, Hosta Glade, and displays of woodland azaleas, lilacs, and colorful annuals. A small building overlooking a marsh serves as a learning center and has classrooms, offices, and a teaching greenhouse. The Margot Picnic Area offers a shelter, tables, fire pits, electric outlets, water, and restrooms. A 3 mile paved road (with numerous parking lots) makes a wandering loop through the rolling hills at the back of the property, passing separate collections of azaleas, nut trees, buckeyes, cork trees, oaks, lindens, pines, poplars, hedges, honeysuckles, barberry, larches, willows, lilies, dahlias, hydranges, elms, old-fashioned roses, ninebark, spirea, potentilla, maples, crab apples, hawthornes, ashes, spruces, small trees, weeping trees, and more.

The 905 acres includes the Horticultural Research Center, a 230-acre tract a half-mile away. Formerly known as the Fruit Breeding Farm, research here includes the development of hardy apple trees and other fruits, breeding of woody ornamentals, development of improved nursery practices, propagation of woody plants, and vegetable breeding.

How to get there: Take State Highway 5 west from Minneapolis or Interstate Highway 494. The Arboretum is located off Highway 5 approximately 9 miles west of 494. Look for the entrance on the left a half-mile past the intersection with State Highway 41.

The arboretum grounds are open all year from 8:00 a.m. to sunset. The Snyder building is open from 8:00 a.m. to 4:30 p.m. on weekdays and from 10:00 a.m. to 4:30 p.m. on weekends. The library hours are the same except that it opens an hour and a half later on weekends. The Gift Shop is open daily from 11:00 a.m. to 4:00 p.m. except on Mondays. The Tea Room is open from 11:30 a.m. to 1:30 p.m. for lunch and from 1:30 p.m. to 3:00 p.m. for snacks. There is a small gate fee for all nonmembers.

Map key: West 85

For additional information:

Minnesota landscape Arboretum
3675 Arboretum Drive, P.O. Box 39
Chanhassen, Minnesota 55317
(612) 443-2460

Minnesota State Canoe Routes

The Land of 10,000 Lakes also contains thousands of miles of rivers. From rock-strewn rapids in pine-clad wilderness areas to marshy backwaters beneath towering bluffs, our rivers are as varied as the landscape they flow through. Minnesota lies near the heart of the continent, and overlaps three of North America's great watersheds. The waters of our state are carried north to the Hudson Bay by the Red River; east to the Atlantic through the Great Lakes and the St. Lawrence seaway; and south to the Gulf of Mexico by the Mississippi.

While the lakes get all of the acclaim, the history of Minnesota is really the history of its rivers. Before there were railroads and highways, the rivers guided explorers to the region, led trappers into the hinterlands, and later brought settlers to a new home. The rivers were used to carry away the virgin timber of the North Woods, to power the mills, and to transport goods to market. It is no surprise that our oldest and largest towns and cities are situated along the banks of our rivers.

In the wilderness, in farm country, and even in the Twin Cities, rivers are also a magnet for wildlife. In spite of the demands we place on them, our river valleys still contain some of the richest wildlife habitat in Minnesota. During spring and fall migrations, the rivers – particularly the Mississippi, Minnesota, and St. Croix – are used as flight corridors by countless ducks, raptors, songbirds, and other species. Over the course of a year the lower Mississippi alone harbors 285 species of birds. There are also 52 species of mammals, 23 species of reptiles, and 13 species of amphibians.

Nineteen rivers in Minnesota have been designated as state canoe routes by the Department of Natural Resources. Scattered throughout the state, the rivers have been carefully mapped, with each map showing access points, campsites, rest areas, parklands, and portages. Hazards such as dams and waterfalls are marked, as are stretches of whitewater rapids. Portions of seven of these rivers are within the scope of this book. In addition to the seven rivers briefly described here, there are other rivers and streams in the metropolitan area that can be canoed – such as the Elk and St. Francis rivers in Sherburne County, the South Fork of the Crow River in Wright and Carver counties, Minnehaha Creek through the western suburbs and the city of Minneapolis, and others.

Cannon River

From the town of Waterville in southeastern LeSueur County, the Cannon River winds eastward for 80 miles to its confluence with the Mississippi River near the historic town of Red Wing. The upper portion of the river twists and turns past rolling farmland, wooded hills and bluffs, old mills and railroad trestles, manmade lakes, and small towns. Below Cannon Falls the river enters a picturesque valley flanked by bluffs up to 300 feet high. Where the Cannon joins the Mississippi it flows through a wildlife-rich maze of backwater lakes, sloughs, and bottomland forest. The stretch from Faribault to the Mississippi was designated a state recreational and scenic river in 1979.

Minnesota River

From its source near Brown's Valley on the South Dakota border to its confluence with the Mississippi at Fort Snelling, the Minnesota River flows through a broad and deep valley carved by the Glacial River Warren. Once a major highway for Indians, explorers, traders, and settlers, the river is now used primarily by recreational boats and commercial barge traffic. Below LeSueur the slow-moving river meanders between distant bluffs past sandy banks and gravel bars, farm fields and river towns, bottomland forests and remnant prairies, and large floodplain lakes and wetlands. Few other river valleys in the state contain such a diversity of habitats – including rare fens and goat prairies – as the Minnesota.

Mississippi River

From its famed headwaters in the pine forests of Itasca State Park, the "Father of Waters" rambles for almost 700 miles across Minnesota. Between St. Cloud and Anoka the river winds past a mixture of farmland and sandy hills covered with hardwoods and pines. In some areas the river is crowded with dozens of forested islands, some of which shelter tree-top rookeries of herons and egrets. Closer to the Twin Cities there are increasing numbers of homes, power plants, and bridges, until eventually the river flows along the edge of downtown Minneapolis and St. Paul. Below Saint Anthony Falls the river is squeezed by high wooded bluffs before joining the much broader Minnesota River Valley at Fort Snelling. Heavy industrial development alternates with urban green spaces through St. Paul and the southern suburbs. The river regains its natural character before joining the waters of the St. Croix near Hastings. Beyond Hastings the Mississippi flows between the bluffs of Minnesota and Wisconsin, winding slowly through a broad lowland of tangled side channels, large backwater lakes, assorted wetland communities, and extensive bottomland forests until reaching Lake Pepin a few miles past Red Wing.

North Fork of the Crow River

From its origins in southeastern Pope County, the North Fork of the Crow River flows generally eastward for about 175 miles until it empties into the Mississippi at Dayton. The state canoe route begins 125 miles upstream at Lake Koronis. Once flanked by the Big Woods and pockets of prairie, the North Fork now winds through a pastoral countryside of rolling farms with stretches of wooded hills and bottomland forest. In the upper portion of the river canoeists must deal with many hidden snags, overhanging branches, fences, and sharp bends. Below Kingston the river deepens and widens, meandering in a wide floodplain and occasionally tumbling over small rapids. The river joins the South Fork at Rockford and forms the border between Hennepin and Wright counties. This stretch of the river – the nearest to the Twin Cities – is deeper and wider still, and is well suited to family trips.

Rum River

After spilling out of Mille Lacs Lake, the Rum River meanders for 145 miles until it reaches the Mississippi River at Anoka. After flowing through a lovely area of wetlands and smaller lakes near Mille Lacs Lake, the river bends south amid dense forests of hardwoods and pines. The stretch of the river between Lake Onamia and Princeton is rocky and contains many rapids. Below Princeton the river flows lazily across the Anoka sandplain, through marshy lowlands, undulating farm country, oak forests, and scattered stands of red and white pine. Scenic and close to the Twin Cities, the lower portion of the Rum River is ideal for an overnight trip or a day trip with the whole family.

St. Croix River

The St. Croix River was one of the eight original rivers included in the National Wild and Scenic Rivers System. With the Namekagon River – a tributary that is likewise protected from its beginnings in the pine forests of northern Wisconsin – the riverway provides some 200 miles of near-wilderness canoeing above Taylors Falls. Between its confluence with the Namekagon and the town of Taylors Falls, the river flows swiftly through a rich valley with large areas of floodplain forest and wooded hills and bluffs covered with second-growth forests mixed with tall red and white pines. Below Taylors Falls and closer to the Twin Cities, the St. Croix is squeezed between towering, pine-clad cliffs known as the Dalles, before becoming a broad and gentle river with lots of channels and backwaters. At Stillwater the river widens and deepens into Lake St. Croix, formed by a natural bar at the river's junction with the Mississippi. Bordered by steep wooded bluffs and many hillside houses, the lake fills the bottomlands from here to the confluence with the Mississippi River at Hastings.

Straight River

Twisting through the farmland of southern Minnesota, the Straight River is a state canoe route from Owatonna to Faribault, where it empties into the Cannon River. Away from these towns, and the other small communities situated on its banks, the river is a narrow, bucolic stream. Cultivated fields, grazing pastures, and farm buildings are screened by a band of woods on either bank. In some places the river is bordered by rock-strewn hills and outcroppings of bedrock sandstone.

Facilities: As mentioned above, pamphlets are available from the Department of Natural Resources that contain a wide variety of detailed information about each of these rivers, including parks and other public lands along the river and outfitters who can rent canoes and provide shuttle service.

For additional information:

Minnesota Department of Natural Resources
Trails and Waterways Unit
Information Center, Box 40
500 Lafayette Road
St. Paul, Minnesota 55155
(612) 296-6699

St. Croix National Wild and Scenic River
Superintendent, P.O. Box 708
St. Croix Falls, Wisconsin 54024
(715) 483-3284

Minnesota Valley
Nature Center

Owned by the Minneapolis Chapter of the Isaak Walton League, the Minnesota Valley Nature Center protects 52 acres of bluffs and bottomlands along the Minnesota River in Bloomington. Because of the varied terrain the small preserve contains a variety of distinct habitats.

The exposed south-facing slope overlooking the river supports a woodland dominated by bur oak and red oak with cottonwood, elm, red cedar, and a dense understory of buckthorn, prickly-ash, sumac, raspberry, and gooseberry. In contrast, a more sheltered stream valley deeply cut into the bluff is shaded by tall sugar maple and basswood with ironwood and hackberry. Watercress grows along the tiny stream that flows into a manmade pond fringed with cattail, sedge, and willow. The surrounding floodplain contains a typical bottomland forest of cottonwood, black willow, and silver maple, as well as elm, green ash, and boxelder. Within this small tract of rich alluvial soil are three of the largest cottonwood trees in the state.

Facilities: Well marked trails lead from the blufftop to the riverbottom and make a loop around the pond. During periods of high water portions of the trail are flooded out. The Red Barn Learning Center here contains a meeting room, exhibits, and resources for naturalist study groups. The trails are open to the public but the learning center is open by appointment only.

How to get there: Heading south on Interstate Highway 35W through Bloomington, exit onto 98th Street and go west. After a short distance veer left onto Old Shakopee Road and continue about 3 miles to Normandale Blvd. (Highway 100 extended). Turn left onto Normandale Blvd. and stay on it as it bends to the right and becomes Auto Club Road. Look for the entrance to the center on the left after crossing the railroad tracks. The nature center is open from sunrise to sunset.

For additional information: *Map key:* West 86

Minnesota Valley Nature Center
6601 Auto Club Road
Bloomington, Minnesota 55438
(612) 944-1423

Minnesota Zoological Garden

Well established as an outstanding and popular public resource, the Minnesota Zoo celebrated its tenth birthday in the spring of 1988. The young zoo is situated in suburban Apple Valley, amid a 500-acre expanse of hummocky, oak-covered glacial hills dotted with numerous ponds and wetlands, small restored prairie remnants, and a bog. A dizzying array of indoor and outdoor exhibits, facilities, and programs serve to educate and entertain visitors throughout the year.

In addition to a multitude of captivating animals from around the world, the zoo is a good place to see and learn about much of the wildlife currently or formerly found in our state. On the Minnesota Trail visitors walk along an enclosed glass passage past native animals living in reproductions of their natural habitat, including beaver, river otter, striped skunk, fox, lynx, puma, loon, great horned owl, and a variety of songbirds and freshwater fish. Some of the native animals that can be viewed in larger outdoor habitats on the Northern Trail are bison, pronghorn, moose, coyote, elk, wolf, and prairie dog. The main building overlooks a shallow, marsh-rimmed lake where trumpeter swans, Canada goose, and other waterfowl abound.

Facilities: Six miles of trails (including parts of the Northern Trail) are groomed for cross-country skiing in winter, and wind through the zoo's natural areas. Skis can be rented. This trail system is not open for hiking the rest of the year. The varied animal trails include the Minnesota Trail and Northern Trail (described above), the Ocean Trail (dolphins, octopus, crabs, anemones, clownfish, and other creatures from both warm and cold water marine regions), the Tropics Trail (a climate controlled environment with gibbons, hornbills, bears, gavials, fruit bats, tapirs, leopards, cobras, macaques, tropical birds, and exotic plants from tropical regions), the Discovery Trail (Japanese snow monkeys, and the Zoolab, Bird Show, and Children's Zoo with tarantulas, armadillos, chinchillas, reindeer, llamas, yaks, parrots, and snakes), and the Sky Trail (a monorail train ride over the Northern Trail and some of the natural habitats. The main building contains the Zoo store, Zoo lab, theater, amphitheater, food service (Dairy Queen), restrooms, offices, a library, and an audio-visual studio. The zoo also has an animal nursery and hospital. There are diaper changing areas, and a limited number of strollers and wheelchairs can be rented. Some picnic sites are situated by the parking lots. The Minnesota Zoo is the headquarters for the International Species Information System.

How to get there: The Zoological Garden is about 20 miles south of downtown Minneapolis and 18 miles southwest of downtown St. Paul. Driving on Interstate 35W, head east on Cliff Road, then south on State Highway 77 and follow the signs to the zoo. Driving on Interstate 35E, head south on Highway 77 and follow the signs.

During the summer the Zoo is open from 10:00 a.m. to 6:00 p.m. Monday through Saturday, and stays open until 8:00 p.m. on Sunday. The Zoo closes a bit earlier in winter. There are moderate fees for parking, admission, and the monorail ride. Members enter free and receive many other benefits.

Map key: East 87

For additional information:

Minnesota Zoological Garden
Apple Valley, Minnesota 55124
(612) 432-9000

Montissippi County Park

Within the city limits of Monticello, in the shadow of the N.S.P. nuclear power plant, are 170 acres of land on the Mississippi River known as Montissippi County Park. The area is a combination of dense second-growth woodlands, old fields, and plantations of pine and spruce. The trails winding through this Wright County Park are good for walking and scenic spots along the river provide opportunities for fishing, birdwatching, or contemplation. A lovely picnic area set amid mature bur oaks overlooks the river and would make a pleasant stop for weary travellers on Interstate Highway 94.

Facilities: Three miles of trails in connected loops are used for hiking and cross-country skiing. The picnic area has tables, grills, water, and toilets. There is also a volleyball court, a boat launch, and an overlook with a bench. The park is adjacent to the Monticello City baseball fields.

How to get there: Heading northwest from the Twin Cities on Interstate Highway 94, take the Monticello exit (State Highway 25) and go north. Before crossing the river turn left on County Highway 75. Proceed about 2 miles to park entrance on right. The park is open daily from 6:00 a.m. to 11:00 p.m.

Map key: West 88

For additional information:

Wright County Parks Department
Route 1, Box 97B
Buffalo, Minnesota 55313
(612) 682-3900, ext. 182
339-6881 (Metro)
1-800-362-3667, ext. 182 (Toll Free)

Mound Springs Park

Mound Springs Park is part of the confusing array of federal, state, and local lands that together protect well over 20,000 acres of diverse habitats along the Minnesota River as it flows into the metropolitan area. Owned and managed by the city of Bloomington, this municipal park is situated between the dense suburbs atop the bluff and Long Meadow Lake in the floodplain. The 270-acre preserve takes its name from the 400-year old Indian burial mounds found here and the cold springs that flow from the base of the hill.

Though some are hidden by vegetation and others have been vandalized, there are more than a dozen unmarked burial mounds of various sizes within the park. The mounds are generally located high on east-facing slopes where the first rays of the rising sun would help guide the spirit on its journey to the other world. The hillsides also contain reminders of more recent activities. There is a gravel pit that operated from 1950 to 1956, the foundation of an old cooling house where milk was stored in spring water pumped from the base of the hill, and scattered apple trees.

The rest of these well-drained slopes range from old clearings giving way to sumac, prickly-ash, buckthorn, red cedar, box elder, aspen, and cottonwood, to mature woodlands dominated by large bur oak and red oak, with some basswood (including one more than 150 years old), ironwood, and an abundance of gooseberry and black raspberry. The tiny O'Dell Creek flows through the area, cutting into the water table and exposing small springs where watercress may be found.

In contrast, the rich, well-watered soil at the base of the bluff supports a typical lowland wood of silver maple, slippery elm, green ash, black willow, and cottonwood. Also plentiful in this swampy habitat are river grape, red-osier dogwood, equisetum (or scouring rush), ferns, arrowhead, skunk cabbage, marsh marigold, and showy aster. Through the foliage here you can see the western end of Long Meadow Lake. This large, shallow lake stretches for more than three miles along the floodplain. Separated from the river channel by natural levees, it is spring-fed and the surface is actually eight feet above the normal level of the Minnesota River. Bordered by sedges, cattails, and bulrushes, with water lillies, duckweed, and pondweed in the open waters, the lake teems with wildlife.

Herons and egrets feed on frogs or minnows in the shallows, ducks and geese nest in the marsh, muskrat and beaver inhabit the waters, red fox and raccoon forage around the edge, and white-tailed deer come to drink. In all, more than 250 species of birds use the river valley, either nesting here or migrating through, and an observant visitor may be suprised by what can be seen in the middle of our growing urban landscape.

Facilities: A little more than 3 miles of trails explore the area from bluff-top to bottomland. These trails are wide but not well marked. Several overlooks along the trail provide excellent views of the river valley. A guide for the area is available from the Bloomington Park and Recreation Department. A small picnic area with tables and a grill is situated near the parking lot. When completed, the Minnesota Valley Trail will pass through the park. You can follow the main trail west along the valley for half a mile to Parker's Picnic Grounds, or two miles to Lyndale Avenue.

How to get there: Take Interstate Highway 35W south from Minneapolis or Interstate Highway 494, and exit at 98th Street. Turn left (east) onto 98th Street, going over the Interstate, then take a right (south) onto Lyndale Avenue. Take the next left at 102nd Street and drive east for a little over a mile to the end of the road.

Map key: West 89

For additional information:

Bloomington Park and Recreation
Department
2215 W. Old Shakopee Road
Bloomington, Minnesota 55431
(612) 887-9601

Murphy-Hanrehan Park Reserve

Increasingly popular with cross-country skiers and birdwatchers alike, the Murphy-Hanrehan Park Reserve is one of the most outstanding natural areas near the Twin Cities. Although the reserve is located in Scott County, it is operated by the Hennepin County Parks system through the Scott-Hennepin Park Advisory Board. Spread out over nearly 3,000 acres of rugged terrain, the park is undeveloped except for trails and offers a remarkable feeling of wilderness only minutes from busy Burnsville Center.

Reaching south and east from the shore of Hanrehan Lake, the northern half of the preserve occupies a range of steep glacial hills dotted with small pothole lakes and numerous wetlands. Except for a scattering of open meadows on the more gently rolling slopes, the rock-strewn uplands are cloaked by what is probably the largest expanse of mature woodlands in the metropolitan area. The forest is dominated by oaks – primarily white oak and red oak with some bur oak and pin oak – alternately mixed with basswood, ironwood, black cherry, bitternut hickory, red cedar, stands of quaking and bigtooth aspen, and some sugar maple. The well lit understory supports a dense growth of small trees and shrubs such as red-elderberry, alternate-leaf dogwood, serviceberry, buckthorn, chokecherry, hazelnut, honeysuckle, prickly gooseberry, blackberry, raspberry, woodbine, and wild grape, as well as an abundance of ferns and flowers. Nestled into low areas between the hills are a variety of watery habitats ranging from open waters rimmed with white and yellow waterlilies, arrowhead, blue flag, and cattail, to stretches of sedges and thickets of willow and red-osier dogwood.

The hills disappear to the south and, beginning with Murphy Lake, the southern half of the park encompasses a more gently rolling landscape split by a small branch of the Credit River. The woods here are basically maple-basswood, although still with a great deal of oak, grading into silver maple, green ash, and black willow in swampy areas. An extensive wetland borders the river where it flows through the park.

On a well-drained tract of about 40 acres, Hennepin Parks employees have worked hard to re-establish a healthy prairie community within the preserve. In recent years they have planted more than seventy varieties of native wildflowers and nine species of prairie grasses.

The rich and varied environments at Murphy-Hanrehan support a profusion of wildlife. The woods and meadows are inhabited by white-tailed deer, coyote, badger, red and gray fox, raccoon, striped skunk, woodchuck, long-tailed weasel, and plenty of rabbits, squirrels, moles, mice, shrews, and bats. Beaver, muskrat, mink, and an occasional otter are found in the lakes, marshes, and river. The preserve is also home to many reptiles and amphibians, including the tiny spring peeper.

Generally more easily seen and heard, it is the wealth of birds that attracts many of the park's visitors. Waves of warblers move through the park each spring and some stay to raise their young, such as the blue-winged warbler, parula warbler, cerulean warbler, hooded warbler, American redstart, yellow warbler, yellowthroat warbler, and ovenbird. Among the numerous raptors that live here are the red-tailed hawk, red-shouldered hawk, broad-winged hawk, Cooper's hawk, kestrel, barred owl, great horned owl, and screech owl. A great variety of other birds reside in the preserve, including the pileated woodpecker, red-bellied woodpecker, wild turkey, ruby-throated hummingbird, scarlet tanager, northern oriole, indigo bunting, rufous-sided towhee, cedar waxwing, blue-gray gnatcatcher, veery, wood thrush, olive-sided flycatcher, yellow-throated vireo, eastern bluebird, and many more. Common loons have been known to nest within the area and yellow-crowned night herons travel here to feed from rookeries on the Mississippi River. In addition, a lot of ducks, grebes, herons, egrets, rails, terns, and other birds are drawn to the park's lakes and wetlands.

Facilities: Unlike most of the larger parks in the metropolitan area, Murphy-Hanrehan contains no recreational facilities except for an extensive system of trails. There are more than 20 miles of trails open to hiking, including about 10 miles of horseback riding trails. Twelve miles of this trail system are groomed for cross-country skiing. There are no ski rentals here but snacks and ski waxes are available at the trailhead building. The trails in this park are not appropriate for unskilled or inexperienced skiers. Portions of the horse trails are used for snowshoeing and snowmobiling in winter. A few picnic tables are located in small openings along the trails. Because the network of trails and old roads is confusing and poorly marked it is a good idea to obtain a map before hiking here. Nearby Cleary Lake Regional Park offers a wide selection of developed facilities.

How to get there: From the Twin Cities take Interstate Highway 35W or 35E south to Burnsville and exit onto County Road 42. Head west on 42 for about 4 miles and turn left (south) onto County Road 27. Follow 27 for almost 2 miles and turn left again onto County Road 68. After a little more than a mile turn right onto a gravel road (still 68) and look for the park entrance on the left. To reach the parking area and trailhead for the horseback riding trails continue farther along 68 and turn left onto Sunset Lake Road. Look for the parking area on the right.

The park is open daily from sunrise to sunset. Horseback riding is prohibited from November 1 to April 1.

Map key: West 90

For additional information:

Hennepin Parks
12615 County Road 9
Plymouth, Minnesota 55411
(612) 559-9000
or (612) 447-2171 (Cleary Lake)

Nerstrand Woods State Park

About an hour's drive south of the Twin Cities, in eastern Rice County, is an inviting expanse of woodlands known as Nerstrand Woods State Park. It is the only state park near the Twin Cities, and one of very few in Minnesota, that doesn't border a river or contain any lakes or wetlands. Instead, Nerstrand Woods encompasses 1,280 acres of rolling hills and valleys traversed by Prairie Creek. An island of trees surrounded by a sea of farms, the park protects a sizable remnant of the "Big Woods," a rich hardwood forest that once covered more than 3,000 square miles of south-central Minnesota.

The rich broadleaf woodland is comprised chiefly of sugar maple, basswood, elm, ironwood, red oak, white oak, bitternut hickory, and pockets of bigtooth aspen; interspersed are green ash, butternut, black walnut, blue beech, bur oak, black cherry, and quaking aspen. Low-lying areas along the creek support black willow, boxelder, silver maple, and cottonwood. The leafy canopy of these trees is unbroken except for grassy bottomlands where Prairie Creek meanders back and forth between wooded slopes, frequently cutting new channels. Downstream the creek straightens out a bit and speeds up before plunging over a picturesque waterfall and shattering the stillness of the forest.

The wild inhabitants of Nerstrand Woods are secretive and easily overlooked, but evidence of their activity is plentiful. Deer, foxes, raccoons, and other animals that roam the forest leave countless tracks in the soft earth. Parallel rows of small holes in live trees are a sure sign of the yellow-bellied sapsucker, while large rectangular cavities chiseled into old trees are the work of the pileated woodpecker. Small stick and mud dams across the stream and stumps of trees with tooth marks reveal the presence of beavers in Prairie Creek.

The park has a unique beauty to offer visitors in every season. Many come in springtime before the trees leaf out, when the forest floor is carpeted by a dazzling display of wildflowers. All along the trail one can admire the blooms of bloodroot, spring beauty, sharp-lobed hepatica, large-flowered bellwort, wild ginger, cut-leaved toothwort, Virginia bluebell, Dutchman's breeches, and wild strawberry, as well as mayapple, jack-in-the-pulpit, blue cohosh, marsh marigold, and numerous others. Nerstrand Woods is also home to the endangered dwarf trout lily, which grows nowhere in the world except a few places in Rice and Goodhue Counties.

In summer the deeply shaded forest provides a cool retreat from the hot sun. The park becomes a popular destination again in the fall when the diverse woodlands burst into a colorful array of reds, oranges, and yellows. Later, in winter, the dense forest is a scenic backdrop for cross-country skiers who enjoy the snowy valleys and steep hillsides.

Facilities: A well maintained trail system leads visitors throughout the forested hills. There are 11 miles of hiking trails, 5 miles of groomed trails for cross-country skiing, and 6 miles for snowmobiling. A wooded picnic area includes an open shelter, tables, grills, and toilets. The park contains 61 semi-modern campsites, 11 rustic sites, and a group camp for up to 200 people.

How to get there: From the Twin Cities take Interstate Highway 35 south to State Highway 19 (Northfield exit). Follow 19 east into Northfield. From downtown Northfield take Division Street south and stay on it as it becomes State Highway 246 and heads out of town. Follow 246 for about 10 miles as it bends east and then turns south again. Where 246 turns east (left) toward the town of Nerstrand, turn right onto County Highway 40. The park is located on both sides of the road after one mile. The parks facilities are located a little farther down the road on the right.

The park is closed from 10:00 p.m. to 8:00 a.m. except to registered campers. Daily or annual permits are required for all vehicles entering a state park. They may be purchased at the park entrance.

Map key: East 91

For additional information:

Nerstrand Woods State Park
Manager
Route 1, Box 80
Nerstrand, Minnesota 55053
(507) 334-8848

Minnesota Department of Natural Resources
Division of Parks and Recreation
Information Center, Box 40
500 Lafayette Road
St. Paul, Minnesota 55155
(612) 296-4776

Oakdale Park

Just a few minutes northeast of St. Paul, this municipal park sprawls over 196 acres of uneven terrain in suburban Oakdale. It includes a broad, shallow lake, dense hardwood forest, abandoned fields, plantations of spruce and pine, and several small pothole marshes.

Acorn Lake, which lies at the heart of the northern half of the park, is really more a marsh than a lake. Its shallow, open waters give way to lush growths of waterlily, arrowhead, cattail, and other aquatic plants. Surrounding the lake and covering the steeper hills within the park is a mature woodland dominated by white oak and red oak. Bur oak and northern pin oak also grow here, as well as aspen, paper birch, and black cherry. Throughout the woods are numerous bowl-like depressions alternately filled with cattail, willow, dogwood, and alder.

The old fields and evergreen plantations that occupy the more gently rolling areas add to the diversity of habitats here. White-tailed deer, red fox, woodchuck, raccoon, gray squirrel, wood duck, pheasant, pileated woodpecker, and great horned owl are among the creatures one might see from the trails that criss-cross the landscape.

Facilities: There are 5 miles of mowed trails with benches placed in scenic spots. The trails are groomed in winter for cross-country skiing. Long term development plans call for an interpretive center and picnic shelter. Currently there are tennis courts, playground apparatus, and a few picnic tables with grills located near the entrance to the park.

How to get there: From Interstate Highway 94, exit north onto Century Avenue one mile east of St. Paul. Proceed 4.5 miles to 45th Street North and turn right (east). The park entrance is one-half mile east at the intersection of 45th Street and Granada Avenue.

Map key: East 92

For additional information:

Oakdale Community Services
1584 Hadley Avenue North
Oakdale, Minnesota 55119
(612) 739-5086

Oakridge Waterfowl Production Area

Scattered throughout St. Croix County in Wisconsin, just across the St. Croix River from Minnesota, are more than two dozen federally owned Waterfowl Production Areas totalling nearly 5,000 acres. These areas are all centered around a marsh complex or several "prairie potholes." The main objective of management is waterfowl production, particularly mallards, blue-winged teal, and wood ducks, but all have other marsh species inhabiting them.

Oakridge Waterfowl Production Area is one of the most interesting of these preserves and is used by a wide variety of wildlife. Located about three miles northeast of New Richmond, Oakridge is at the center of a number of such areas strung out to the north and south. Although it includes more than 600 acres of varied topography and habitats, it is Oakridge Lake that is the main attraction.

Lying at the base of a wooded ridge, the lake is really two large pools connected by a narrow marshy channel. Broad sweeps of shallow open water are dotted with "islands" of hardstem bulrush and surrounded by a wide fringe of cattail. The gently rolling upland between the lake and the road is planted in grasses, such as bromegrass, switchgrass, bluegrass, and quackgrass, to provide nesting cover for waterfowl. Across the lake a mature oak forest blankets the ridge for which the area is named.

An array of birds find the environs of Oakridge Lake to their liking. Mallard, wood duck, and blue-winged teal are common, as well as ruddy duck, ring-necked duck, coot, and pied-billed grebe. The area contains one of only three nesting colonies of the red-necked grebe in Wisconsin. Red-winged blackbird, kingfisher, sora rail, Forster's tern, and black tern also live here. Caspian terns are occasional visitors, while great egrets and double-crested cormorants can be seen feeding throughout the summer. Because Oakridge is closed to waterfowl hunting, large numbers of migrating ducks and geese concentrate on the lake in the fall. At that time of year bald eagles have often been observed.

The Amscher Waterfowl Production Area is directly across the road from Oakridge. It occupies an additional 500 acres of slightly rolling grassland punctuated by numerous small lakes and marshes.

Facilities: There are no developed facilities, with the exception of small parking areas, at any of the Waterfowl Production Areas. Hunting is allowed at most of these areas but it is prohibited at Oakridge. Other activities, such as hiking and birding are permitted

How to get there: To reach New Richmond, take State Highway 64 east from Stillwater, or take State Highway 65 north from Interstate Highway 94. From New Richmond, take State Highway 64 east of town for 3 miles after diverging from State Highway 65. Turn left (north) onto 170th Street (formerly Meadowdale Road). Proceed 3 more miles and turn left (west) again at the first intersection after crossing the railroad tracks. Oakridge is north of this road and Amscher is to the south. After about a mile there is a small parking area on the left.

Map key: East 93

For additional information:

Area Wildlife Manager
Department of Natural Resources
Box 61
Baldwin, Wisconsin 54002
(715) 684-2914

Ojibway Park

Ojibway Park contains 119 acres of open space in the rapidly growing suburb of Woodbury. While a good portion of the area has been developed for a variety of recreational activities, the park also includes a small pond, some open grasslands, an extensive wetland, and a lovely stretch of mature woodlands.

The forest here is characterized by a mixture of tall oaks — red oak, bur oak, and pin oak — and basswood, along with elm, black cherry, red maple, and box elder. The understory supports a dense growth of shrubs such as elderberry, gray dogwood, gooseberry, bittersweet, woodbine, and wild grape. A number of footpaths wind through the woods, passing a few tiny woodland marshes, and leading to the edge of a broad wetland choked with cattails, sedges, willow, and red-osier dogwood, and bordered by groves of quaking aspen.

Facilities: A paved trail for hiking and biking makes a big loop from the parking lot and connects with a network of woodchip nature trails that explores the forest. Small interpretive exhibits are situated in various spots along the trails. The parks trails are used for cross-country skiing in winter. The rest of the park contains a picnic area, playground equipment, restrooms, a soccer fields, baseball diamonds, a hockey rink, a pleasure rink, volleyball courts, and a horseshoe pit.

How to get there: Head east from St. Paul on Interstate Highway 94, then south on Interstate Highway 494. After almost one and a half miles on 494, exit at Valley Creek Road. Turn left, crossing over the Interstate, and take the first right, heading south on Woodlane Drive. Go almost a mile, then turn left onto Courtly Road. The parking lot is located at the end of this residential street.

Map key: East 94

For additional information:

Department of Parks and Recreation
Woodbury City Hall
2100 Radio Drive
Woodbury, MN 55125
(612) 739-5972

Ottawa Bluffs

Ottawa Bluffs is a 62 acre remnant of native prairie and woods in Le Sueur County. Owned by the Minnesota Chapter of The Nature Conservancy, the preserve occupies a west-and south-facing slope overlooking the broad Minnesota River Valley. Although small, the area is diverse and protects several plants and animals of note.

Woodlands cover about two-thirds of the tract and include bur oak, northern red oak, and red cedar. Red cedar is particularly abundant, occasionally forming dense groves where it has successfully invaded prairie areas. Prescribed burns are used to control the advancing red cedar and sumac, and restore the open prairie. Prairie grasses and flowers have been able to maintain a hold on much of the drier west-and south-facing hillsides. Grasses such as side-oats grama, little bluestem, and prairie dropseed, as well as big bluestem and Indian grass, provide a backdrop for leadplant, ground plum, prairie ragwort, and a variety of other wildflowers.

Among the grasses and flowers is a relatively small gray-green plant only 3 or 4 inches tall, with inconspicuous cream-colored flowers. This is the low milkvetch, a western species generally found more than a hundred miles further west, but present at Ottawa Bluffs as an isolated outpost. Also living here is the harvest mouse, a prairie rodent with a very localized distribution in the state.

Another feature is a tiny but constant spring that gives rise to a shallow sedge-filled pool and drains through a small gully that dissects the bluff. The sheltered gully is shaded by cottonwood, elm, boxelder, and aspen.

The view from atop Ottawa Bluffs is outstanding, taking in the distant opposite bluffs, the town of St. Peter, extensive wetlands and woods on the floodplain, and the meandering Minnesota River.

Facilities: There are no developed facilities at Ottawa Bluffs. As with all Nature Conservancy preserves, the protection of the natural plant and animal communities is the highest priority. Although you are invited to observe and enjoy the preserve, please use care to minimize the impact of your visit.

How to get there: From St. Peter, go east on State Highway 99 for about one mile. Turn left onto County Road 23 and proceed about 4 miles north. Look for small Nature Conservancy signs on the right. Park along the road. Note: If you cross railroad tracks, you have gone too far.

Map key: West 95

For additional information:

The Nature Conservancy
Minnesota Chapter
1313 Fifth Street, S.E.
Minneapolis, Minnesota 55414
(612) 379-2134

Otter Lake Regional Park

Encompassing 884 acres in the northeastern corner of Ramsey County, Otter Lake Regional Park is comprised of three distinct tracts of land. One of these, the 335-acre Tamarac Nature Center, is managed separately and listed elsewhere. The remaining acreage lies on opposite sides of Bald Eagle Lake. Nearly all of the facilities are located east of the lake in what is known as Bald Eagle Park. Stretching between the west side of this popular lake and the shores of Otter Lake is a 408 acre expanse of wildlands that the county plans to develop for nature oriented activities.

This undeveloped area is an attractive combination of wet lowlands, forested hills, and old fields. Mature upland woods are made up of red oak, white oak, northern pin oak, red maple, black cherry, basswood, and ironwood, with aspen, red cedar, and paper birch advancing into abandoned open areas. There are also swampy woodlands with black willow, cottonwood, aspen, boxelder, and elm, as well as small stands of tamarac. The wetlands are primarily cattail marsh bordered by thickets of red-osier dogwood and willow. Otter Lake itself is fringed with sizable beds of bulrushes and attracts an abundance of waterfowl. Among the many birds that inhabit the park are the American bittern, sora rail, wood duck, brown thrasher, warbling vireo, eastern wood pewee, short-billed marsh wren, red-headed woodpecker, and rose-breasted grosbeak.

Facilities: The only development at this time in the Otter Lake "unit" is a boat launch off Otter Lake Road. Bald Eagle Park, however, offers a variety of lakeshore activities. There is a picnic area with a shelter, tables, grills, water, and toilets; a swimming beach with lifeguards; playground equipment; and a boat launch.

How to get there: Bald Eagle Park is located on the west side of U.S. Highway 61 about 6 miles north of Interstate Highway 694. To reach the opposite side turn west onto County Road 6 south of the lake and follow Bald Eagle Blvd. along the shoreline. Otter Lake can also be reached by exiting off Interstate Highway 35E at the county line and going southeast on County Road 60.

Map key: East 96

For additional information:
Ramsey County Parks and
Recreation Department
2015 N. Van Dyke Street
Maplewood, Minnesota 5109
(612) 777-1707

Palmer Lake Nature Area

Shingle Creek weaves through heavily developed suburban communities before flowing into the Mississippi River in north Minneapolis. Where it crosses from Brooklyn Park into Brooklyn Center it flows through a low, marshy basin known as the Palmer Lake Nature Area. The preserve includes more than 200 acres in Brooklyn Center and additional acreage in Brooklyn Park. Most of the area is occupied by shallow, open waters and extensive stretches of cattail. Around the edges the slightly higher land supports small stands of cottonwood, willow, green ash, and aspen. There are no trails or boardwalks that penetrate the marsh but there is an overlook from which you can view the mallards, egrets, gulls, and other birds that feed here.

Facilities: The nature area, which is undeveloped, is adjacent to West Palmer Park and East Palmer Park. West Palmer Park has softball fields, basketball and tennis courts, playground apparatus, and picnic tables. East Palmer Park has a ball field, basketball court, and play area. A paved trail being developed around the perimeter of the area will eventually hook up with other trails in the northern suburbs.

How to get there: The parking lot for the nature area is located on 69th Street North just east of Shingle Creek Parkway. To reach West Palmer Park, go west on 69th Street and turn right on West Palmer Lake Drive. To reach East Palmer lake Park, go east on 69th Street and turn left on Oliver Avenue and proceed two blocks to 71st Avenue.

Map key: West 97

For additional information:
Brooklyn Center Parks and
Recreation Department
6301 Shingle Creek Parkway
Brooklyn Center, Minnesota 55430
(612) 561- 5448

Patrick Eagan
Municipal Park

As the name implies, Patrick Eagan Municipal Park is located in the fast growing suburb of Eagan, about three and a
half miles south of Interstate Highway 494. Undeveloped except for two miles of trails, the 102 acre park is situated in a
secluded basin surrounding small McCarthy Lake.

Small pockets of mature trees can be found here, particularly
cottonwood, black willow, and silver maple in the low marshy
areas, but most of the terrain is characterized by a mixture of
grassy meadows, second-growth woodlands, and planted evergreens. What open meadows do remain are giving way to
invaders such as sumac, boxelder, and elm, as well as eye-pleas-
ing groves of quaking aspen and paper birch. Larger red oak,
bur oak, and black cherry are scattered about, often standing
above dense thickets of chokecherry, prickly-ash, hazelnut,
buckthorn, raspberry, and wild grape.

A variety of conifers, mostly red pine and Scotch pine with
some white pine, have been planted singly and in groves. The
Scotch pine, an attractive tree native to the Scottish highlands,
has become one of the most widely planted trees in the world.

Though somewhat unruly in appearance, this combination of
plants and habitats makes the park a haven for many songbirds
and small mammals that thrive amid the suburban neighborhoods.

Facilities: There are 2 miles of wide trails here that are mowed for hiking most of the year and groomed for cross-country skiing in winter.

How to get there: The entrance to the park is located on Lexington Avenue, one-half mile north of Diffley Road.. From the Twin Cities take Cedar Avenue (Highway 77) or Interstate Highway 35E south to the Diffley Road exit. Go east on Diffley Road one mile past Pilot Knob Road, then turn left (north) on Lexington and look for the park entrance on the left. The driveway to the park passes a private residence and could easily be missed.

Map key: East 98

For additional information:

Eagan Parks and Recreation
Department
3830 Pilot Knob Road
P.O. Box 21199
Eagan, Minnesota 55121
(612) 454-8100

Paul Hugo Farm Wildlife Management Area

At first glance the Paul Hugo Farm Wildlife Management Area may seem more like an abandoned farm than a rich wildlife habitat. From the dirt parking lot all that is visible are separate stands of boxelder and aspen and an old field grassland with a few red cedar trees. A walk down the old farm road, however, will lead you beyond the open fields and through a swampy thicket of small trees and shrubs to a mature woodland bordering Rice Lake. Here the 360 acre preserve spreads out to encompass most of the lake and the extensive wetlands along the shoreline. Tall hardwoods such as basswood, red oak, and white oak, stand with sugar maple, butternut, bur oak, black cherry, and ironwood on well-drained hillocks. Aspen, elm, ash, and even tamarac, prosper in the wetter lowlands before giving way to a belt of cattail marsh which rims the lake. An abundance of waterfowl finds food and shelter in the wetlands and open waters of Rice Lake while ruffed grouse, raccoon, red fox, and other animals find refuge in the woods and thickets.

Facilities: There are no developed facilities here other than a designated parking area and the old road which serves as a foot trail. Though you can observe the marsh and lake from shore, good vistas are rare and the best way would be by small boat or canoe. State Wildlife Management Areas are managed for three primary reasons: wildlife production, public hunting, and trapping. Other activities, such as birdwatching and canoeing are also encouraged but should probably be avoided during the hunting season.

How to get there: Take U.S. Highway 61 north from St. Paul, State Highway 36, or Interstate Highway 694. Two miles after crossing from Ramsey County into Washington County, turn right onto County Road 8A. Follow County 8A east for 2.6 miles and turn left onto Homestead Ave. N. Go north for .7 miles and look for a small dirt parking area on the left.

Map key: East 99

For additional information:

Resident Manager
Carlos Avery WMA
Forest Lake, Minnesota 55025
(612) 296-5200

Minnesota Department of Natural Resources
Section of Wildlife, Box 7
500 Lafayette Road
St. Paul, Minnesota 55155
(612) 296-3344

Pine Point County Park

About three miles northwest of Stillwater, Pine Point County Park contains nearly 300 acres of gently rolling land bordering on two small lakes – Loon Lake and Lake Louise. A combination of oak woods, evergreen plantations, and wetlands occupy the hills and low-lying areas, while the rest – 130 acres of level uplands – is currently leased for farming. Plans call for portions of the croplands to be restored to prairie and oak savanna, with the remainder to be used as an agricultural production study area. The Minnesota-Wisconsin Boundary Trail passes through the heart of the park on an old Soo Line railroad grade.

Facilities: Five miles of trails in numerous interconnecting loops allow hikers, cross-country skiers, and horseback riders to explore the entire park. There are small stationary maps located where the trails intersect. Future development of the park may include an outdoor classroom, a trailhead center, and facilities for picnicking and camping.

How to get there: From St. Paul take State Highway 36 east toward Stillwater. About 5 miles past Interstate Highway 694 turn left (north) onto County Highway 15. Proceed for just over 6 miles and turn right onto County Road 61. After one mile turn right again. The park entrance will be on the left directly across from the Washington County Highway Department.

Map key: East 100

For additional information:

Washington County Parks
Department
11660 Myeron Road North
Stillwater, Minnesota 55082
(612) 731-3851

Poplar Lake Open Space

Poplar Lake is one of eleven undeveloped open space areas scattered about Ramsey County. Extending for a mile and a half along the northern edge of the County, this 432 acre tract is the largest of these sites, most of which occupy wet, low-lying areas important for groundwater regeneration. In addition to providing this service, these areas conserve open vistas and valuable wildlife habitat in the most thoroughly developed county in Minnesota.

The preserve takes its name from Poplar Lake, a shallow expanse of open water bordered by stretches of cattail, sedges, willow, alder, and dogwood. The surrounding landscape is a fairly flat composite of woodlands, old fields, and scattered marshes. Small patches of oak woods are found on drier sites but much of the area is flooded during wet years and supports a mixture of aspen, birch, elm, cottonwood, and some tamarac. Observant visitors who want to explore the area may be surprised by the variety of wildlife that finds refuge here.

Facilities: Although there are no marked trails or other facilities, hiking, cross-country skiing, and snowshoeing are permitted.

How to get there: Take Interstate Highway 35E north from St. Paul or Interstate Highway 694. About 6 miles north of 694 (at the county line), take the exit for County Road 81. Cross back over the Interstate then take a right onto County Road 59. Go a short distance and take a left onto County Road 32. Follow 32 (County Road J) as it bends left, then right. The preserve is on the left after the intersection with County Road 4 and extends to Western Avenue. There are no designated parking areas.

Map key: East 101

For additional information:

Ramsey County Parks and
Recreation Department
2015 North Van Dyke Street
Maplewood, Minnesota 55109
(612) 777-1707

Rice Creek—Chain of Lakes Regional Park Reserve

This sprawling Anoka County Park Reserve stretches for seven miles along the course of Rice Creek as it flows through Lino Lakes and parts of Centerville, Circle Pines, and Blaine. The reserve takes in about 2,500 acres of flatlands and low hills encompassing one sizable lake—George Watch—and partially surrounding six others—Peltier, Centerville, Marshan, Reshanau, Rice, and Baldwin. The landscape between these lakes is made up primarily of vast tracts of wet lowlands and old fields, with pockets of upland woods, some planted evergreens, and a restored prairie.

The park's watery habitats are extensive and diverse. There are broad sweeps of shallow, open water, patches of emergent bulrush and waterlily, cattail marshes, sedge meadows, and thickets of willow and red-osier dogwood. The woodlands are also varied, ranging from water tolerant stands of tall black willow and cottonwood with boxelder, aspen, ash, and elm, to well-drained oak forests dominated by red oak and bur oak with basswood, white oak, and black cherry. Nearly 100 acres of remnant prairie and oak savanna have been restored between George Watch Lake and Marshan lake.

Wildlife is plentiful throughout the area, but particularly in and around the wetlands and lakes. The park contains a treetop rookery where dozens of great blue herons raise their young. Many other birds are drawn here to nest or feed, including the great egret, black-crowned night-heron, double-crested cormorant, American bittern, and a host of ducks, geese, grebes, rails, gulls, terns, and shorebirds.

Facilities: There is no developed trail system in the park at this time and many of the more interesting areas are not easily reached. A number of roads and informal trails, however, do penetrate the park. Perhaps the best way to explore the area is by boat or canoe. There are boat launches on Peltier, George Watch, and Centerville Lakes that provide access to miles of shoreline. Canoes can follow the course of Rice Creek from one lake to another and travel the entire length of the park. Many people fish here from boats and from shore. A swimming beach and picnic area on Centerville Lake has tables, grills, water, horseshoe pits, playground equipment, and a bathhouse with toilets. There is also an 18 hole golf course. Plans call for the extensive development of the park in stages over the next few years. This will include paved parkways and parking lots, a major nature center and a network of nature trails, additional picnic areas with shelters, and a variety of camping facilities.

How to get there: From St. Paul or Interstate Highway 694, head north on Interstate Highway 35E. Nearly 10 miles north of 694, exit onto County Highway 14 and turn left (west). Stay on 14 (Main Street) through Centerville and follow it into the park. The boat launches on Peltier and George Watch Lakes are located off this road. Turn left onto the park road which bends around Centerville Lake to reach the other boat launch, picnic area, and swimming beach. The golf course is not accessible from these roads.

Map key: East 102

For additional information:

Anoka County Parks Department
550 Bunker Lake Boulevard
Anoka, Minnesota 55304
(612) 757-3920

Richter Wood County Park

Richter Wood County Park is an 80 acre tract of wild land amid the agricultural landscape of eastern Le Sueur County. The park protects one of the surviving remnants of a vast forest, known as the "Big Woods," that carpeted the region little more than a century ago. Today it stands in sharp contrast to the cultivated fields that are plowed up to the park's boundary. Acquired in the 1860s by August Richter, the woodland escaped conversion to cropland because it provided another sort of harvest. For a few decades the property was selectively logged of its giant elms, which were used to produce headings and staves for a barrel-making operation in nearby Montgomery. Although this practice, and the later infestations of Dutch elm disease and oak wilt, have left their mark on the woods, it remains a good example of the area's natural heritage.

Generally flat and poorly drained, the well watered terrain is cloaked by a high leafy canopy broken only by small woodland marshes. Both American elm and slippery elm can still be found alongside green ash, black ash, and silver maple in wet, marshy areas. However, it is a combination of sizable sugar maple and basswood trees that characterizes most of the forest. The sugar maples are particularly abundant here, as they have aggressively replaced the lost elms and oaks. A few tall red oaks are scattered about, as are ironwood, hackberry, and bitternut hickory. Each spring, before the trees leaf out, the forest floor comes alive with colorful wildflowers. Bloodroot, Dutchman's breeches, spring beauty, and dogtooth violet, as well as trilliums, toothworts, and trout lillies, are some that may be seen.

Facilities: The park is managed by the Le Sueur County Parks Committee and has a fulltime caretaker living on the premises. A network of interconnecting loops are maintained for hiking and cross-country skiing through the woods. An old barn serves as a picnic shelter with tables, water, and toilets. Outside there are additional tables with grills and water.

How to get there: Head south from the Twin Cities on Interstate Highway 35. A few miles into Rice County exit onto State Highway 19 and drive west towards Lonsdale. After 19 bends north outside of Lonsdale, turn left onto County Road 2. Stay on 2 as it becomes County Road 28 in LeSueur County. Three miles past the county line turn left onto State Highway 13 and drive south to Montgomery. From State Highway 13 in Montgomery, go west on County Road 26 about 11 miles. Turn left (south) onto dirt road and proceed .65 miles to the park entrance on right.

Map key: East 103

For additional information:

Le Sueur County Parks Committee
c/o County Auditor
Le Center, Minnesota 56057
(612) 364-5000 (caretaker)

Ritter Farm Park

Until 1971 Ritter Farm Park was a working farm in a rural setting. Today it is a public park in the rapidly developing suburb of Lakeville. Located just west of Interstate Highway 35 on the shore of Lake Marion, the park is a pleasant combination of natural and man-made habitats amidst rolling moraine hills. The 313-acre municipal park includes old fields, a remnant apple orchard, a grove of spruce and pine, marshes, ponds, and mature oak woodlands. White-tailed deer, red fox, muskrat, raccoon, woodchuck, cottontail rabbit, and gray squirrel are among the mammals that live here. The varied landscape and open spaces are also home to birds such as the rose-breasted grosbeak, cardinal, mourning dove, white-breasted nuthatch, goldfinch, northern oriole, yellow-shafted flicker, meadowlark, green-backed heron, and yellow-bellied sapsucker. Some of the old farm fields have been allowed to go wild and provide a good opportunity to observe various stages of natural succession. The park includes a lovely picnic area on a grassy knoll overlooking Lake Marion that is shaded by large wide-spreading oaks.

Facilities: An extensive network of cross-country ski trails is groomed throughout the winter and mowed for hikers in the off season. Although there are few other facilities within the park, the city plans to construct a variety of amenities, such as a boat launch, picnic shelter, playground equipment, and a horseshoe court. There are satelites by the picnic area. Among other things, the park is a popular spot for fishing and sledding.

How to get there: Heading south from the Twin Cities on Interstate Highway 35, take the Orchard Trail/185th Street exit. Follow the frontage road 10 blocks south to 195th Street. Turn west here, crossing over the Interstate, and follow the signs to the parking lot. There is a nominal parking fee during the winter.

Map key: East 104

For additional information:

Lakeville Park and Recreation
Department
City Hall
Lakeville, Minnesota 55044
(612) 469-4431

Riverbend Nature Center

The Riverbend Nature Center is a 600 acre outdoor classroom on the outskirts of Faribault. Over the centuries the landscape here has alternated several times between forest and prairie. This natural cycle was interrupted by the arrival of settlers who converted the forests, prairies, and marshes into an agricultural landscape of plowed fields, grazing land, and scattered woodlots. Today the Nature Center is assisting Mother Nature to re-create an example of the area's natural heritage.

The Straight River meanders through the entire length of the preserve. Although Straight may seem an odd name for this twisting, turning stream, it is actually a loose translation of "Owatonna," a Dakota Indian word meaning morally strong or honest. The floodplain here supports a typical lowland forest of silver maple, cottonwood, elm, green ash, and black willow. In the rich alluvial soil of these bottomlands, the extremely rare Minnesota dwarf trout lily can be found blooming in springtime. This small flower, which exists only in Rice and Goodhue Counties, grows in record numbers near the banks of the river.

Pockets of well-developed upland forests are comprised primarily of black sugar maple, basswood, red oak, and ironwood, with some bitternut hickory, butternut, and swamp white oak. Surrounding acres of once-cultivated clearings are giving way to dense growths of small trees and shrubs such as sumac, prickly-ash, buckthorn, serviceberry, black raspberry, Virginia creeper, and riverbank grape. In other areas this slow process of succession has been hastened by the planting of thousands of seedlings, including red oak, black walnut, white cedar, and Norway pine. Among the many birds attracted to the mature woodlands and brushy thickets are the warbling vireo, red-headed woodpecker, wood thrush, ovenbird, eastern wood pewee, black-billed cuckoo, rose-breasted grosbeak, brown thrasher, and indigo bunting.

An additional 21 acres of abandoned cropland are being restored to tallgrass prairie. Though lacking the diversity of an undisturbed prairie, it provides valuable habitat for birds like the dickcissel, bobolink, vesper sparrow, field sparrow, bluebird, meadowlark, and ring-necked pheasant.

The last remaining agricultural field has been returned to its original condition — a pond. By blocking old drainage tiles and constructing a three foot high dike, more than 15 acres of shallow open water, marsh, and swampy thickets were created. Common yellowthroat, yellow warbler, red-winged blackbird, and long-billed marsh wren may be seen here, as well as wood duck, teal, mallard, and coot.

In all, more than 260 species of birds have been sighted within the Nature Center. A sizable herd of white-tailed deer shares the area with raccoon, red and grey fox, beaver, mink, and other small mammals. Innumerable species of fish, reptiles, amphibians, and insects are also an integral part of the diverse environs.

Facilities: The Nature Center has a small interpretive building with a classroom, exhibits, and restrooms. About six miles of well-marked trails explore the numerous habitats. These range from blacktop and limestone to woodchip and grass. A few dozen benches have been installed along the trails. There is a small picnic area with a restroom located by the upper parking lot. The Center's main office and a gift shop are located in the basement of City Hall.

The Nature Center is open every day of the year between 8:00 a.m. and sunset, and the office is open weekdays from 9:00 a.m. to 3:00 p.m..

How to get there: Take Interstate Highway 35 south to Faribault and exit onto State Highway 60. Follow 60 east through Faribault toward Kenyon. Two blocks past the viaduct, turn right at Shumway Avenue and follow Nature Center signs to the lower parking lot.

Map key: East 105

For additional information:

River Bend Nature Center
P.O. Box 265
Faribault, Minnesota 55021
(507) 332-7151

Riverside Park

Riverside Park is a small, undeveloped preserve situated along a secluded stretch of Mississippi River backwaters in St. Paul Park. Although the park itself covers less than 20 acres, it borders on an extensive bottomland of swamp forests and marshes rich in wildlife. The park's rocky soils support a woodland dominated by basswood and red oak, with bur oak, ironwood, hackberry, butternut, elm, red cedar, and ash. The dense, sunlit understory is dense with prickly-ash, buckthorn, hazelnut, honeysuckle, raspberry, poison ivy, woodbine, and wild grape.

A short but steep drop exposes the underlying bedrock and separates the dry upland terrace from the floodplain. Narrow footpaths here provide a pleasant vantage point for observing the plentiful birds and other animals that abound near the river. White-tailed deer, raccoons, muskrats, pileated woodpeckers, great egrets, wood ducks, kingfishers, and dozens of songbirds are among the wildlife you might see.

Facilities: There are no developed facilities here but a number of unmarked trails of various sizes criss-cross the area.

How to get there: From Interstate Highway 94 in St. Paul or Interstate Highway 494 just east of the Mississippi River, head south on U.S. Highway 61. Proceed a bit more than two miles and exit at Summit Avenue. Drive south through St. Paul Park on Summit, then turn right at Pullman Avenue. The small parking lot for the park is located at the western end of the street.

Map key: East 106

For additional information:

Parks Department
City Hall
900 3rd Street
St. Paul Park, MN 55071
(612) 459-9785

Robert E. Ney Memorial County Park Reserve

The Robert E. Ney Memorial County Park Reserve in Wright County occupies 320 acres of rambling wildlife habitat just north of the town of Maple Lake. Bordering the western shore of 232 acre Lake Mary, the reserve is a patchwork of mature hardwoods, dense second-growth woodlands, brush-choked old fields, lowland forest, and wetlands. Deer, fox, woodchuck, rabbit, ruffed grouse, wood duck, and an assortment of songbirds live here. A small pond within the park drains into Silver Creek, which flows through rolling farmland to Lake Maria in nearby Lake Maria State Park.

Facilities: Near Lake Mary, a small brick chapel dedicated to the memory of Robert Ney occupies a grassy clearing set amid tall shade trees. There is a picnic table and a fire ring located here. While plans call for the development of a trail system, at this time there is only a short trail that begins near the chapel. A boat launch provides access to Lake Mary.

How to get there: From the Twin Cities take State Highway 55 northeast to the town of Maple Lake. In town, turn right (north) onto County Highway 8. Just less than 2 miles from town turn right onto a gravel road. The road passes a few residences before coming to a Y intersection by the lake. Turn left here and look for the small parking area on the left.

Map key: West 107

For additional information:

Wright County Parks Department
Route 1, Box 97B
Buffalo, Minnesota 55313
(612) 682-3900, ext. 182339-6881 (Metro)
1-800-362-3667, ext. 182 (Toll Free)

Roberts Bird Sanctuary

Sandwiched between Lake Harriet and Lakewood Cemetery in south Minneapolis is a 13 acre strip of wetlands and woods known as Roberts Bird Sanctuary. This small parcel of wild land is fenced off from the heavy traffic near the lake and stands in stark contrast to the manicured landscape around it. The area was designated as a refuge in 1936 and later named after Thomas Sadler Roberts, who was the first curator of the Museum of Natural History at the University of Minnesota. Dr. Roberts is considered to be the father of Minnesota ornithology. Over the years a combination of human encroachment, disease, exotic plants, and storm damage has greatly altered the natural character of the area, but today the Minneapolis Park Board is working to restore some of its beauty and value to wildlife.

The sanctuary originally contained a tamarac swamp but the tamaracs were toppled in 1925 by a severe wind storm that also destroyed one of the five bandstands that have occupied the north shore of lake Harriet. Many elms replaced the tamaracs and thrived for decades before they succumbed to Dutch elm disease in the late 1970's. Then a straight line windstorm in 1979 and a tornado in 1981 wiped out the remaining elms and many other large trees near the east entrance. In addition to other unwelcome invaders, the colorful, but pernicious, purple loosestrife has infested the disturbed area.

224

Inside the east entrance, the few large cottonwood and black willow trees that remain stand above a thicket of boxelder, ash, buckthorn, red elderberry, mulberry, bittersweet nightshade, and wild grape. More than 100 trees have been planted in this area to restore the canopy lost during the tornado; these include silver maple, green ash, sugar maple, basswood, swamp white oak, black cherry, river birch, serviceberry, hackberry, and ironwood. The cattail marsh that extends to the west has recently been dredged to create shallow ponds and improve the habitat for aquatic birds.

West of the marsh is a small hill with tall bur oak and sugar maple mixed with ash, red oak, and basswood. Young woods and swampy areas make up the remainder of the sanctuary. A surprising variety of birds may be seen here, including wood duck, mallard, black-crowned night heron, indigo bunting, northern oriole, cowbird, goldfinch, yellow-shafted flicker, rose-breasted grosbeak, red-eyed vireo, hairy woodpecker, red-headed woodpecker, sora rail, and sparrow hawk.

The recently reconstructed Lake Harriet Rock Garden is adjacent to the east entrance and the popular Lake Harriet Rose Garden is located just across the road.

Facilities: Currently there is a single trail that traverses the area while numerous informal trails detour into the woods and thickets. A marsh trail is being developed to provide visitors a close up look at the recovering wetland community. The surrounding parklands offer an abundance of facilities and activities, including picnic tables, grills, paved trails for walking and biking, swimming beaches, and restrooms.

How to get there: Parking is located off Roseway Road between King's Highway (Dupont) and the Lake Harriet Parkway. Enter the sanctuary through the turnstyle gate beyond the Rock Garden. Additional parking is next to the west entrance near the Lake Harriet Bandstand.

Map key: West 108

For additional information:

Minneapolis Park and Recreation Board
310 Fourth Avenue South
Minneapolis, Minnesota 55415
(612) 348-2226

Roseville Central Park

This 240-acre municipal park stretches for more than a mile through the heart of suburban Roseville. Most of the park is highly developed and contains a wide variety of entertainment and athletic facilities laid out around 12 acre Lake Bennet and a few small cattail marshes. Fringed with a narrow strip of cattails, weeping willows, and other trees, Lake Bennet is home to a few trumpeter swans that were donated to the city. These spectacular birds have been clipped and live year round on the small lake, which is aerated to maintain open water.

In contrast, the 65-acre section east of Dale Avenue has been set aside as the "Joe Mogg Memorial Boardwalk and Nature Area." Less than thirty years ago this area was a truck farm where celery was grown in the fertile soil of an old lakebed. Since then however, the basin has been remade into an attractive wildlife habitat by the efforts of the local community. Today storm run-off supplies water to a productive wetland choked with willow, cattail, sedge, red-osier dogwood, arrowhead, horsetail, swamp honeysuckle, and wild cucumber. The Roseville Wildflower Club has helped reclaim the land by planting dozens of native flowers throughout the area. Marsh marigold, common skullcap, tufted loosestrife, daisy fleabane, swamp milkweed, forget-me-not, and showy lady slipper are just some that have been established in the boggy lowland. In order to further improve the habitat, five ponds have been dredged with small islands where waterfowl can nest.

To the north the wetland is bordered by a steep hill cloaked by large oaks, while on the south side there is a dense growth of black willow, boxelder, aspen, silver maple, cottonwood, elm, buckthorn, and wild grape. The uplands along the southern edge of the nature area were planted with rows of red pine (the state tree) about two decades ago.

Facilities: Visitors can get a close-up look at the wetland on the floating boardwalk that leads to an elevated observation deck with benches. A short trail also winds through the upland south of the marsh. A guide for the nature trail can be obtained at City Hall. Between Lexington and Victoria Avenues there is a fishing dock on Lake Bennet, a paved trail for hiking and biking around the lake, two picnic areas with shelters, tables, grills, and restrooms, an exercise course, a bandshell, playground equipment, bocceball courts, tennis courts, and a softball field. Between Victoria and Dale Avenues there is a picnic shelter and fields for softball and football.

How to get there: Less than 2 miles from St. Paul, the Mogg Nature Area is most easily reached by exiting off State Highway 36 (between I35W and I35E) onto Dale Avenue. Look for the entrance to the small parking lot on the right about half a mile north of the highway. The rest of the park stretches west between Dale and Lexington Avenues. To park near Lake Bennet take the Lexington Avenue exit instead and look for the entrance on the right as you head north.

Map key: East 109

For additional information:

Roseville Park and Recreation
Department
2660 Civic Center Drive
Roseville, Minnesota, 55113
(612) 490- 2200

Rum River Central Park

Along the meandering river from which it takes its name lies Rum River Central Park, a scenic expanse of low, sandy hills and floodplain just a few miles upstream from Anoka and the confluence with the Mississippi River. Currently the park encompasses 434 acres on the west side of the river but the county plans to acquire an additional 246 acres between the opposite bank and Cedar Creek.

The park's well drained uplands were once a combination of prairie and scattered oaks known as an oak savanna, but years of agricultural use have greatly altered the landscape. Today the former savannas are well-developed oak woodlands, small pine plantations, or abandoned fields, while other reminders of the park's settled past include small clearings, overgrown foundations, old roads, and lilac bushes.

Mature red oaks and bur oaks still dominate the dry areas, but instead of shading prairie grasses and flowers they overshadow thickets of aspen, cherry, boxelder, red cedar, elm, and prickly-ash. Dispersed throughout the low areas of the park are wetlands of various size rimmed with aspen, willow, dogwood, and alder. The floodplain along the river is well forested and contains an unusually large amount of silver maple with lesser numbers of cottonwood, black willow, and green ash. White-tailed deer share the woods and fields with foxes, raccoons, woodchucks, rabbits, and squirrels. Wood ducks, mallards, great egrets, and green-backed herons may be seen on the river and marshes where muskrats and painted turtles make their home.

The park is situated halfway between the St. Francis Canoe Base (Rum River North Park) and the Rum River South Canoe Base (in Anoka), which makes it an ideal picnic or camping spot for those canoeing down the river.

Facilities: An extensive network of trails for hiking, cross-country skiing, and horseback riding winds along the river and crisscrosses the park. Fishing is popular along the banks of the river. "North Star Tubing and Canoeing," located within the park, rents tubes and canoes and provides a launch and shuttle service. Development of the park's facilities is in its early stages. Plans call for separate picnic areas with shelters, tables, and grills, a large family campground, a smaller canoe campground, playfields, restrooms, and additional parking lots along the park's roads.

How to get there: The park is reached by taking State Highway 47 north from the junction with U.S. Highway 10 in Anoka. After about 7 miles turn right onto County Highway 7, which leads to the park entrance.

Map key: West 110

For additional information:

Anoka County Parks and
Recreation
550 Bunker Lake Blvd.
Anoka, Minnesota 55304
(612) 757-3920

Rum River North Park

At the edge of the little town of St. Francis in northern Anoka County is Rum River North Park. Although comprised of just 80 acres, this out-of-the-way park stretches for a full mile along the east bank of the meandering river. Most of the small preserve is carpeted by a combination of mature oak woodlands, mixed second-growth forest, and planted evergreens. Two small streams that drain local wetlands flow through the woods and empty into the river within the park.

Situated seventeen miles upriver from Anoka and the confluence with the Mississippi, Rum River North Park is a good launching site for a one day canoe trip on the gentle water. Recognizing its beauty and value as a natural resource, the county has made efforts to prevent additional residential or commercial development along its entire shoreline.

Facilities: A number of mowed trails wind through the woods and along the riverbank. The park provides a canoe launching and shuttle service. A wooded campsite is being developed for canoeists coming down the river. There are separate picnic areas available with shelters, tables, grills, restrooms, drinking water, and a ballfield. The park has a resident caretaker.

How to get there: From the Twin Cities take State Highway 65 (Central Avenue) north from Interstate Highway 694 for about 23 miles to County Highway 24. Turn left (west) onto 24 and follow it for about 7 miles (as it turns south and again to the west) to St. Francis. The park entrance is on the right, at the public library, just before the bridge over the Rum River. An additional entrance (picnic shelters, ballfield) is reached by turning right onto County Road 72.

Map key: West 111

For additional information:

Anoka County Parks and
Recreation
550 Bunker Lake Blvd.
Anoka, Minnesota 55304
(612) 757-3920

Rush River State Wayside

The Rush River State Wayside straddles the final stretch of the surging country stream for which it is named. Plans call for the park to encompass 1,200 acres but at present a little less than half has been acquired. This small river drains the farm-land of southeastern Sibley County and as it nears the Minne-sota River it drops into a narrow valley and flows between steep bluffs. The valley has been created by erosion and throughout the park there are many fresh examples, including whole hill-sides bordering the river. A number of dry tributary ravines cut into the sides of the valley, creating a ragged landscape that supports a variety of plant communities.

The sheltered ravines and fertile soil above the valley are shaded by a spacious woodland dominated by tall sugar maple and basswood, with red oak, ironwood, bitternut hickory, hackberry, elm, and butternut. Typical of such woods, spring wildflowers abound, such as bloodroot, rue anemone, yellow violet, wild ginger, Jack-in-the-pulpit, sharp-lobed hepatica, and cutleaf toothwort. In contrast, more exposed slopes and abandoned pastures are characterized by wide-spreading bur oak, groves of aspen, a few paper birch, red cedar, ash, red elderberry, prickly-ash, and sumac. A small remnant of native prairie has managed to survive on one very dry, south-facing hillside. The frequently flooded lowlands along the river support tall cottonwood trees, with silver maple, boxelder, elm, and dense willow thickets.

Facilities: While the park lacks a marked trail system, plenty of well-worn, informal trails wind through the hills and along the river. There are two picnic area with tables, firerings, and pit toilets. One has a shelter and playground equipment and the other a water pump. Steps lead uphill from the playground to a scenic overlook with a bench. Camping is permitted on Knob Hill but reservations are required and there is a fee.

How to get there: From the Twin Cities, head southeast to Shakopee and then along the Minnesota river Valley on U.S. Highway 169. Where 169 crosses from Scott County into Le Sueur County, turn right (west) onto State Highway 19. Follow 19 across the river and into the small town of Henderson. In town turn left (south) onto State Highway 93 and go a short distance before turning right onto Ridge Road. Take Ridge Road uphill and turn right again at South Street. From the intersection of South Street and Ninth Street, head south out of town on the unpaved township road. Stay on this road for about a mile and a quarter and look for the park entrance on the left.

Map key: West 112

For additional information:

Park Manager
19825 Park Blvd.
Jordan, Minnesota 55352
(612) 492-6400

Minnesota Department of Natural Resources
Division of Parks and Recreation
Information Center, Box 40
500 Lafayette Road
St. Paul, Minnesota 55155
(612) 296-4776

Sakatah Lake State Park

This 842-acre park stretches for 3.5 miles along the southern shoreline of Sakatah Lake, which straddles the line between Rice and Le Sueur Counties. Heavily wooded with a mature hardwood forest, the park's rolling topography also includes second-growth woodlands, old fields, and wetlands. This combination of habitats amid the surrounding farmland makes Sakatah Lake State Park a valuable sanctuary for many of southern Minnesota's wildlife species. Deer, red fox, raccoon, woodchuck, striped skunk, cootontail rabbit, muskrat, mink, and an abundance of birds live here.

Situated at the southern edge of the "Big Woods," the park preserves remnants of this once vast forest. The rich woodland is alternately dominated by tall basswood, bur oak, and sugar maple, with lots red oak, white oak, ironwood, and ash, as well as bitternut hickory, elm, black walnut, and hackberry. Open areas are slowly being reclaimed by sumac, prickly-ash, aspen, boxelder, cottonwood, raspberry, wild grape, and Virginia creeper. Colorful wildflowers adorn the forest floor in springtime before the trees leaf out.

Covering more than 1000 acres, Sakatah Lake is a natural widening of the Cannon River. Along the upper reaches of the Cannon River Valley, huge blocks of ice left by receding glaciers formed depressions that filled with water, creating lakes such as Sakatah. Seventy-nine miles upstream from the Mississippi River, Sakatah Lake is the beginning of the Cannon River State Canoe Route.

The Sakatah Singing Hills State Trail passes through the park on an abandoned railroad grade that parallels the lakeshore. This 42-mile-long multiple use trail provides a limestone hard surface between Mankato and Faribault for bicyclists, hikers, skiers, and snowmobilers.

Facilities: Five miles of well-maintained trails lead hikers through the wooded hills. In winter, two miles of trails are groomed for cross-country skiers and an additional two miles are available for snowmobilers. There are 60 semimodern campsites set into the woods with a dumping station, showers, and flush toilets. A separate group camp is also available. In various spots along the lakeshore the park offers: a small interpretive center, a swimming beach, a boat launch, and an attractive picnic area with tables, grills, fire rings, water, and toilets.

How to get there: Take Interstate Highway 35 south from the Twin Cities to Faribault. Just after crossing the Cannon River, exit onto State Highway 60 and head west. Follow Highway 60 for a little more than a dozen miles and look for the park entrance on the right after crossing into Le Sueur County.

The park is closed from 10:00 p.m. to 8:00 a.m. except to registered campers. Daily or annual permits are required for vehicles entering a state park. They may be purchased at the park entrance.

Map key: East 113

For additional information:

Sakatah Lake State Park Manager
Route 2, Box 19
Waterville, Minnesota 56095
(507) 362-4438

Minnesota Department of Natural Resources
Division of Parks and Recreation
Information Center, Box 40
500 Lafayette Road
St. Paul, Minnesota 55155
(612) 296-4776

Sand Dunes State Forest

The Sand Dunes State Forest lies adjacent to the southern edge of the Sherburne National Wildlife Refuge about thirty-five miles northwest of the Twin Cities. While the forest's official boundaries take in 10,800 acres of the Anoka sandplain on both sides of the St. Francis River, less than half of that acreage is owned by the state or federal government and open to the public.

The area derives its name from the unstable soil conditions that have characterized the region since the meltwater streams of the retreating glaciers formed the sandplain some 12,000 years ago. In places, sand dunes were later superimposed on the exposed plain by local wind action. By the time of settlement the landscape here was made up of oak forests, oak savannas, and prairies with small areas of open shifting sands and numerous shallow lakes and marshes.

Long considered unproductive, the sand dunes became a serious concern during the drought years of the 1930s when drifting sands and sand storms threatened local communities. Since then most of the native vegetation has been replaced by extensive plantings of red pine and jack pine, which grow naturally on sandy soils farther north. In fact, the first tree planted by a machine in Minnesota grows here. In addition to timber management and fire prevention, the Department of Natural Resources digs small potholes and plants cover crops and food plots for wildlife.

The pine plantations have stabilized the dunes so completely that only one sand dune within the forest remains in its natural state. Scattered pockets of natural woodland, grassland, and wetland persist here. (This is particularly true in areas along the meandering St. Francis River, which is actually part of the National Wildlife Refuge.)

Facilities: The State Forest is used for a wide variety of recreational purposes, including hunting, camping, picnicking, hiking, fishing, and water sports on Ann Lake. Extensive trails for hiking, horseback riding, and snowmobiling are maintained in the two largest parcels of state land within the forest. On the shore of mile-long Lake Ann there is a 24-unit campground, a picnic area, a boat landing, and access to the trail system. There is also a fire lookout tower which is open to the public and offers an expansive view of the area.

How to get there: From the Twin Cities head northwest to Elk River on U.S.Highway 10 or Interstate Highway 94 and State Highway 101. From Elk River go north on U.S. Highway 169 a little more than 10 miles to Zimmerman and turn left (west) onto County Highway 4. After about 6 miles turn left onto County Road 15, which bisects the forest. Take the first right and follow the signs to reach the facilities at Lake Ann.

Map key: West 114

For additional information:

Minnesota Department of Natural
Resources
Trails and Waterways Unit
Information Center, Box 40
500 Lafayette Road
St. Paul, Minnesota 55155
(612) 296-6699

Schaefer Prairie

On a quarter-section of land surrounded by miles of cultivated corn fields in McLeod County, Schaefer Prairie protects
one of the few intact remnants of blacksoil prairie existing on
the rich loamy soils of south-central Minnesota. Virgin tallgrass
prairie occupies nearly half of the 160-acre preserve, while the
rest is composed of pothole marshes, small ponds, floodplain
and creek, and old fields.

The several potholes and a low, gravelly ridge running north-
south down the center of the tract would have made early 20th
century farming difficult and help explain why the land was not
cultivated. At that time there was a market for wild hay and
the prairie was mowed almost every year by horse-drawn
equipment. In order to ensure its continued survival, the Minnesota Chapter of The Nature Conservancy purchased the
prairie in 1967 and it was named to commemorate the pioneer
Schaefer family.

Since then, prescribed burning has been used to manage the
grassland in the absence of the grazing and wildfires that
helped shape it. While the number of pests such as ticks are
decreased by the burning, studies show that wild mammals and
birds have adapted to prairie fires and virtually all escape the

flames. Small animals go underground while larger ones move away temporarily or jump unharmed across the fire line. More importantly, since fire is the best known method for maintaining the native prairie, in the long run it is essential to the survival of prairie animals.

The Nature Conservancy burns only a portion of the preserve in any one year, leaving food and shelter for animals immediately after the fire. Before long the burned areas will have taller grasses that produce more seed and a greater variety of prairie plants. These tracts will then attract abundant wildlife, including deer and many kinds of birds.

Nearly 300 plant species have been recorded at Schaefer Prairie, and an observant visitor should find several dozen wildflowers in bloom on any summer day. Among the grasses and flowers that occur in a wide range of moisture conditions are big bluestem, Indian grass, rough blazing star, blue-eyed grass, purple prairie clover, and golden alexander. Wet, lowlying areas are characterized by cordgrass, Indian paint brush, yellow star-grass, mountain mint, water hemlock, closed gentian, vanilla grass, saw-tooth sunflower, woundwort, prairie loosestrife, great lobelia, and prairie blazing star. Species generally restricted to mesic or moist soils include smooth aster, Kalm's brome grass, northern bedstraw, wild pea, and stiff-leaved goldenrod. Many other plants are best suited for the driest sites, such as the gravelly ridge, including side-oats grama, blue grama grass, prairie dropseed, pasque flower, prairie false dandelion, upland and silky aster, buffalo bean, alum root, dotted blazing star, and tooth-leaved evening primrose.

Visitors may find it interesting to compare the undisturbed prairie (generally the northern and eastern acreage) with the abandoned fields (much of the southern half of the preserve). Buffalo Creek flows through the area behind a green wall of boxelder, green ash, cottonwood, willow, elm, hackberry, and a variety of shrubs.

Facilities: There are no developed facilities at Schaefer Prairie. As with all Nature Conservancy preserves, the protection of the natural plant and animal communities is the highest priority. Although you are invited to observe and enjoy the preserve, please use care to minimize the impact of your visit.

How to get there: Schaefer Prairie is located in southwestern McLeod County a little more than an hours drive west of Minneapolis. From the Twin Cities, take U.S. Highway 212 west through Carver County toward Glencoe. Continue west past Glencoe for about seven miles and turn left onto a gravel road. This road is unnumbered, but is opposite County Road 4, which is marked. Go about half a mile to the first intersection. This is the northeast corner of the preserve. Look for Nature Conservancy signs posting the area. To park, proceed to the southeast corner of the preserve to a field road where you can pull off.

Map key: West 115

For additional information:

The Nature Conservancy
1313 Fifth Street S.E.
Minneapolis, Minnesota 55414
(612) 379-2134

Sherburne National Wildlife Refuge

At 30,600 acres, the Sherburne National Wildlife Refuge is the largest preserve of any kind within an hour's drive of the Twin Cities. Stretching across almost 50 square miles of the Anoka Sandplain in Sherburne County, the refuge encompasses much of the St. Francis River Valley. The moderately rolling terrain was created at the end of the last ice age when the glaciers were in retreat. Torrents of meltwater flowing from the sea of ice deposited immense quantities of sand, known as outwash, over the freshly exposed earth. Scattered hills represent glacial formations, such as kames and eskers, not completely buried by the outwash, or sand dunes formed by strong winds soon after the meltwater streams ran dry. The lakes and marshes were produced when blocks of ice were stranded by the retreating glaciers, leaving depressions when they melted.

When settlers arrived little more than a century ago, the St. Francis River Basin was considered one of the finest wildlife areas in the state of Minnesota. These pioneers found a patchwork landscape where windswept prairies broken by oak forests and savannas were interspersed with tamarac swamps, expansive wetlands, and shallow lakes. Dramatic changes came quickly as the settlers reshaped the land for agriculture. The thin topsoil of the sandy prairies was plowed and oak forests were logged; wetlands were ditched and drained; and savannas were invaded by woody vegetation.

By the 1940s most of the natural habitat, and the wildlife it supported, was gone. However, local organizations of sportsmen and conservationists recognized the valley's potential and stirred interest in preserving and restoring it as a wildlife area. The Minnesota Conservation Commission, forerunner of the Department of Natural Resources, realized the difficulty of dealing with 300 individual landowners and turned to the Federal Bureau of Sport Fisheries and Wildlife for help, requesting that they consider the area for a National Wildlife Refuge. When the refuge was established in 1965 it became part of an invaluable network of United States lands managed specifically for wildlife. Today the National Wildlife Refuge System includes more than 400 refuges, which total nearly 90 million acres in 49 states and five trust territories.

True to its purpose, Sherburne is home once again to an exceptional array of wildlife, but it has required a great deal of habitat restoration and manipulation to undo much of the damage done during the first seventy years of settlement. Each of the three major types of habitat here – wetlands, woodlands, and grasslands, including oak savannas – has its own distinct problems, and each has its own management program.

The first priority of the refuge is to restore and maintain habitat for migratory birds, primarily waterfowl. Twenty-three impoundments combine with natural lakes and marshes to cover some 12,000 acres – over one-third of the refuge. The St. Francis River supplies the water and a system of control structures regulates the water levels in the impoundments. By controlling the depth of the water in these manmade wetlands, refuge managers are able to provide a diversity of habitats for the great variety of birds that nest here or stop over during migration. For example, some pools will have shallow waters and exposed mudflats, which benefit shorebirds and allow aquatic vegetation to grow, while others are kept a bit deeper to create an ideal habitat for surface-feeding ducks. Wild rice, an excellent food for wildlife, is able to thrive where a depth of two feet is maintained. Still other areas are flooded with as much as six feet of water to meet the needs of diving birds.

Any visitor will quickly see that these management techniques have been a success. The wetlands abound with wildlife. The most spectacular symbol of this success is the bald eagle, which began nesting here a few years ago after a long absence. Some of the more conspicuous species include Canada goose, mallard, wood duck, blue-winged teal, great blue heron, pied-billed grebe, coot, red-winged blackbird, muskrat, leopard frog, and painted turtle, but patient observers may see a great deal more. The common loon, red-necked grebe, northern shoveler, canvasback, ring-necked duck, green-winged teal, redhead, hooded merganser, and black-crowned night heron raise their young here, as do the American bittern, sora rail, spotted sandpiper, black tern, belted kingfisher, long-billed marsh wren, yellow-headed blackbird, and swamp sparrow. Among the many other birds that are not known to nest here but might be seen, particularly during spring and fall migration, are the double-crested cormorant, American wigeon, pintail, ruddy duck, lesser scaup, bufflehead, snow goose, and an occasional whistling swan. Beaver, mink, Blanding's turtle, and the blue-spotted salamander also inhabit the marshes.

Like the original wetlands, most of the prairie was destroyed; however, unlike the wetlands, restoring the native grasses and flowers is a long-term project. About 10,000 acres of disturbed grasslands and remnant prairies carpet the well-drained, sandy uplands. While the re-introduction of native species is sometimes necessary, the most important tool used to re-establish the prairie is fire. Prescribed burning every few years encourages the growth of native flowers, such as hoary puccoon, blue lupine, and Indian paintbrush, and warm season grasses, such as big bluestem, little bluestem, Indian grass, switchgrass, and side-oats grama. It also reduces competition from non-native cool season grasses, as well as encroaching trees and shrubs.

As the health of this habitat improves, it becomes more attractive to wildlife. The grasslands are the preferred haunt of the coyote, badger, woodchuck, pocket gopher, and thirteen-lined ground squirrel, as well as a growing number of birds, including the sandhill crane, ring-necked pheasant, kingbird, horned lark, bobolink, vesper sparrow, lark sparrow, eastern bluebird, and sharp-tailed grouse. Other animals, such as white-tailed deer, red fox, raccoon, striped skunk, and birds of prey, move back and forth between the woodlands and open areas. Cooper's hawk, red-tailed hawk, marsh hawk, screech owl, and long-eared owl are some of the raptors that nest in the woods but are often seen hunting over the grasslands.

A few thousand acres of woodlands are scattered about the well-drained uplands. Most of these areas represent oak savannas which, in the absence of fire, have developed into thick forest. Mature oaks – bur oak, red oak, northern pin oak, and some white oak – stand above boxelder, black cherry, aspen, birch, elm, red maple, and a dense growth of shrubs, ferns, and flowers. These woodlands are now self-sustaining communities except for several plantations of pine and spruce which are gradually being removed. Wildlife found here includes squirrel, chipmunk, rabbit, broad-winged hawk, woodcock, ruffed grouse, black-billed cuckoo, red-headed woodpecker, great crested flycatcher, red-eyed vireo, black and white warbler, and American redstart. Black bear and bobcat, both rare this far south, occasionally find shelter in the woods.

Facilities: Visitors should make their first stop at the information stations located where the county roads enter the refuge. Two separate natural areas offer self-guided nature trails. The Mahnomen Trail has 2.5 miles of trails with an observation tower and a boardwalk. Restrooms, a water pump, and picnic tables are located next to the parking area. The Blue Hill Trail has another 6.25 miles of trails. Both trails are open for cross-country skiing but are not groomed. The entire refuge is open for snowshoeing in winter. In addition to the county roads that cross the refuge there is an excellent 12 mile Wildlife Drive with interpretive exhibits. When the water is high enough a 12-mile stretch of the St. Francis River is used for canoeing. For visiting groups, there is an old school house with displays, a library, movie projector, slide projector, drinking water, and restrooms. Fishing is allowed in some areas and much of the refuge is open to hunting.

How to get there: From the Twin Cities take Interstate Highway 94 and County Highway 101 to Elk River. Take U.S. Highway 169 north from the junction of Highways 101, 10, and 169 in Elk River. After 11 miles turn left onto County Road 9 and drive 4 miles west to the refuge.

Map key: West 116

For additional information:

Refuge Manager
Sherburne National Wildlife
Refuge
Route 2
Zimmerman Minnesota 55398
(612) 389-3323

Springbrook Nature Center

Once destined to become a golf course, the Springbrook Nature Center was rescued twice by the efforts of local citizens who recognized its natural beauty and diversity. Situated just five miles from Minneapolis on the northern edge of Fridley, the center preserves a representative parcel of the vast Anoka sandplain. The slightly undulating, sandy terrain was formed by shifting streams of glacial meltwater that deposited their loads of sand and gravel across the region. Within its 127 acres Springbrook contains several distinct habitats that are characteristic of this region. An extensive trail system fans out from the interpretive center and winds through oak forest, oak savanna, aspen groves, prairie, old fields, ponds, and wetlands.

On July 18, 1986 the landscape here was dramatically altered by another natural phenomenon when a tornado crossed the Mississippi River and became almost stationary, spending about ten minutes within the boundaries of the nature center. While some plant communities, such as the prairies and wetlands, were hardly affected by the twister, the forest and savanna were devastated. Approximately 5,000 trees, including rock-solid oaks and supple aspens, were severed, shredded, or uprooted. Most of the downed trees were hauled away, new trees were planted, and man-made structures and trails have been rebuilt, but for years to come the preserve will provide visitors a glimpse of what a tornado can do.

The remaining upland woods are composed primarily of oaks – red oak, bur oak, northern pin oak and some white oak – mixed with basswood, black cherry, paper birch, red cedar, and other trees. The well-lit understory is packed with smaller trees and shrubs, such as buckthorn, prickly-ash, serviceberry, wild plum, chokecherry, smooth sumac, red elderberry, hazelnut, honeysuckle, blackberry, raspberry, woodbine, and wild grape. The center embraces a few scattered parcels of undisturbed and restored prairie, including the savanna where almost all of the old, wide-spreading oaks were ripped apart by the storm. A constantly changing array of wildflowers brings color to these small prairies throughout spring and summer. The native grasses are interspersed with pasque flower, prairie smoke, prairie violet, blue-eyed grass, hoary puccoon, wild rose, prairie larkspur, butterfly weed, Culver's root, lead plant, rough blazing star, and a great many more.

For about two decades a beaver colony was active here, creating a complex of wetlands where a stream had flowed through a soggy lowland. They abandoned the site in 1980, probably moving downstream to the Mississippi River. Without their constant efforts, a substantial area of open water was reduced to two small ponds while trees and shrubs moved in around the edges. In order to re-establish the valuable habitat the beavers had created, the center has constructed an earthen dam of similar proportions. Herons, egrets, ducks, geese, are once again common sights from the boardwalks and overlooks that provide easy access to the area.

Springbrook's diverse landscape makes it a good spot for birdwatching. Broad-winged hawks, long-eared owls, and great horned owls are raptors known to nest here. Bluebirds, northern orioles, scarlet tanagers, rose-breasted grosbeaks, meadowlarks, indigo buntings, catbirds, and a few warblers are among the songbirds that can be seen. White-tailed deer, red and gray fox, raccoon, pocket gopher, and a variety of reptiles and amphibians also inhabit the area.

Facilities: Visitors should make their first stop at the partially earth-sheltered interpretive center which has exhibits, an auditorium, a classroom, a workroom, and offices. The building houses an exhibit displaying the effects of the tornado, including a videotape of the tornado itself. There is an outdoor amphitheater near the building. A combination of paved trails (handicapped accessible), woodchip trails, and boardwalks wind throughout the area.

How to get there: From Interstate Highway 694 just east of the Mississippi River, exit onto University Avenue (State Highway 47) and head north. After about 3 miles turn left (west) onto 85th Avenue. The entrance is on the left .3 miles west of University.

Map key: West 117

For additional information:

Springbrook Nature Center
6431 University Avenue N.E.
Fridley, Minnesota 55432
(612) 784-3854

Spring Lake Park Reserve

Spring Lake Park Reserve is located on the Mississippi River about 10 miles downstream from St. Paul. The park overlooks scenic Spring Lake, a huge pool created by the construction of Lock and Dam Number 2 at Hastings. Although plans call for the reserve to eventually encompass 1,200 acres and four miles of shoreline, only about two-thirds of that has been acquired, in five noncontiguous parcels.

Trails and picnic facilities are found in the accessible easternmost section of the park known as Schaar's Bluff. While much of this area is composed of old farm fields, it is defined by the high rocky bluffs that drop sharply to the water's edge. More than two miles of hiking trails wind through the woodlands that line the bluff-tops and fill the ravines. The well drained uplands are dominated by red oak, bur oak, and basswood with smaller ironwood and red cedar abundant as well. These open woods support a dense understory of shrubs such as elderberry, prickly-ash, black raspberry, chokecherry, and wild grape. Elm, ash, boxelder, and butternut thrive in the more sheltered ravines. Many spots along the trail offer expansive views of Spring Lake and the surrounding countryside. Bald eagles and turkey vultures are often seen from the bluffs here.

Near the river at the base of the bluffs is a substantial grove of black walnut trees. The stand grows upon a sloping fan of alluvial deposit coming out of a large ravine cut into the bluff.

Facilities: The park's well-maintained trails are ideal for a leisurely walk along the bluff. Most of the trails (away from the blufftop) are groomed for cross-country skiers in the winter. There is a spacious picnic area overlooking the river with shelters, tables, grills, firerings, and restrooms. Fields adjacent to the picnic area are mowed for ball playing, frisbee throwing, etc. Other sections of the park contain a boat launch and an archery range.

How to get there: To get to Schaar's Bluff, take County Highway 42 east from State Highway 55 (just over 4 miles east of the intersection with U.S. Highway 52 in Rosemount) or west from U.S. Highway 61 in Hastings. Go north at Idell Avenue (a dirt road), which leads to the park.

For additional information:

Dakota County Parks Department
  8500 127th Street East
  Hastings, Minnesota 55033
  (612) 437-6608

Stanley Eddy Memorial County Park Reserve

The Stanley Eddy Memorial County Park Reserve contains four separate "units" totalling 620 acres in western Wright County. The park is managed as a natural area, and developed trails and a few other facilities are limited to the northern and southern units, which together make up most of the reserve.

The northern unit occupies 250 acres of scenic rolling hills, small lakes, and marshes. Most of the hilly terrain is blanketed by a lovely hardwood forest dominated by mature sugar maple, red oak, basswood, and ironwood, along with bitternut hickory, white ash, elm, red cedar, and scattered stands of paper birch and bigtooth aspen. Each spring the woodland floor is sprinkled with such wildflowers as bloodroot, blue cohosh, wild ginger, spring beauty, jack-in-the-pulpit, Virginia waterleaf, and Solomon's seal. A small swamp adjoining Pickerel Lake is filled with tamarac, paper birch, sensitive fern, marsh marigold, and other water-tolerant plants.

A little more than two miles away by road, the southern unit protects an additional 275 acres of wooded hills. This tract includes an overlook which, at 1,232 feet above sea level, marks the highest spot in Wright County.

Facilities: The northern unit has about 4 miles of trails for hiking and cross-country skiing in interconnected loops. There is a stationary map of the trails at the parking lot and smaller ones at trail intersections. A few picnic sites, each with a table and grill, are located off the trail. Two primitive hike-in campsites, each with a table, fire ring, and pit toilet are also available. There is a water pump and a toilet at the parking lot.

The southern unit has a little more than 2 miles of trails for hiking, about half of which are groomed for skiers. There are picnic sites located here as well.

How to get there: From the Twin Cities, take State Highway 55 west through Hennepin County and most of Wright County. A little more than 4 miles west of Annandale, is the town of South Haven, turn south onto County Highway 2. Follow Highway 2 for about 5 miles, twice turning left. After the second left look for the park entrance on the left. To reach the southern unit, continue on Highway 2 for just over a mile and a half before turning left onto a smaller township road. After a short distance the entrance will be on the right.

Map key: West 119

For additional information:

Wright County Parks Department
Route 1, Box 97B
Buffalo, Minnesota 55313
(612) 682-3900, ext. 182
339-6881 (Metro)
1-800-362-3667, ext. 182 (Toll Free)

Starring Lake Park

Across the road from Flying Cloud Airport in rapidly growing Eden Prairie, this municipal park includes approximately 160 acres of open space and recreational facilities wrapped around scenic Starring Lake. Oak-covered hills separate the park's well developed uplands from the lake, which is a popular spot for local fishermen. A paved trail circles the shallow lake, twice crossing Purgatory Creek as it flows in and out of the lake on its way to the Minnesota River.

Facilities: Three miles of paved trails for hiking and biking encircle the lake and an additional mile or so is groomed for cross-country skiing. There is a small building that can be reserved by groups for picnics, as well as outdoor sites with tables and grills that are set amid large bur oaks and overlook the lake. There is also a fishing dock, a creative play area, and facilities for tennis, volleyball, basketball, and softball. The Department of Natural Resources maintains a public access to the lake off Research Road.

How to get there: Heading towards Shakopee on U.S. Highway 169 (Flying Cloud Drive), turn right (at the light) onto Pioneer Road (County Road 1). Look for the entrance on the right before the intersection with Research Road.

Map key: West 120

For additional information:

Eden Prairie Park and Recreation
Department
7660 Executive Drive
Eden Prairie, Minnesota 55344
(612) 937-2262

Suconnix Wildlife Management Area

The Suconnix Wildlife Management Area stretches over 1,021 acres of diverse habitats amid the rolling farms of northwestern Wright County. The combination of woodlands, thickets, old fields, food plots, lakes, and marshes, supports abundant wildlife. There are no facilities and the area is managed primarily for hunters, but birdwatchers, berry-pickers, and others, will enjoy it here if they don't mind the lack of trails.

The most level land, which was long cultivated or grazed, remains open except where thickets of sumac, aspen, chokecherry, boxelder, red cedar, and wild grape, advance outward from the woodland's edge. Most of the old fields are maintained as non-native grasslands but native prairie grasses have been planted in a few spots and some areas are cultivated and left as food plots for wildlife.

Covering the hills and gullies that drain into the lakes and marshes is a mixed woodland dominated by mature bur oak along with sizable basswood and red oak. Ironwood is abundant in the understory which is thick with shrubs such as elderberry, prickly-ash, hazelnut, gray dogwood, gooseberry, witch-hazel, and raspberry. Quaking aspen and paper birch are common around the margins of the pothole lakes and wetlands. These watery habitats range from open waters to expanses of cattails and sedges to thickets of willow and red-osier dogwood.

Many species of wildlife benefit from the intermingling of different habitats. Great horned owls, barred owls, red-tailed hawks, and red foxes, which nest or den in the forest, hunt in the open meadows where woodchucks, rabbits, pheasants, thirteen-lined ground squirrels, and other small mammals and birds are found. The grasslands provide browse for deer and nesting cover for some waterfowl. Mallards, blue-winged teal, wood ducks, American bitterns, sora rails, yellow-headed blackbirds, and kingfishers share the lakes and marshes with beavers, muskrats, and mink.

Facilities: There are no developed facilities here except for the designated parking areas. State Wildlife Management Areas are managed for three primary reasons: wildlife production, public hunting, and trapping. Other activities, such as hiking, birdwatching, and berry-picking are also encouraged but should probably be avoided during the hunting season.

How to get there: Suconnix WMA is most easily reached by taking Interstate Highway 94 northwest toward St. Cloud. At the edge of Wright County, take the Clearwater exit and head south on State Highway 24. Stay on Highway 24 for 4 miles and then take a left onto the unpaved township road. Follow this road through a right turn and a left turn before looking for small parking areas along the road. The WMA is on both side of the road but it is oddly shaped, so one should observe the signs and take care to stay off private property. There are seven separate parking areas.

Map key: West 121

For additional information:

Department of Natural Resources
Minnesota Department of Natural Resources
Area Wildlife Manager
P.O. Box 370
St. Cloud, Minnesota 56302
(612) 255-4279

Minnesota Department of Natural Resources
Section of Wildlife, Box 7
500 Lafayette Road
St. Paul, Minnesota 55155
(612) 296-3344

Tamarac Nature Center

Located seven miles north of St. Paul, the Tamarac Nature Center occupies 320 acres of scenic land adjacent to Interstate Highway 35E. Although technically a part of Otter Lake Regional Park, the center is separated from the rest of the park and is managed as a distinct unit. The landscape ranges from flat lowlands to rolling uplands with a few steep hills, and encompasses a variety of habitats, including oak forest, tamarac swamp, prairie, old fields, cattail marsh, and two small lakes connected by a stream.

The larger of the two lakes, Tamarac Lake, is at the heart of a swampy area characterized by water-tolerant trees and shrubs such as tamarac, paper birch, quaking aspen, alder, highbush cranberry, and red-osier dogwood. Marsh marigold, blue flag, swamp saxifrage, and sensitive fern prosper here. Usually found in moist to boggy soils, the soft green tamarac tree is a deciduous conifer that grows as far north as the Arctic Circle.

The trails here also pass through two separate oak woodlands interesting for their dissimilarity. Bordering the swamp is a dry, sandy area dominated by mature red oaks with scattered black cherry and red maple, as well as an abudance of red elderberry in the understory. In contrast, the steep hill that rises behind Fish Lake supports wide-spreading white oak and bur oak along with the same paper birch and quaking aspen that thrive in the swamp.

The remainder of the preserve is comprised primarily of old fields and prairie remnants. During the spring and summer something is always blooming in these grasslands. Butterflyweed, prairie phlox, sunflower, and blazing star are a few flowers found in the dry prairie, while jewelweed, white turtlehead, great blue lobelia, and bittersweet are among those found in the wet prairie and fens. The old fields too, support their own array of flowers, including milkweed, morning glory bindweed, hoary alyssum, and evening primrose. A variety of trees, such as sumac, red cedar, wild plum, and boxelder, can be seen invading the open areas. These hardy pioneers represent the early stages of succession and only burning or selective cutting prevents the woodlands from gradually taking over most of the area.

Wildlife is abundant. White-tailed deer, red fox, raccoon, striped skunk, woodchuck, muskrat, and mink live here, in addition to rabbits, squirrels, gophers, chipmunks, weasels, shrews, voles, and mice. Birds are also plentiful. Bluebird, meadowlark, bobolink, and kestrel are among those easily seen in the open areas. Ruby-throated hummingbird, woodcock, ruffed grouse, pileated woodpecker, Cooper's hawk, belted kingfisher, great horned owl, green-backed heron, and least bittern are a few more of the over 70 summer residents.

A grove of black locust trees, particularly lovely when blooming in springtime, is located next to the parking lot.

Facilities: There are 3.4 miles of woodchip trails with floating boardwalks, a teaching station at Tamarac Lake, trail signs, and benches. Trails are groomed for cross-country skiers in winter. Currently a trailer acts as a temporary interpretive center - a large interpretive building is planned. Picnic tables are available.

How to get there: Driving north on Interstate Highway 35E from either St. Paul or Interstate Highway 694, exit at State Highway 96 (County Road G). Go east to Otter Lake Road (first light) and turn left. Drive north for 1.3 miles and look for parking lot on the left.

The trails are open every day from a half hour before sunrise until a half hour after sunset. The building is open weekdays 8:30 a.m. to 5:00 p.m.

Map key: East 122

For additional information:

Tamarac Nature Center
5287 Otter Lake Road
White Bear Lake, Minnesota 55110
(612) 429-7787
or (612) 777-0393 (Ramsey County Parks)

Tamarac Nature Preserve

The Tamarac Nature Preserve occupies an 80-acre slice of boggy lowlands wedged between residential neighborhoods in suburban Woodbury. The tract is maintained as a natural area and is undeveloped except for a loop trail that provides a close-up look at an otherwise inaccessible mixture of wetland communities. A narrow belt of upland woods borders the bottomland, which is crammed with a rich diversity of water-tolerant plants. Attractive stands of mature tamaracs mixed with paper birch are surrounded by stretches of cattails and dense thickets of willow, speckled alder, and red-osier dogwood, along with Joe-Pye weed, arrowhead, jewelweed, horsetail, marsh marigold, and a variety of ferns. The adjacent woods are comprised of red maple, ironwood, paper birch, and stands of aspen on the south side, while rows of planted spruce serve as a buffer to the north.

Facilities: Woodchip paths, floating walkways, and a portion of a paved bike trail combine to make a loop through the area. There is some playground equipment on a grassy knoll adjacent to the parking lot.

How to get there: Head east from St. Paul on Interstate Highway 94. Roughly a mile and a quarter beyond the intersection with Interstate Highway 494, exit onto Radio Drive and turn right (south). After 2 miles turn right onto Valley Creek Road and go west almost half a mile before turning right again at Tower Road. Look for the parking area on the right.

Map key: East 123

For additional information:

Department of Parks and
Recreation
Woodbury City Hall
2100 Radio Drive
Woodbury, MN 55125
(612) 739-5972

Terrace Oaks West Park

Terrace Oaks West Park is a scenic municipal park operated by the city of Burnsville. Though surrounded by suburban neighborhoods and skirted by Interstate 35E, the 230 acre park is maintained in a natural state and provides an unexpected sense of solitude. An extensive network of wide trails winds through a landscape of steeply rolling hills blanketed by mature woodlands and punctuated by numerous marshes and small ponds.

The forest cover is primarily oak, with stands of red oak and white oak mixed with lesser amounts of aspen, black cherry, and ironwood. Characteristic of this forest type, there is a dense understory of small trees and shrubs, such as serviceberry, buckthorn, prickly-ash, hazelnut, and raspberry, which provide food and shelter for many birds and small mammals.

Atop some of the hills, where it is drier and more exposed, you can find large bur oaks standing apart above small remnants of native prairie. With the suppression of fire however, the prairie flowers and grasses such as little bluestem and side-oats grama, are giving way to encroaching sumac and prickly-ash. The hill just to the north of the parking area is perhaps the most accessible example and is a nice spot from which to view the area.

In contrast, the swampier sections, particularly around the cattail marshes and ponds, support a lot of elm and boxelder. Unfortunately, like elsewhere, a great many of the elms have been killed by Dutch elm disease.

Facilities: A number of interconnecting loops for hiking and cross-country skiing lead visitors throughout the park. Next to the parking lot, there is a picnic shelter and a building with tables, grills, playground equipment, and a bathroom. The building is used in winter as a warming house with ski rental and concessions.

How to get there: The park occupies the southeast corner of the intersection of County Road 11 and Burnsville Parkway. From Minneapolis take Interstate Highway 35W south across the Minnesota River, then take State Highway 13 east just over 2 miles to County Road 11. Take a right (south) and go about a mile. Look for the park on the left. From St. Paul take Interstate Highway 35E south to County Road 11. Go north and look for the park on the right.

Map key: East 124

For additional information:

Burnsville Department of Parks
and Recreation
1313 East Highway 13
Burnsville, Minnesota 55337
(612) 431-7575

Theodore Wirth Park

Acquired in sections from 1889 to 1917, Wirth Park is the largest park in the city Minneapolis. The 743 acre park straddles the line between Minneapolis and Golden Valley and extends from the railroad tracks on the south side of Brownie Lake to the northern end of Theodore Wirth Parkway at Lowry Avenue. Originally called Saratoga Springs, then Glenwood Park, it was given its current name in 1938 to honor the man who was responsible for convincing the city to purchase the property. Although it is crossed by railroad tracks, highways, and parkways, and contains a golf course and numerous other facilities, the park protects several natural attractions.

West of the golf course an extension of the park, known as the Back 40, reaches into Golden Valley to include a stretch of rolling hills wrapped around the south end of Twin Lake. Secluded from roads and houses, this quiet area is unknown to most visitors of the park. A sandy beach on Twin Lake lies next to a marsh that shelters muskrats and turtles, as well as waterfowl and other birds. The adjacent uplands are a mixture of woodlands and meadows, except for a small remnant of native prairie.

Situated at the center of the park, Wirth Lake is geologically connected to the chain of larger, better-known lakes to the south. These lakes all occupy a preglacial river valley that was filled with debris by the glaciers. Similar valleys carved deep into the bedrock and later buried during the Ice Age are marked by other chains of lakes across the state. In spite of Highway 55, which runs along the north side of the lake, and the recreational facilities along the east side, Wirth Lake is home to beavers and other wildlife that find refuge in the wetlands and woods to the west. A trail here leads past the famous Rockwood Oak, whose silhouette is seen on the Wirth Park signs.

Several small ponds and marshes are found along Bassett Creek, which meanders across the northern half of the park on its way from Medicine Lake to the Mississippi River. The most undeveloped section of the park is located on either side of Wirth Parkway between Glenwood Avenue and Highway 12. This area, which surrounds the Eloise Butler Wildflower Garden and Bird Sanctuary (described separately), is comprised of heavily wooded hills and steep-sided depressions. One of these depressions is filled by Birch Pond, a small but scenic, marsh-rimmed pond set into the woods just east of the parkway. The dense woods are dominated by oaks, mixed with a wide variety of other trees, including many sizable evergreens planted decades ago. The largest red maple in Minneapolis, about thirteen feet around at shoulder height, can be found on the east side of the parkway across from the horseshoe-shaped parking lot.

Tucked away amid the woods west of the parkway is a five-acre basin occupied by a tamarac bog. For a few years efforts have been made to restore the long-forgotten bog by eradicating non-native shrubs and reestablishing native bog plants, including various species of orchids and carnivorous plants such as sundew and pitcher plants. The mature tamarac trees standing above a carpet of sphagnum moss represent a tiny outpost of the north woods at the edge of Minneapolis.

At the southeast corner of Wirth Parkway and Golden Valley Road is a boulder with a bronze plaque that marks the 45th parallel of north latitude, the midway point between the equator and the North Pole.

Facilities: A paved bicycle trail follows the parkway the length of the park, while a separate paved trail for pedestrians takes a less direct route. Both connect to the system of trails that lead around the lakes, along Minnehaha Creek, and along the Mississippi River. A number of other unpaved trails wind throughout the southern half of the park and the Back 40. Plans call for the development of a circular trail with a boardwalk to provide better access to the tamarac bog. A short blacktop path leads from the parking lot just south of Glenwood Avenue to a small shelter built over a natural spring reputed to be from the same source as Glenwood-Inglewood water. Many facilities are located off Glenwood Avenue in the vicinity of Wirth Lake, including a picnic area with a shelter (available for a fee), tables, and grills; a swimming beach with bathhouse and totlot; a fishing dock, tennis courts, an information kiosk, a Finnish memorial, and a 4H children's garden. An eighteen-hole golf course and a par-3 course take up most of the park north of Highway 55. A miniature version of a Swiss chalet, the clubhouse sells snacks and drinks. The Chalet can be rented for private use. In winter the Chalet and golf courses are transformed into the Wirth Winter Recreation Area, featuring downhill and cross-country skiing, ski jumping, tubing and sledding, and snowshoeing.

How to get there: The park is located a short distance west of downtown Minneapolis. Exit off U.S. Highway 12 (Interstate 394) onto Wirth Parkway and turn north into the park. Glenwood Avenue, State Highway 55 (Olson Memorial Highway), and Golden Valley Road all intersect the parkway as they cut through the park.

Map key: West 125

For additional information:

Minneapolis Park and Recreation
Board
310 Fourth Avenue South
Minneapolis, Minnesota 55415
(612) 348-5702

Thomas Lake Park

Lying along the sinuous shoreline of 52 acre Thomas Lake, this natural area offers visitors a taste of suburban Eagan's presettlement landscape. Containing approximately 60 acres, Thomas Lake Park is comprised of oak woods, prairie, and wetlands. The most noteworthy feature here is the "Native Prairie Area," a 12-acre expanse of rolling prairie dotted with small marshes. Growing among the prairie grasses — Indian grass, big and little bluestem — are dozens of flowering plants, such as leadplant, purple prairie-clover, wild bergamot, alum-root, tall cinquefoil, yarrow, blue aster, and rough blazing star. The marshy depressions support a separate array of grasses and flowers, including cordgrass, Muhly grass, smartweed, climbing false buckwheat, monkey-flower, water plantain, boneset, and blue flag. Encroaching groves of sumac, pin cherry, and aspen exemplify the ongoing competition between the prairie and the woodlands that cover the rest of the park. These woodlands are dominated by red oak, white oak, and bur oak, with a lot of quaking aspen and some black cherry.

Facilities: A paved trail with benches placed in scenic spots makes a short loop through the prairie. Informal but well-worn dirt paths explore the rest of the area. Other facilities – two tennis courts, playground equipment, and a ball field – are located in the adjacent Evergreen Park.

How to get there: Heading south of the Twin Cities on either the Cedar Avenue Freeway or Interstate Highway 35E, take the exit for Cliff Road and drive east. At Pilot Knob Road turn left (north). Take the next left at Walfrid Street and another left after one block onto Sequoia Drive. Bend to the right onto Lodgepole Drive and park along the road near Evergreen Park. From here walk across the mowed ballfield toward the power-line where you can pick up the paved trail.

Map key: East 126

For additional information:

Eagan Parks and Recreation
Department
3830 Pilot Knob Road
P.O. Box 21199
Eagan, Minnesota 55121
(612) 454-8100

Timber Shores Park

Timber Shores Park protects 34 acres of wetlands and woods adjacent to Bass Lake in suburban Plymouth. Most of the small park is comprised of shallow open water and cattail marsh fed by Bass Creek, which flows out of the lake here. Cottonwood, willow, ash, aspen, and dogwood thrive in the water-logged soils, while a narrow stretch of uplands along the lake supports large red oak, bur oak, and white oak, as well as basswood, ironwood, and paper birch.

Facilities: A combination of gravel and paved trails and a stretch of floating boardwalk lead through the marsh to the woods by the lake where other facilities are located. These include a fishing dock, a canoe launch, and a small picnic area with a shelter, table, and play apparatus. A softball field and playground are found by the parking area.

How to get there: The park is located just south of Bass Lake Road in northeastern Plymouth. One mile west of County Highway 18 on Bass Lake Road turn left (south) onto Zachary Lane. After a short distance turn right onto 53rd Avenue N. and pull into parking lot on the right.

Map key: West 127

For additional information:

Parks and Recreation Department
Plymouth City Hall
3400 Plymouth Blvd.
Plymouth, Minnesota 55447
(612) 559-2800 (ext. 265)

Townsend Woods

Hidden away amid the farms of southwestern Rice County is a small but special tract of land known as the Townsend Woods Scientific and Natural Area. Situated a quarter-mile from the nearest road, the 80-acre preserve contains a rare fragment of the "Big Woods" that once blanketed much of the region. Because of agriculture and other commercial pressures very few remnants of this original forest still remain.

The best of Townsend Woods is found on the steep north-facing hill that runs through the property. The sloping woodland here is a striking mixture of stately sugar maple, basswood, and red oak, with ironwood in the open understory. Unlike an oak forest, with its dense understory of small trees, shrubs, flowers, and ferns, the leafy canopy of the maple-basswood forest allows very little direct sunlight to reach the ground. In fact, the light intensity in summer is so low that most plants are unable to carry on photosynthesis and either die back or use food reserves stored in corms, tubers, bulbs, or rhizomes. The distinctive ground layer is made up primarily of spring and early summer herbs that flower before the trees have leafed out. At Townsend Woods the warm sunlight of springtime stimulates the growth of wildflowers such as bloodroot, Dutchman's breeches, white trout lily, cut-leafed toothwort, nodding trillium, sharp-lobed hepatica, wild ginger, Virginia waterleaf, and blue phlox.

To the south of this undisturbed grove, away from the steep slope, the original forest is gone. In its place is a young woodland of much greater diversity where elm, ash, hackberry, bitternut hickory, bur oak, butternut, and other trees compete for space. Given enough time and the absence of fire, this varied woodland will be supplanted by the shade-tolerant sugar maple and basswood trees. This stable, self-maintaining phase of development is called the "climax" stage.

A variety of other habitats, including a sedge-filled marsh, a seasonal stream at the base of the hill, and a few acres of old fields add diversity to the preserve and make it an attractive refuge for wildlife.

Facilities: There are no developed facilities of any kind at Townsend Woods. The area has been set aside to protect natural plant and animal communities for scientific and educational purposes. You are invited to observe and enjoy the area, but please remember that your visit can have an impact on the natural community. Picnic areas, restrooms, and other facilities are available at nearby Sakatah Lake State Park.

How to get there: From the Twin Cities take Interstate Highway 35 south. At Faribault, exit onto State Highway 60 west and proceed towards Morristown. Less than a mile after the junction with County Highway 16 in Morristown, turn right onto County Road 99. Almost immediately 99 turns to the left and heads west, soon following the south shore of Lower Sakatah Lake. At the intersection with Leroy Avenue turn right, staying on 99 and passing between Upper and Lower Sakatah Lakes. Turn right again at the next intersection and head north. The state-owned, walk-in, right-of-way is located on the right side of the road near a farmstead about three quarters of a mile north of 240th St.

The right-of-way is marked only by a few small signs. Park here along the road and follow the right-of-way as it bends around the farmstead and then follows the edge of a field almost a quarter of a mile to the woods. The edge of the woodland appears to be a nearly impenetrable thicket but once inside the forest is generally open and airy.

Map key: East 128

For additional information:

Scientific and Natural Areas
Program
Box 7, Minnesota Department of
Natural Resources
500 Lafayette Road, DNR Building
St. Paul, Minnesota 55155
(612) 297-3288

Valley Park

Lying adjacent to Interstate Highway 35E in Mendota Heights, less than a mile from St. Paul, this 90 acre municipal park stretches along a small stream as it flows toward the nearby Mississippi River. Except for a few facilities located by the parking lot, the valley is maintained as a natural area.

The main trail follows the stream as it flows from an open water marsh rimmed with sedges through plantings of evergreens, old fields, and lowland woods. Beyond the planted white pine and white spruce, the once open hillsides are growing over with groves of sumac and aspen and thickets of other pioneer species. Farther down the valley the stream cuts through a woodland of cottonwood, black willow, green ash, elm, and boxelder.

On the exposed hillside above the stream, large bur oaks and red oaks stand amid dense growths of buckthorn and prickly-ash. In contrast, a hidden and sheltered tributary ravine is shaded by basswood, sugar maple, ironwood, hackberry, and butternut hickory.

Facilities: A good trail with a small bridge follows the stream through the park. Plans call for paving this trail for bicycling. Informal trails lead off in other directions. Near the parking lot there is a small picnic area with a shelter and tables, as well as a softball field, playground equipment, 2 tennis courts, and a satellite toilet.

How to get there: From Minneapolis take State Highway 55 across the Mendota Bridge to State Highway 110 and head east. From St. Paul go south on Interstate Highway 35E to State 110 (second exit after crossing the river) and exit east. Half a mile east of I35E take a left onto Dodd Road (State 149) and go north just over half a mile to Marie Avenue. Take a left onto Marie and after a few blocks look for the park entrance on the right.

Map key: East 129

For additional information:

Mendota Heights City Hall
Park and Recreation Department
750 South Plaza Drive
Mendota Heights, MN 55120
(612) 452-1850

Valley Municipal Park

Split into Valley Park North and Valley Park South by a local thoroughfare, this municipal park totals 140 acres of open space and recreational facilities in the suburb of Inver Grove Heights. The park is aptly named, as it occupies a small valley set apart from the surrounding community by steep hills on both sides.

In Valley Park South portions of the hillsides support attractive woods of red oak and bur oak mixed with groves of quaking aspen, along with some planted pine trees. The valley bottom is largely open with scattered thickets of cottonwood, boxelder, elm, red cedar, and sumac. A tiny pond provides a watering hole for the small mammals and other wildlife that find refuge here. The landscape in the northern section of the park is similar but is generally more open and grassy.

Although it is unmarked and overgrown, the foundation of the first homestead in Inver Grove Heights is situated within the park. A date on the old well shows that it was dug in 1842, sixteen years before Minnesota was granted statehood.

Facilities: A paved pathway with benches placed along it cuts through both sides of the park. Valley Park South has a picnic area with a shelter, tables, grills, restrooms, playground equipment, and a softball field. Additional picnic tables and grills are situated along the path. Valley Park North contains two softball fields and a few tennis courts. There are also a few picnic tables and grill on this side.

How to get there: From Interstate Highway 494 in south St. Paul, take the 7th Avenue Exit and proceed south on Cahill Avenue (County 75). Go south to 70th Street and take a right at the light. There are separate entrances and parking on both sides of the road.

Map key: East 130

For additional information:

Inver Grove Heights City Hall
Park and Recreation Department
8150 Barbara Avenue
Inver Grove Heights, MN 55075
(612) 457-2111

Warner Nature Center

Like a handful of other nature centers in the metropolitan area, the Warner Nature Center is only open to organized groups with reservations. The center is located about 25 miles northeast of St. Paul in Washington County. The Lee and Rose Warner Foundation owns 513 acres, while the Science Museum of Minnesota owns two noncontiguous tracts, which add another 235 acres. Altogether the separate parcels include steeply rolling, forested hills, portions of two major lakes, a coldwater stream, a small sphagnum bog, a backwater access to the St. Croix River, and abandoned pasture land.

Facilities: The nature trail here includes a 350 foot boardwalk through the bog. A trailside museum houses a classroom, laboratory, group meeting area, reference library, kitchen, garage, and restrooms. An outdoor shelter with bleacher seating is used for programs.

How to get there: Head north from the Twin Cities on Interstate Highway 35E. Almost 10 miles north of Interstate Highway 694 take the exit for Hugo (County Road 8 after crossing into Washington County) and drive east 2 miles to U.S. Highway 61. Go north on 61 for 2.5 miles, then turn right (east) onto County Highway 4. Continue east on 4 for roughly 7 miles and turn right (south) onto County Road 55. The main entrance is on the left side of this road after about 1.5 miles.

There are no charges for school groups but there is a fee for all other groups.

Map key: East 131

For additional information:

Warner Nature Center
c/o Science Museum of Minnesota
30 East 10th Street
St. Paul, Minnesota 55101
(612) 433-2427

Westwood Hills Environmental Education Center

Scarcely a stone's throw from busy Highway 12, in the northwest corner of St. Louis Park, is the Westwood Hills Environmental Education Center. The center encompasses only 160 acres but like many of our suburban nature centers it contains a surprising variety of habitats. Three interconnected trails lead visitors through cattail marsh, restored prairie, an evergreen plantation, and mature upland forests.

The Marsh Trail, which features a quarter-mile stretch of floating boardwalk, circles a shallow 60-acre lake with a wide fringe of cattail and pockets of purple loosestrife. Scattered stands of boxelder, black willow, hackberry, and cottonwood thrive in the low, wet areas surrounding most of the lake. A portion of this trail passes through a boggy area that was part of a golf course until a few years ago. Natural succession has reclaimed the area but has been assisted by the planting of tamarac trees among the thickets of red-osier dogwood.

The Basswood Trail leads through a mature woodland that rises from the water's edge to the highest point in St. Louis Park. The trail is aptly named, as large basswood trees are abundant, sharing the canopy with tall red oak and some white oak, red maple and ash. Ironwood is plentiful in the shaded understory along with prickly-ash, alternate-leaf dogwood, ferns, and flowers. At the north end the woods grade through a dense woodland of black walnut, black cherry, buckthorn, honeysuckle, and wild grape to an open area with old apple trees, chinese elm, and sumac.

The Prairie Trail winds through an aromatic plantation of spruce, pine, and cedar to a restored hillside prairie. After the woodland flowers have come and gone in spring, the prairie offers a continuously changing variety of colorful native flowers throughout the summer months.

The varied habitats here provide a home to many mammals, including red fox, raccoon, woodchuck, rabbit, squirrel, chipmunk, muskrat, and an occasional mink or white-tailed deer. Many songbirds and waterfowl also find a haven in the woods, thickets, and wetlands, making Westwood Hills a popular place for birdwatchers.

Facilities: There is a partially earth-sheltered education center with exhibits, classrooms, offices, and restrooms. The well-maintained trail system includes about 4 miles of woodchip trails and floating boardwalks with an overlook, an observation dock, and benches.

How to get there: The center is located just south of State Highway 12 (Interstate Highway 394) and east of County Highway 18. Take Texas Avenue south from 12 or north from Cedar Lake Road to Franklin Avenue. Go west .3 miles to the entrance on the right.

The Education Center is open 8:00 a.m. to 4:30 p.m. on weekdays, and noon to 5:00 p.m. on weekends and holidays. The trails are open from dawn to dusk.

Map key: West 132

For additional information:

Westwood Hills Environmental
Education Center
8300 West Franklin Avenue
St. Louis Park, Minnesota 55426
(612) 924-2544

Wild River State Park

Wild River State Park takes its name from the St. Croix River, which was designated a National Wild and Scenic River by the U.S. Congress in 1968. One of our newest and largest state parks, this heavily wooded preserve encompasses about 7,000 acres stretching for nearly twenty miles along the pristine river. The area is within easy driving distance of the Twin Cities and lures urban dwellers who can explore the beautiful valley on more than forty miles of uncrowded trails.

For thousands of years this tranquil valley was home to native Americans – nomadic people at first, and later the Sauk, Fox, Dakotah, and Chippewa tribes – who left it essentially unchanged. Then, less than 150 years ago, the construction of two British fur posts here ushered in a period of bustling economic activity and dramatic change. Military roads were built along the river when Minnesota became a territory in 1849. During the following years the lumbermen arrived and in a few short decades the valley was stripped of its vast stands of red and white pines. Two small towns were built within the park's boundaries: Sunrise, complete with a sawmill, gristmills, hotels, schools, saloons, and houses; and Amador, which had only a sawmill, hotel, and ferry dock. In 1889-1890, the St. Croix Dam and Boom Company constructed a dam here to aid the transportation of logs down the river. The Nevers Dam was thought to be the largest wooden pile-driven dam in the world and spanned the river until it was dismantled in 1954-1955.

As the wildlife and forests disappeared, the trappers and lumbermen moved on, and the towns dwindled away. Farmers settled the level uplands and the valley began a slow process of recovery. Remnants of old roads and settlements remain but a richly varied second-growth woodland has replaced the pine forests. Frequently flooded lowlands, particularly in the northern part of the park, support a typical bottomland forest characterized by silver maple, black willow, elm, and other water-tolerant species. Carpeting flat terraces and gentle slopes, the remaining woodlands vary considerably from place to place, reflecting differences in soil, sunlight, moisture, and stage of succession. A short walk may pass more than half the tree species native to Minnesota, including bur oak, red cedar, northern pin oak, quaking and bigtooth aspen, paper birch, white oak, boxelder, red maple, black cherry, basswood, sugar maple, red oak, white ash, American elm, bitternut hickory, ironwood, blue beech, witch hazel, butternut, alternate-leaf dogwood, hackberry, yellow birch, and some white pine and red pine. Old field grasslands, evergreen plantations, and a few scattered marshes add to the diversity of habitats.

With the return of the forests has come the return of wildlife. Today the entire valley is an invaluable sanctuary winding from northern wildlands to the edge of the Twin Cities. About 200 birds have been identified within the park. Quiet backwaters and uplands marshes offer food and protection to many ducks, herons, bitterns, rails, terns, and gulls. Raptors nesting in the area include bald eagles and ospreys, as well as the broad-winged hawk, sharp-shinned hawk, northern harrier, long eared owl, saw-whet owl, and others. Among the many other resident birds are ruffed grouse, woodcock, yellow-billed cuckoo, ruby-throated hummingbird, yellow-bellied sapsucker, purple martin, tufted titmouse, wood thrush, yellow-throated vireo, northern waterthrush, scarlet tanager, and rufous-sided towhee. Spring and fall bring multitudes of migrants to the park, including some that stay through the winter, such as evening grosbeak, common redpoll, pine grosbeak, and pine siskin. The park is also home to black bear, white-tailed deer, coyote, fisher, badger, porcupine, raccoon, striped skunk, woodchuck, snowshoe hare, and flying squirrel, as well as beaver, mink, muskrat, and river otter.

Facilities: Hikers and cross-country skiers can wander through the area on 45 miles of trails, which run the length of the park. More than half of this trail system is open to horseback riding. Most of the remaining facilities are located in the broader southern portion of the park. A Trail Center near the park entrance offers ski rentals, warmth, and concessions through the winter. The McElroy Interpretive Center contains exhibits, offices, and restrooms. This building is set in the woods atop a hill and has a wooden deck that overlooks the valley. The main picnic area has enclosed and open shelters, tables, grills, water, and toilets. Two boat launches are situated on the river about 10 miles apart. There are a variety of camping areas: a large semimodern campground with a dump station, showers, and flush toilets; a horseback rider's campground; a primitive group camp for up to 300 people; and 4 separate isolated sites along the river for either canoeists or backpackers. Both horses and canoes can be rented near the park.

How to get there: From the Twin Cities head north on Interstate Highway 35W or 35E. Twenty miles after these highways merge, exit onto State Highway 95 and turn right (east). Stay on 95 for 11 miles to Almelund and turn left onto County Highway 12. Follow 12 to the park entrance.

The park is closed from 10:00 p.m. to 8:00 a.m. except to registered campers. Daily or annual permits are required for all vehicles entering a state park. They may be purchased at the park entrance.

Map key: East 133

For additional information:

Wild River State Park Manager
Route 1, Box 75
Center City, Minnesota 55012
(612) 583-2125

Minnesota Department of Natural
Resources
Division of Parks and Recreation
Information Center, Box 40
500 Lafayette Road
St. Paul, Minnesota 55155
(612) 296-4776

William O'Brien State Park

William O'Brien State Park is situated on the beautiful St. Croix River just north of Marine-on-St. Croix, the oldest logging settlement in Minnesota. Like most of the State Parks near the Twin Cities, William O'Brien was not carved out of the wilderness so much as pieced together out of old farms that had long been stripped of their stately white pine forests. In 1945, Alice O'Brien donated 180 acres in memory of her father, for whom the park is named, and thirteen years later David Greenberg gave the state an undeveloped island in memory of his parents. Since then, the acquisition of additional lands in the hills to the west has enlarged this popular park to its present 1,343 acres.

Stretching from riverbottom to the highest point in Washington County, the park contains a surprising diversity of habitats and the abundant wildlife they attract. Below the bluffs and sandstone outcroppings east of State Highway 95 is a rich lowland where many of the park's facilities are located. At the base of the wooded bluff is manmade Lake Alice, a 15-acre, spring-fed lake that is used for fishing and swimming. Lake Alice is stocked with panfish, but park visitors also fish the St. Croix River for northern pike, walleye, bass, and brown trout.

Across a narrow channel of the river from the picnic area and accessible by boat is 66-acre Greenberg Island. A trail here winds through a floodplain forest of tall silver maple, cottonwood, black willow, and green ash, and past a number of small ponds. Great blue herons nest in the trees by a backwater lake at the southern end of the island. Otter slides can be seen along the muddy banks and signs of beaver activity are everywhere. At times, both ospreys and bald eagles may be observed in the area.

On the other side of the highway is an entirely different landscape comprised of open plateaus and wooded hills. Most of the once-farmed flatlands are now grassy meadows inhabited by woodchuck, badger, gopher, and garter snake. There is a broad wetland complex at the center of the park where muskrat, mink, and duck thrive amid a patchwork of tamarac trees, willow thickets, cattails, sedges, bulrushes, red-osier dogwood, alder, arrowhead, and waterlily.

Most extensive in the steeper hills beyond the marsh, the park's woodlands range from maple-basswood forest with ironwood and hackberry to oak-dominated stands with black cherry, shagbark hickory, bitternut hickory, red cedar, aspen, and paper birch. In addition, there are scattered plantations of white pine, red pine, and spruce. Red squirrel, gray squirrel, and fox squirrel share the forest's bounty, while other animals, such as white-tailed deer, red fox, raccoon, and striped skunk benefit from the combination of wood, thicket, marsh, and meadow. Though secretive and seldom seen, bobcats occasionally wander down the valley as far as the park.

Facilities: Nearly 10 miles of well-marked hiking trails wind throughout the park and lead to scenic vistas in the hills. There is a trail center with seasonal exhibits located by the park entrance. Almost all of the trails are groomed for cross-country skiing in winter. A picnic area by the river contains 200 tables as well as grills, water, a snackbar, and toilets. Lake Alice has a swimming beach and there is a nearby boat launch on the river where canoes can be rented. The park has two modern campgrounds (one on each side of the highway), which offer electricity, a dump station, showers, and flush toilets. There is a separate canoe campground with toilets and a primitive group camp (reservations required). Winter camping is permitted.

How to get there: From the Twin Cities take Interstate Highway 94 or State Highway 36 east toward the St. Croix River. Then follow State Highway 95 north along the river, passing through Stillwater and Marine-on-St. Croix. The park entrance is on the left about two miles beyond the center of Marine-on-St. Croix.

The park is closed from 10:00 p.m. to 8:00 a.m. except to registered campers. Daily or annual permits are required for all vehicles entering a state park. They may be purchased at the park entrance.

Map key: East 134

For additional information:

William O'Brien State Park
Manager
16821 O'Brien Trail North
Marine-on-St. Croix, MN 55047
(612) 433- 2421

Minnesota Department of Natural Resources
Division of Parks and Recreation
Information Center, Box 40
500 Lafayette Road
St. Paul, Minnesota 55155
(612) 296-4776

Willow River State Park

Scarcely twenty miles from St. Paul, Willow River State Park is one of the most popular Wisconsin parks and the closest to the Twin Cities. The park encompasses 2,800 acres of richly varied habitats stretching for about five miles along the Willow River. While portions of the river still rush through scenic gorges carved into the rolling landscape, much of it has been drowned beneath the waters of three man-made lakes – Little Falls Lake, Mill Pond, and Mound Pond – which total more than 300 acres. The surrounding hills are comprised of mixed woodlands, bottomland forest, scattered prairie remnants, small marshes and woodland ponds, pine plantations, and abandoned fields.

The woodlands here are dominated by oaks – primarily black oak and bur oak, with some northern pin oak and white oak – mixed with black cherry, quaking and bigtooth aspen, paper birch, ash, elm, and other trees. The well-lit understory and forest edges support a dense growth of shrubs favored by wildlife, including buckthorn, elderberry, prickly-ash, gray dogwood, viburnum, hazelnut, blackberry, raspberry, and wild grape. A few tall white pines stand singly and in small groves in the highlands above the river. Sugar maple and basswood are beginning to replace the oaks on some sheltered hillsides.

Barely more than a century ago, much of the park's uplands were carpeted by prairie grasses and flowers, but most of these areas were plowed or grazed for decades. Nevertheless, areas of open prairie can still be found where tall grasses are interspersed with dozens of colorful flowers, such as pasque flower, prairie smoke, bush clover, cinquefoil, black-eyed Susan, blazing star, and various asters, goldenrods, and sunflowers. A number of tiny prairie remnants persist as openings in the forest and contain hoary puccoon, hairbell, leadplant, and spiderwort. Many of the once-cultivated parcels are giving way to pioneer trees like red cedar, cottonwood, boxelder, bur oak, chokecherry, and groves of sumac.

The park also has a variety of watery habitats, including emergent vegetation at the upper end of the dammed lakes; numerous wetlands and beaver ponds scattered about the hills; and swampy woods around the marshes and along the floodplain below the dams. Rarely found this far south, northern white cedar prospers in the moist soils along with black willow, silver maple, cottonwood, green ash, and boxelder. The gorge areas support a rich growth of jewelweed, ferns, mosses, liverworts, and other plants that like damp, cool ravines and cliff faces.

Such a diversity of habitats supports a diversity of wildlife. Ducks, herons, and kingfishers share the lakes, wetlands, and river with beaver, muskrat, mink, and an occasional otter. The park is enlivened by white-tailed deer, coyote, badger, raccoon, red fox, woodchuck, and striped skunk, in addition to cottontail rabbit, 13-lined ground squirrel, gray squirrel, red squirrel, fox squirrel, flying squirrel, chipmunk, pocket gopher, prairie vole, star-nosed mole, jumping mouse, white-footed mouse, and long and short-tailed weasel. Among the many birds that nest here are sharp-shinned hawk, marsh hawk, screech owl, long-eared owl, ruffed grouse, whip-poor-will, bob white, nighthawk, blue-winged warbler, blue-gray gnatcatcher, bobolink, wood pewee, ovenbird, indigo bunting, cliff swallow, and purple martin. There is also a host of reptiles and amphibians, including hognose snake, blue racer, fox snake, bull snake and garter snake, as well as leopard frog, green frog, wood frog, gray tree frog, chorus frog, spring peeper, and many toads. The woodland edges are home to the prairie skink, a fairly rare lizard with black and white stripes.

Facilities: A Visitors Center contains exhibits, a classroom, offices, and an outdoor amphitheater. About 8 miles of well-marked trails in interconnecting loops explore the various habitats, including 2 short self-guided nature trails. The trails are groomed for cross-country skiing in winter. The major picnic area is located on the shore of Little Falls Lake and has tables, grills, water, toilets, and playground equipment. There is a guarded, sandy swimming beach close by with a bathhouse and a concession stand. Boat launches on all 3 lakes provide access to nonmotorized boats. A small picnic area is located next to the boat launch on Mill Pond. Fishing is popular in the lakes and the river and continues through the winter. There is a modern campground on Little Falls Lake that offers fire rings, grills, electricity, a dump station, showers, drinking water, flush toilets, and a telephone. A rustic group camp is also available for organized groups. Hike-in sites are open in winter.

How to get there: From the Twin Cities, head east to Wisconsin on Interstate Highway 94. About 3.5 miles after crossing the St. Croix River take the exit for U.S. Highway 12 and drive north. When 12 turns right just less than 2 miles down the road, continue straight on County Road U, crossing the railroad tracks. Turn right onto County Road A and look for the park entrance on the left after almost 2 more miles.

The park is closed from 11:00 p.m. to 6:00 a.m. except to registered campers. Daily or annual permits are required for all vehicles entering a state park. They may be purchased at the park entrance.

Map key: East 135

For additional information:

Willow River State Park
Route 2, County Road A
Hudson, Wisconsin 54016
(715) 386-5931

Wolsfeld Woods Scientific and Natural Area

Less than three miles north of Lake Minnetonka on the fringe of a sprawling metropolitan area is the exceptional Wolsfeld Woods Scientific and Natural Area. Although this little-known preserve contains just 185 acres, it is perhaps the premier example of the "Big Woods" in Minnesota. One of the state's 18 major landscape regions, the "Big Woods" has been reduced to scattered remnants by agriculture and urban development. It might have happened here as well.

The tract was settled in 1855 by the Wolsfeld brothers, who cleared several areas for agricultural purposes. Much of the forested hillsides, however, were cut selectively to provide wood for furniture, barrels, tools, and wagon parts, and the sugar maples were largely spared for the production of maple syrup. While other activities, such as collecting firewood and grazing cattle, also had an impact, the forest survived. In 1961 the land was purchased for development, but the owners recognized the unique qualities of the area and donated the woods to The Nature Conservancy, who then transferred the property to the state's Scientific and Natural Areas Program.

Today Wolsfeld Woods is a rare treasure that offers visitors a glimpse of what has been lost elsewhere. Wrapped around scenic Wolsfeld Lake, the preserve contains steeply rolling, forested hills, wooded swamps, pothole marshes, and narrow stream valleys. The primary forest is dominated by lofty sugar maple and basswood, with lesser numbers of tall red oak, some more than 200 years old. Ironwood is abundant in the spacious understory. The largest bitternut hickory in Minnesota is found here and many of the sugar maples reach near-record height. Each spring, before the budding trees cast a summer-long shadow on the forest floor, the fallen leaves are pushed aside by the vigorous growth of colorful wildflowers. The ground is dotted with bloodroot, rue anemone, spring beauty, trout lily, sharp-lobed hepatica, large-flowered bellwort, Dutchman's breeches, large-flowered trillium, Virginia waterleaf, and patches of wild ginger, yellow violet, and cutleaf toothwort.

Sections of the preserve that were once cleared are going through the process of succession and provide an interesting contrast to the less disturbed maple-basswood forest. These areas are easily identified by the absence of tall trees and the presence of pioneering and sun-loving trees such as bur oak, black cherry, red cedar, stands of aspen, and thickets of sumac and prickly-ash. In some places sugar maple and basswood seedlings have already become established in the understory.

Wetlands of various size occupy depressions throughout the hills, and range from cattail marshes and sedge meadows to seasonally wet swamps with red-osier dogwood, elm, silver maple, green ash, and boxelder. These basins, including Wolsfeld Lake, were created more than 10,000 years ago when the glaciers retreated, leaving blocks of ice buried in the glacial debris. As these blocks of ice melted, they left the depressions that later became lakes and marshes.

Facilities: There is an extensive trail system that explores most of Wolsfeld Woods. Two miles of trails are incorporated into a system of community horse trails. Stationary maps with interpretive information are located at the trailhead and by the lake. An excellent guide is available from the Department of Natural Resources. Wolsfeld Woods has been set aside to protect natural plant and animal communities for scientific and educational purposes. You are invited to observe and enjoy the area, but please remember that your visit can have an impact on the natural community and stay on the trails.

How to get there: From the Twin Cities head west on U.S. Highway 12 to the town of Long Lake (about 6 miles west of Interstate 494). Just beyond the stoplight, turn right (north) onto Brown Road. Drive about 3/4 of a mile to the intersection of Brown Road and County Highway 6, where Trinity Lutheran Church is located. The church has allowed the use of its parking lot. The trail begins at the northeast corner of the lot.

Map key: West 136

For additional information:

Scientific and Natural Areas
Program
Box 7, Minnesota Department of
Natural Resources
500 Lafayette Road, DNR Building
St. Paul, Minnesota 55155
(612) 297-3288

Wood Lake Nature Center

Every day thousands of motorists on Interstate Highway 35W speed past an opening in the sound barriers just south of the Crosstown Highway that briefly reveals an inviting expanse of fields, marshes, and woodlands. Located only four blocks from Minneapolis in densely populated Richfield, the Wood Lake Nature Center is an urban sanctuary for both the wildlife that lives there and the people who visit.

The heart of the preserve is composed of large areas of cattail marsh and shallow open waters, while restored prairie, old fields, and mature woodlands add diversity to its 160 acres. More than three miles of wide trails and floating boardwalks, in addition to blinds, mounds, and observation docks, provide easy access to the wetlands and other habitats and offer excellent opportunities for viewing wildlife.

During a single walk an observant visitor may see a family of Canada geese grazing in the grass; painted turtles sunning themselves on a log; red-winged blackbirds noisily defending their territory; a cottontail rabbit darting for cover; a Forster's tern diving for small fish; or a great egret stalking the shallows. An abundance of other birds inhabit the productive wetlands, including wood duck, blue-winged teal, mallard, ruddy duck, coot, least bittern, Virginia rail, and yellow-headed blackbirds.

These and other residents are joined by many migrants in the spring and fall, bringing the total number of species sighted at Wood Lake since 1971 to 230. Additional wildlife includes red and gray fox, raccoon, woodchuck, spotted and striped skunk, mink, muskrat, long and short-tailed weasel, white-tailed jackrabbit, plains pocket gopher, and eastern chipmunk. There are also numerous species of squirrels, bats, voles, shrews, and mice.

The marshes are secluded from the surrounding houses by a belt of mature woodland that makes up the perimeter of the preserve. Stately cottonwoods stand above boxelder, silver maple, and black willow on one side and red oak, bur oak, aspen, and Chinese elm on the other. Elderberry, honeysuckle, raspberry, and wild grape grow thick in the understory.

Facilities: Situated next to the entrance is a spacious interpretive center with exhibitions, an auditorium (80 to 100 persons), offices, and restrooms. The trails are well maintained and include a floating boardwalk, viewing blinds, observation mounds and docks, and benches. Snowshoes and cross-country skis can be rented during winter.

How to get there: Heading south from Minneapolis on Interstate Highway 35W take the 66th Street exit just south of the Crosstown Highway. Go east a few blocks to Lake Shore Drive and turn right. The parking lot is on the right.

The trails are open daily from dawn to dusk. The interpretive center is open on weekdays from 8:30 a.m. to 5:00 p.m.

Map key: West 137

For additional information:

Wood Lake Nature Center
735 Lake Shore Drive
Richfield, Minnesota 55423
(612) 861-4507

Woodland Wildlife Management Area

The Woodland Wildlife Management Area could hardly have a more misleading name. Located in, and named for, Woodland Township in southern Wright County, only a tiny portion of the area is forested. Instead, this 726-acre preserve encompasses a large open basin of wetlands and grasslands surrounded by rolling farmland. Yet this has not always been the case. Years ago the creek that meandered in and out of the basin was transformed into a straight ditch; this drained the wetlands and created an expansive sedge meadow. Still too wet to plow, the basin was mowed for "marsh hay." Since then, a small dam has been constructed to control the water level and rehabilitate the marsh.

Today the area contains a healthy complex of wetland communities that provide protection, shelter, and food for many wildlife species. Broad sweeps of open water interspersed with dense stands of cattail occupy the heart of the basin, giving way around the edges to extensive stretches of sedge meadow and willow fen. Narrow strips of woodland cover the steeper hills to the east and south, but most of the surrounding upland is characterized by grassland with only scattered trees and shrubs.

Among the birds that make their home here are mallard, blue-winged teal, coot, ruddy duck, and Canada goose, as well as yellow-headed blackbird, marsh wren, and yellowthroat warbler. Trumpeter swans are occasional visitors and white pelicans are commonly seen in late summer. Muskrat and mink remain active throughout the year in the marsh, while raccoon and red fox forage around the fringe.

Facilities: There are no developed facilities here other than a boat access and two designated parking areas. Though you can observe the marsh from uplands to the east and west, the best way to explore the area would be by small boat or canoe. State Wildlife Management Areas are managed for three primary reasons: wildlife production, public hunting, and trapping. Other activities, such as birdwatching and canoeing are also encouraged but should probably be avoided during the hunting season.

How to get there: From the Twin Cities go west on U.S. Highway 12. About 7 miles after crossing the Crow River in Delano, take a left (south) onto State Highway 25 in the town of Montrose. Look for the parking area on the left after about one mile. To reach the opposite side and the boat ramp turn south off Highway 12 one mile east of Montrose. Proceed .4 mile to the parking area on the right.

Map key: West 138

For additional information:

Department of Natural Resources
Area Wildlife Manager
P.O. Box 370
St. Cloud, Minnesota 56302
(612) 255-4279

Minnesota Department of Natural Resources
Section of Wildlife, Box 7
500 Lafayette Road
St. Paul, Minnesota 55155
(612) 296-3344

Index

The Author

Born in Minnesota but raised on the east coast, KAI HAGEN returned in 1976 to attend St. Olaf College in Northfield. He has spent a great deal of time since exploring the back roads and wild spaces of the upper Midwest with his wife and friends. As a frequent volunteer, an intern with The Nature Conservancy, and a staff member of the Clean Water Action Project, Kai has worked to protect the beauty and diversity of his adopted home state. This book grew from his belief that we will not preserve what we do not understand, and that familiarity with our natural heritage is its own reward.

The Illustrator

STEPHANIE TORBERT is an artist, a photographer, an illustrator, a teacher and a naturalist. Her photographs and drawings are represented in museums, galleries, and collections around the world. She has been the recipient of numerous grants and fellowships for her art work from such places as the Bush Foundation, the McKnight Foundation, and the Minnesota State Arts Board. She has been employed as a Naturalist at Eloise Butler Wildflower Garden since 1985.

Stephanie met Kai Hagen one very rainy October morning at Eloise Butler Wildflower Garden in 1987, and sitting in front of a toasty fire in the fireplace decided she would like to illustrate this book.

East Metro Area

(West Metro Area inside front cover)